Library of
Davidson College

The Transformation of a Sacred Town: Bhubaneswar, India

Westview Replica Editions

This book is a Westview Replica Edition. The concept of Replica Editions is a response to the crisis in academic and informational publishing. Library budgets for books have been severely curtailed; economic pressures on the university presses and the few private publishing companies primarily interested in scholarly manuscripts have severely limited the capacity of the industry to properly serve the academic and research communities. Many manuscripts dealing with important subjects, often representing the highest level of scholarship, are today not economically viable publishing projects. Or, if they are accepted for publication, they are often subject to lead times ranging from one to three years. Scholars are understandably frustrated when they realize that their first-class research cannot be published within a reasonable time frame, if at all.

Westview Replica Editions are our practical solution to the problem. The concept is simple. We accept a manuscript in camera-ready form and move it immediately into the production process. The responsibility for textual and copy editing lies with the author or sponsoring organization. If necessary we will advise the author on proper preparation of footnotes and bibliography. We prefer that the manuscript be typed according to our specifications, though it may be acceptable as typed for a dissertation or prepared in some other clearly organized and readable way. The end result is a book produced by lithography and bound in hard covers. Initial edition sizes range from 500 to 800 copies, and a number of recent Replicas are already in second printings. We include among Westview Replica Editions only works of outstanding scholarly quality or of great informational value, and we will continue to exercise our usual editorial standards and quality control.

The Transformation of a Sacred Town: Bhubaneswar, India

edited by Susan Seymour

Results of the Harvard-Bhubaneswar Project are related for the first time by several anthropologists, two sociologists, a scholar of comparative religion, and a regional planner. The project was initiated in 1961 to study rapid urbanization and consequent sociological change in Bhubaneswar, Orissa, India--an ancient temple town which became the new capital city of the state of Orissa in 1947. This book presents a series of studies illustrating the changes and adaptations that have occurred in the Bhubaneswar area. The final chapter reviews and synthesizes the studies, compares the results with those of other studies of urbanization in India, and raises broad questions about the study of socio-cultural change in complex societies.

Susan Seymour is associate professor of anthropology at Pitzer College (Claremont Colleges).

The Transformation of a Sacred Town: Bhubaneswar, India

edited by Susan Seymour

Westview Press • Boulder, Colorado

A Westview Replica Edition

All rights reserved. No part of this publication may be reproduced or transmitted in any form or by any means, electronic or mechanical, including photocopy, recording, or any information storage and retrieval system, without permission in writing from the publisher.

Copyright © 1980 by Westview Press, Inc.

Published in 1980 in the United States of America by
    Westview Press, Inc.
    5500 Central Avenue
    Boulder, Colorado 80301
    Frederick A. Praeger, Publisher

Library of Congress Cataloging in Publication Data
Main entry under title:
The Transformation of a sacred town.
    (A Westview replica edition)
    Includes index.
    1. Urbanization--India--Bhubaneswar--Addresses, essays, lectures. 2. Bhubaneswar, India--Social conditions--Addresses, essays, lectures. 3. Bhubaneswar, India--Economic conditions--Addresses, essays, lectures.
    I. Seymour, Susan.
    HT147.I5T7   307.7'6'095413   79-26726
    ISBN 0-89158-768-3

Printed and bound in the United States of America

This volume is dedicated to

CORA DU BOIS

in very grateful recognition of her guidance and inspiration throughout this enterprise. It was she who conceived the Harvard-Bhubaneswar Project and encouraged each of us to participate in it. Not only did she help direct our individual research projects, carefully reading and commenting upon all field notes and guiding us through our dissertations, but she has since continued to read and offer penetrating criticism of our writings and has been a continual source of stimulation and encouragement. It is not usual for a senior professor and scholar to serve as both dedicated teacher and friend to her younger students and colleagues, but in both of these respects Cora Du Bois has succeeded.

Contents

List of Figures and Tables. xi
Acknowledgements. xiii

INTRODUCTION - Susan Seymour. 1

PART 1
THE NEW CITY

1 THE SETTING 9
   Peter Grenell

2 PLANNING THE NEW CAPITAL OF BHUBANESWAR . . 31
   Peter Grenell

PART 2
RELIGIOUS ADAPTATIONS

3 LINGARAJ TEMPLE: ITS STRUCTURE AND
   CHANGE, CA. 1900-1976. 69
   Manamohan Mahapatra

4 RELIGIOUS INSTITUTIONS AND POLITICAL
   ELITES IN BHUBANESWAR 83
   David Miller

5 TWO URBANIZING ORISSAN TEMPLES. 97
   James M. Freeman & James Preston

PART 3
EDUCATIONAL ADAPTATIONS

6 PATTERNS OF CHILDREARING IN A CHANGING
   INDIAN TOWN 121
   Susan Seymour

7 INDIAN EDUCATION: A VIEW FROM THE
   BOTTOM UP 157
   Alan Sable

PART 4
ECONOMIC ADAPTATIONS

8   THE WIDENING ECONOMIC GAP: AN URBAN
INDIAN EXAMPLE. 185
    James M. Freeman

9   THE ECONOMY OF AN URBANIZING VILLAGE. . . . 217
    Harish C. Das

10 CUTTACK ENTREPRENEURS 235
    Doris L. Taub & Richard P. Taub

PART 5
TRADITION IN TRANSITION

11 SOME CONCLUSIONS: SOURCES OF CHANGE
AND CONTINUITY. 257
    Susan Seymour

   INDEX 275

Figures and Tables

Figures

1.1 Map of Orissa 10
1.2 Map of Bhubaneswar. 20
1.3 The Three Governmental Hierarchies
     and Their Lines of Responsibility 29

Tables

3.1 Traditional Roles of Temple Servants. . . . 74
3.2 Main Occupations of Priestly
     Groups in 1976. 78
6.1 Sample of Households: Old Town 124
6.2 Sample of Households: New Capital. 125
6.3 Sample of Children (Birth to
     Ten Years). 126
6.4 Maternal Nurturance: Age-Grade of
     Child by Location of Residence. 138
6.5 Seeking Nurturance: Age of Child
     by Location of Residence. 139
6.6 Seeking Nurturance: Age of Child
     by Household Size 139
6.7 Proportion of Nurturant Acts
     Performed by Mothers and Mother-
     Surrogates by Location of Residence . . . 140
6.8 Proportion of Nurturant Acts
     Directed to Different Age-Grades
     of Children by Socioeconomic Status . . . 141
6.9 Seeking Nurturance: Age of Child by
     Socioeconomic Status. 141
6.10 Responsible Acts Performed by Older
     Children (Six to Ten Years) by
     Socioeconomic Status 142
7.1 Girls' Attrition Rates by Fathers'
     Occupations 165
7.2 Respondents' Assessment of the
     Importance of Various Factors
     in Accounting for Success in Life 168

7.3	Choices Between Instrumental and Non-instrumental Attitudes Toward Schooling	169
7.4	Occupation and School Enrollment: Neighborhood Schools	177
7.5	Caste Composition of the Neighborhood Schools	177
7.6	Examination Pass Rates in Neighborhood Schools	179
7.7	Primary School Attrition Rates by Section of the City and Type of School	179
7.8	Primary School Attrition Rates by Fathers' Occupations	180
8.1	The Caste Distribution of Households in Kapileswar, 1972	187
8.2	Household Occupations of Six Castes Whose Earners Resided in Kapileswar in 1971	192
8.3	Acres of Cultivable Land Owned per Household	196
8.4	Wealth Owned Other Than Land per Household	197
8.5	Annual Income per Household Based on Average Number of Adults per Household	198
8.6	Cumulative Wealth per Household Scale	199
8.7	Households Owning Above and Below the Land Survival Figure of .7 Acre per Adult	199
8.8	Total Acres Owned by Landowners of Different Size Holdings	200
8.9	Comparison of the Wealth of Six Castes of Kapileswar	202
9.1	Distribution of Livestock in Nuapalli in 1964	222
9.2	A Sample Working-Age Population of Nuapalli Engaged in Agricultural and Urban Wage Labor in 1964	223
9.3	Approximate Annual Incomes from Shopkeeping in Nuapalli in 1964	225
9.4	Approximate Annual Incomes from Wood Cutting in Nuapalli in 1965	227

Acknowledgements

The preparation of this volume has been a cooperative enterprise in many respects. First, I want to thank the South Asia Regional Council of the Association of Asian Studies which supported a Harvard-Bhubaneswar Project conference in 1976. Nine of the Project collaborators, including Cora Du Bois, gathered in Chicago at the home of Richard and Doris Taub to discuss and plan a volume that would bring together and integrate some of the findings of the Harvard-Bhubaneswar Project. I am grateful to all my colleagues for their participation in that conference and their continued advice and help in the preparation of this volume.

I want to take this opportunity to thank the Government of India, the Government of the State of Orissa, and the residents of Bhubaneswar and its environs who made possible the research upon which this volume is based. We are all greatly appreciative of the warmth and hospitality that we experienced while residing and working in Orissa. While it would be impossible to identify all the individuals in Orissa who contributed to this enterprise, I do want to express my gratitude to Gagan N. Dash for his excellent Oriya language instruction. In collaboration with Dr. D. P. Pattanayak, Professor Dash developed a training manual in conversational Oriya (*Conversational Oriya*, Myore, India: Kapila Power Press, 1972) and instructed six of the American collaborators in the Harvard-Bhubaneswar Project.

For editorial and typing assistance I am indebted to several persons. Eleanor Gorman and Ellen Riley helped with the copy editing and preparation of the manuscript. Beverly Scales and Celeste Basehart typed early drafts of it, and Diane Mosher and Beverly Wachel typed the final draft.

Finally, I especially want to express gratitude to my husband, Laurence Graham, for his continual encouragement and support throughout this enterprise. In addition, he has carefully read and criticized several chapters and has helped in the technical preparation of the volume. His assistance has been invaluable.

The Transformation of a Sacred Town: Bhubaneswar, India

Introduction
Susan Seymour

Until 1947 Bhubaneswar, Orissa, India, was a small, ancient, temple town noted for its sacred Hindu complex largely controlled by the major temple of Lingaraj and its temple servants. In that year, however, jungle that covered public territory two miles north of the Old Town was selected as the site for a new capital city for the state of Orissa. The New Capital was conceived as a planned city to be devoted to administrative, educational, and other government institutions. By 1961 the first stage of construction of the New Capital had been completed, government servants had arrived, and Bhubaneswar's population had jumped from an estimated 10,000 to over 38,000. The Old Town's religiously-oriented and agriculturally-based population had been brought into contact with a set of Western-educated government officers, and the process of urbanization was well underway.

Bhubaneswar seemed thus an ideal context in which to examine rapid urbanization and consequent sociocultural change and adaptation. This was particularly so since Orissa was recognized as one of India's least developed states, but one with considerable untapped resources for development. In 1961 Cora Du Bois of Harvard University initiated a pilot investigation[1] to explore the feasibility of Bhubaneswar as a site for such a study. As a consequence, an extended study involving many persons in research was undertaken which came to be known as the "Harvard-Bhubaneswar Project." This volume represents the first effort to integrate and synthesize some of the findings of that project.[2]

The Harvard-Bhubaneswar Project was conceived as a long-term, multidisciplinary, and essentially ethnographic approach to the study of urbanization and sociocultural change in India. It initially

spanned more than a decade (1961-73), but some of
the project's collaborators have continued to do
work there since that time and plan yet further
studies. Bhubaneswar and its environs are, therefore, becoming an unusually well documented case in
the literature on urbanization and sociocultural
change in a complex society. Further, these changes
have been examined from a variety of perspectives.
From 1962 to 1973 six Orissan and eight American
Ph.D. candidates, representing a variety of fields
(anthropology, sociology, comparative religion, and
regional planning) undertook research in Bhubaneswar
under Professor Du Bois' guidance. The Old Town,
the New Capital, the five villages that have been
incorporated into the administrative area of Bhubaneswar, and Cuttack, the former capital and chief
commercial center of Orissa twenty miles away, have
all been foci of research.

Collaborators in the Harvard-Bhubaneswar Project had access to one another's field notes, as well
as to newspaper clippings and unpublished analytic
summaries of relevant writings and publications, all
of which were gathered and filed by Professor
Du Bois. In this way, ideas and information were
shared, and each investigator was able to build upon
the work of his colleagues. The project "archives"
have recently been transferred to the Joseph
Regenstein Library of the University of Chicago and
are available there to interested scholars.[3]

The ethnographic, intensive fieldwork approach
of the Harvard-Bhubaneswar Project was intended to
document change in Bhubaneswar and its environs in
as nonjudgmental a way as possible. As Srinivas
(1972: viii) has aptly noted, "The availability of
data of sufficient richness on selected periods of
a civilization might prove crucial for the understanding of social change." Reliance upon repeated
informal interviews and observations was also intended to supplement and in some instances counteract
Western stereotypes of Indian culture derived largely from scholarly Sanskritic views based upon traditional texts. For example, views of Indian religion
founded upon textual and ritualistic Hinduism tend
to predict a decline in religious practices and
beliefs with rapid urbanization and sociocultural
change. To the contrary, however, in Bhubaneswar
and its environs certain forms and institutions of
Hinduism have proved to be highly adaptive and
resilient (see Chapters 4 and 5).

The essentially ethnographic orientation of the
project also helped counteract tendencies to apply

to Bhubaneswar such Western-based dichotomous formulations as "modernity" and "tradition." Without such an approach, the overt and striking physical differences between the old and new parts of Bhubaneswar might have led to the simplistic view that the Old Town represents "traditional" India and the New Capital "modern" India and to a concern with preconceived oppositions between a rural and religious center, on the one hand, and an expanding urban metropolis, on the other. Such formulations have dominated the social science literature on urbanization and sociocultural change since the work of Wirth (1938) and Redfield (1941) and tend to encourage static categorization rather than concern with process—i.e., concern with the *adaptive strategies* that people adopt when faced with changing circumstances. This volume, as representative of the Harvard-Bhubaneswar Project, takes the more current view that sociocultural change is a complex, nonlinear process of adaptation and, accordingly, tries to identify patterns of adjustment of old institutions and ways of life to the introduction of new ones. Changes and adaptations in family organization, socialization practices, formal schooling, status hierarchies, economic and religious institutions are all described. While some contrasts between the old parts of Bhubaneswar (the Old Town and the five contiguous villages) and the new parts are evident, it has rarely been appropriate to view them in opposition to one another. If one examines the educational institutions in Bhubaneswar, for example, it becomes apparent that despite overt differences in school buildings and teachers' dress, there are not important differences in children's performances between the Old Town and the New Capital. Rather, other variables that cross-cut the Old Town and the New Capital appear to determine whether children stay in school and how well they do there (see Chapter 7).

Notwithstanding efforts to avoid static categorization in this volume, however, it has at times been expedient to refer to "traditional" Bhubaneswar and to the effects of "modernization." We do so with the awareness that what is now called "traditional" simply refers to an arbitrary, time-bound series of adaptations in Indian culture as observed in the mid-twentieth century and that "modernization" implies a whole complex of recent adaptations to the intrusion of Euro-American civilization into the Indian context. The implications of these terms for the understanding of sociocultural change in

India and elsewhere are explored further in Part Five.

The volume is organized as follows: Part One focuses on the New Capital—the entity that gave rise to rapid urbanization and sociocultural change in Bhubaneswar and its environs. Chapter 1 describes the physical, economic, and political setting of the new city. Chapter 2 then traces the actual process by which the New Capital was planned and constructed. It raises perennial questions about the urban planning process and suggests some of the effects the new city was to have on the already existing settlements in the area.

Part Two shifts perspective to the Old Town, one of its adjoining villages, and the city of Cuttack in order to examine some of the religious adaptations that have occurred since establishment of the New Capital. Chapter 3 focuses on the dominant temple in the Old Town, Lingaraj, and its attendants, outlining that institution's recent history and the impact of the New Capital upon it. Chapter 4 describes the range of Hindu monasteries that exist in the Old Town and the interrelationships of Old Town gurus and members of the New Capital government elite. Chapter 5 extends the discussion of religious institutions beyond the boundaries of the Old Town. It compares the recent growth of a temple in Cuttack with the decline of a temple in Kapileswar, a village adjacent to the Old Town.

Part Three is concerned with educational adaptations in Bhubaneswar. Using "education" in its broadest sense, Chapter 6 compares family organization and childrearing practices for a set of Old Town and New Capital households, suggesting the range and variation that exist in child care practices and how they relate to dimensions of family organization and socioeconomic status. Chapter 7 focuses upon schools and formal education in Bhubaneswar, stressing the rational and flexible approaches that Old Town and New Capital families have used in adjusting to a new array of educational institutions.

Part Four illustrates some of the economic changes that have occurred since establishment of the New Capital and the adaptations that residents in the Bhubaneswar area are making. Chapters 8 and 9 examine these economic adaptations from the perspective of two villages that have been incorporated into the Bhubaneswar municipality. Chapter 10 then extends the discussion of economic change and development to the nearby city of Cuttack.

In conclusion, Part Five (Chapter 11) synthesizes some of the findings of the previous chapters and examines them from a broader perspective, suggesting how they might contribute to our understanding of sociocultural change and adaptation in such complex societies as India.

NOTES

1. The two-year pilot project was supported by a National Science Foundation grant, G17913. Subsequent research by Professor Du Bois was also supported by the National Science Foundation.
2. The Harvard-Bhubaneswar Project has already produced a number of publications, as indicated in the reference sections of chapters, but to date results of the project have not been integrated or synthesized. Other publications are planned and will continue to be produced by both the Indian and American collaborators in the project.
3. The Harvard-Bhubaneswar "archives" include a small library of relevant printed materials on Orissa (e.g. gazeteers, newspapers, government publications, histories), a set of completed Ph.D. dissertations, and an incomplete bibliography of publications on Orissa in addition to some six file drawers of annotated field notes.

REFERENCES

Redfield, Robert. 1941. *The Folk Culture of Yucatan*. Chicago: University of Chicago Press.
Srinivas, M. N. 1972. Foreward to *When a Great Tradition Modernizes* by Milton Singer. New York: Praeger Publishers.
Wirth, Louis. 1938. Urbanization as a way of life. *American Journal of Sociology* 54:1-24.

Part 1
The New City

Peter Grenell has lived in India for over five years, one year as a student at the Tata Institute of Social Sciences, Bombay, nearly two years as an American Institute of Indian Studies fellow in Bhubaneswar, one as a Ford Foundation consultant in Calcutta, and nearly two more as consultant and project officer for the United Nations Children's Fund in New Delhi. Trained as a city planner, he has worked on new town plans in India, the United States, and Venezuela for public and private sector clients. He has also contributed to numerous housing studies and programs for federal and city governments, with special emphasis on self-help and other approaches to lower cost housing. He is currently acting as a consultant to the State of California Coastal Conservancy. Mr. Grenell attended Antioch College, Yellow Springs, Ohio, and the Massachusetts Institute of Technology. He has published several articles in professional journals and co-authored FREEDOM TO BUILD, Macmillan, 1972, with John F. C. Turner and Robert Fichter et al. He now lives in San Francisco.

Chapters 1 and 2 are based upon Mr. Grenell's careful two-year investigation (1964-66) of the city planning process in Bhubaneswar. Chapter 1 briefly describes the state of Orissa, Bhubaneswar, and its environs. Chapter 2 then outlines the long, complex process by which the New Capital was established, planned, and gradually constructed. Mr. Grenell concludes by identifying some of the factors that have affected the urban planning process in Bhubaneswar and that appear to have cross-cultural application as well.

1

The Setting

Peter Grenell

THE REGION

Coastal Orissa is a fertile rice-growing area in eastern India, midway between Calcutta and Madras (see Figure 1.1). Much of the rice produced in the Orissa delta is shipped north to Bengal, along with many tons of fish from the region's rivers and tidal waters. Despite the area's fecundity, however, life is not always easy for the mainly rural inhabitants. Although the temperature range and rainfall patterns are less extreme than in other parts of India, this rich agricultural area is subject to cyclones, floods, and droughts which devastate the land roughly six years out of every ten.

Almost half of Orissa's 22 million people live in the coastal region along the Bay of Bengal, which encompasses four of the state's thirteen administrative districts. These coastal districts, with between 400 and 800 people per square mile, are the most densely settled areas in the state. The region's population has grown considerably during the past century. This growth has led to a rise in the number of landless families. For landowners, increasing fragmentation of holdings through inheritance has resulted in parcels barely large enough to support a household. Periodic natural disasters further burden the population, especially the poorest sector.

The state's interior is an area of hills, plateaus, and forests. This region was divided into twenty-six independent princely states until 1948, when these states were absorbed into the Indian Union. The inland region is not as fertile as the coast and often suffers from severe drought. In recent years, the government has begun mining the extensive mineral deposits there and has established

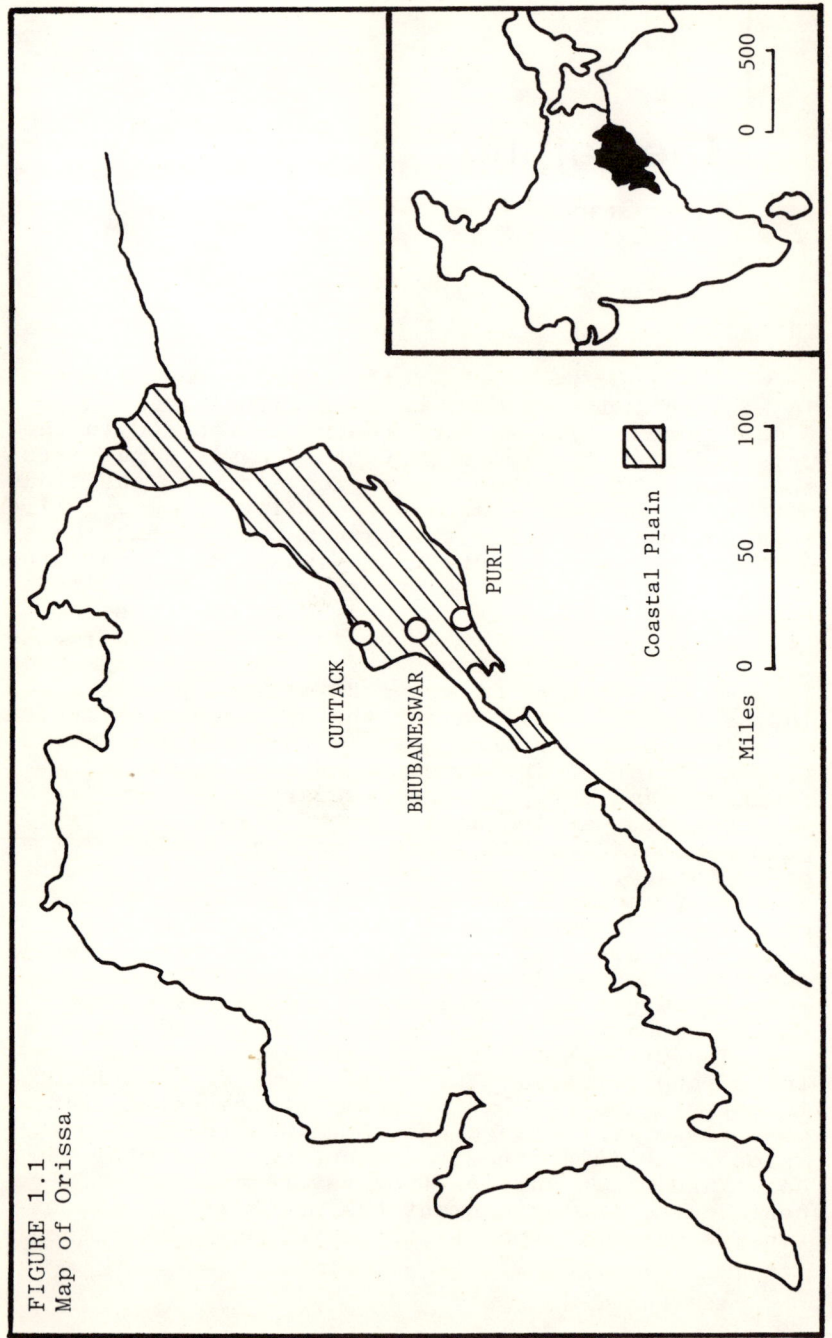

FIGURE 1.1
Map of Orissa

several industrial enterprises in the hinterland. Despite these attempts at industrialization, however, the different tribes of the inland region are still generally poorer than the lowlanders. The area lacks the coast's productivity, comparatively better climate, urban concentrations, and better access to other states.

Orissa is primarily an agricultural state—94 percent of its population is classified as rural, more than that of any other state—and there is relatively little industrial activity compared to neighboring West Bengal and Bihar. There are two large sector factories, the Rourkela steel plant and a MIG fighter plane factory. The state built a port on the coast a few years ago at Paradip to be used in exporting iron ore. And there are a few more industries located near Rourkela in the northwestern part of the state and around the commercial city of Cuttack near the coast.

PRINCIPAL CITIES

Orissa is one of the least urbanized states in India. In 1961 Cuttack was the only city with a population greater than 100,000. By 1971 only three cities had exceeded 100,000: Cuttack, still the largest at nearly 200,000; the capital city of Bhubaneswar; and the new steel-manufacturing city of Rourkela (*Census of India*, 1971). Cuttack, Bhubaneswar, and Puri, an important religious center, are all located in the coastal region within fifty miles of one another (see Figure 1.1). This central area in and around Bhubaneswar and Cuttack is the locale for the research reported in this book.

The city of Puri is one of India's holiest places for it is the site of the temple of Lord Jagannath, an important incarnation of Vishnu. Each year, several hundred thousand pilgrims and other visitors crowd this city of 60,000 to watch Lord Jagannath make his annual trip to visit his aunt in a nearby temple. The image of Lord Jagannath is carried in a hugh wooden chariot hauled by devotees (hence the English word "juggernaut"), accompanied by representations of his brother, Balaram, and his sister, Subhadra, also pulled in chariots. The origin of the worship of Lord Jagannath is unknown, but it probably has tribal roots. Although it is now mainly a Vaishnavite temple, the Puri Jagannath Temple has incorporated many elements of Shiva worship into its rituals. This ritual breadth has enabled Puri to exert a powerful religious influence on the coastal region and beyond for centuries. More recently, Puri, with its coastal location and beautiful beaches, has become a tourist center.

    A little more than halfway from Puri to Cuttack lies Bhubaneswar, another ancient temple town and pilgrimage place. The temple of Lord Lingaraj, the most sacred Shivaite temple in eastern India, is located here. At one time, the temple priests controlled vast paddy lands from which the temple derived much of its income and its servants their sustenance; in recent times, however, the holdings have diminished. Besides its religious importance, Bhubaneswar has a rich historical tradition. It was the seat of the great Orissan kings and temple builders of the eighth to the thirteenth centuries, many of whose temples still dot the landscape in and around the Old Town. Five miles south of Bhubaneswar, on the plain below the Dhaulagiri Hills, the Emperor Ashoka defeated the Kalinga army in a bloody battle that took place two centuries before Christ. It was in reaction to the horrors of the slaughter that Ashoka is said to have become a Buddhist. In addition, because of its location at the edge of the fertile delta ricelands on the region's main north-south communications corridor, Bhubaneswar has long been a way-station for pilgrims en route to Puri as well as a destination in its own right.

    Bhubaneswar is also Orissa's capital. Cuttack had been the state capital, but over a period of years beginning in 1948, when construction of a new town began on a vacant site across the railway line from the old temple town, the location of the capital shifted. The visible contrast between the new planned government settlement (the New Capital), with its broad straight streets and rows of neat official residences, and the densely and irregularly settled old temple town (the Old Town) was one of the original stimuli for the research presented in this book.

    Cuttack, twenty miles northeast of Bhubaneswar, is the former capital, chief commercial center, and largest city of Orissa. It is squeezed between two branches of the Mahanadi River and even in the 1930s was crowded. In spite of its size and economic importance, Cuttack seems more a collection of small towns huddled together than a true city. Behind its broad, shop-lined main streets, hundreds of narrow, unpaved paths wind their way through village-like enclaves. As in Puri and Bhubaneswar, the principal means of transportation are bicycles, bicycle-rickshaws, and feet. The chief urban characteristic of the place is its crowded streets.

HISTORICAL AND POLITICAL OVERVIEW

Because of its geographic isolation and relatively good climate and soil, coastal Orissa passed through successive periods of Hindu, Muslim, and British rule with little economic or social disruption. During this long time-span the inland hill region remained under the suzerainty of a series of ruling princes, some of whom had long been powerful leaders and others of whom were little more than tribal adventurers. After its native Hindu dynasties declined and were finally overthrown in the fifteenth century (Panigrahi 1961), coastal Orissa itself had no unique identity in contrast to, say, the Rajput kingdoms in the West.

While under British rule, what is now the state of Orissa was a part of Bengal. In 1912 Orissa and Bihar were separated from Bengal, and Orissa was then governed from Patna in Bihar. Around the turn of the century an active Oriya nationalist movement developed. This movement was rooted in feelings of cultural and linguistic identity and harkened back to the days of the great Kalinga kings and temple builders of a thousand years earlier (Bailey 1963). It had several objectives; chief among them were the recognition of Oriya as one of the official languages of India and the creation of a separate Oriya-speaking province. Both goals were reached in 1936 with the establishment of Orissa Province[1] by the Government of India. It was composed of the four coastal districts of Cuttack, Puri, Balasore, and Ganjam, the interior districts of Sambalpur and Koraput, and the two small enclaves of Angul and the Khondmal Hills. The remaining territory consisted of twenty-six princely states. Even with the recognition of Oriya as an official Indian language and the creation of Orissa as a state, feelings of antagonism toward their ex-rulers in Bihar and Bengal still linger in many Orissans today.

Once the new province was established, the Orissa Government began to consider the question of whether or not to build a new administrative capital, as Cuttack was already crowded and had little room for expansion. In 1937 the first elected Legislative Assembly of the new province voted after heated debate to retain the provincial headquarters at Cuttack, then the only city of any size in Orissa. Before any final action could be taken, Freedom Movement politics and World War II intervened. In 1945

Bindu Sagar and
Lingaraj Temple(right).

OLD TOWN

Lingaraj Temple.

Bathing ghats,
Bindu Sagar.

Orissa Secretariat.

NEW CAPITAL

Orissa Legislative Assembly.

Public Works Department.

Outskirts of town, Lingaraj Temple.

OLD TOWN

Market.

Street with temple ruin(right).

Outskirts of town,
government flats.

NEW CAPITAL

Main Market.

Raj Path
(a main avenue).

under a caretaker government, an alternate capital site near Bhubaneswar was investigated. In addition to being near the famous religious center, the site was uninhabited, government-owned, well-drained, suitable for construction, and relatively accessible to the rest of the province. Publicity given the site selection studies, however, rekindled the old regional animosities which had lain dormant since 1937, particularly those of Cuttack inhabitants who felt that they would incur a substantial loss if the capital were moved. Eventually, in 1946 the interim Orissa Government, led by the famous Freedom Fighter, Harekrushna Mahtab, unanimously decided to locate the new administrative capital at Bhubaneswar (*Orissa Legislative Assembly Proceedings* (1946:964).

The New Capital was designed by Otto Koenigsberger, who had served as architect and planner to the government of Mysore and who had also prepared a development plan for the Tata family-owned steel town of Jamshedpur in Bihar. In 1946 the population of what was to become the Bhubaneswar Notified Area,[2] a region of some thirteen square miles, did not exceed 10,000. By 1951, after three years of construction, it reached 17,000; by 1961 it had swelled to over 38,000; and it had exceeded 100,000 by 1971 (*Census of India* 1971:46). A decade after construction had begun, the government recognized that the town would expand beyond the limits of the old Koenigsberger Plan, and new planning activity was undertaken. Preliminary assistance was sought from the Ford Foundation Urban Planning team then being consulted by the Government of India on the Delhi Regional Plan. Eventually, the planning was completed by the Orissa State Town Planning Organization with the help of the Government of India's Town and Country Planning Organization.

Since World War II, Orissa politics have gone through two main stages. From 1947 to 1958 power was divided between two groups—the Congress Party, composed of coastal people, and the Ganatantra Parishad (now the Swatantra Party), dominated by ex-rulers of Orissa's former princely states. The latter rarely lost an election in their own areas. From that time on, however, the Orissa political scene has been characterized by shifting coalitions of political leaders of different persuasions and highlighted by periodic government collapses; when no local leader has been able to govern, there have been temporary take-overs by the Government of India.

BHUBANESWAR: A SNAPSHOT

In 1965, roughly the midpoint of the Harvard-Bhubaneswar Project, Bhubaneswar's population was about 50,000 people, two-thirds of whom lived in the New Capital. The rest lived in the Old Town and the five surrounding villages of Kapileswar, Laxmisagar, Baragad, Nuapalli, and Siripur (see Figure 1.2).

There are several striking contrasts between the New Capital and these other settlements, especially the Old Town. In the Old Town, houses are densely clustered around a set of medieval temples; the most prominant of these, the Lingaraj Temple, is at the town center along with the communal water rank. A measure of Orissa's conservatism is the attitude of the people toward those who would visit their temples. Although the Orissa temples are important tourist attractions, they remain among the very few Indian temples that do not permit foreigners—including those certified by the Indian authorities to be orthodox Hindus—inside even the outer walls. That this rule has persisted, despite national legislation to the contrary and, on occasion, great political pressure, indicates the strength of these traditional feelings and the power of those who hold them.

By contrast, the New Capital is laid out in broad intersecting avenues which form neighborhood blocks on which rows of government quarters were built after the British cantonment model. Large government buildings and a marketplace are at the town center. In the Old Town, houses are built in a variety of styles, many of them having dirt floors, thatched roofs, and no modern amenities such as running water and electricity. By contrast, New Capital houses follow only a few designs, which vary mostly by number of rooms, and are provided with these amenities. In addition, unlike Old Town houses, most New Capital quarters are surrounded by western-style fenced yards.

The old and new towns differ in population and social structure as well. Old Bhubaneswar is dominated by several subcastes of Brahman priests who have little formal education but who operate the temples and own much of the surrounding agricultural land. Below them in rank are a variety of service castes and outcastes with whom the Brahmans are linked by traditional occupational and economic ties. Most Old Town neighborhoods, or wards, are organized according to caste and kinship patterns (see Appendix A). The New Capital, on the other hand, consists

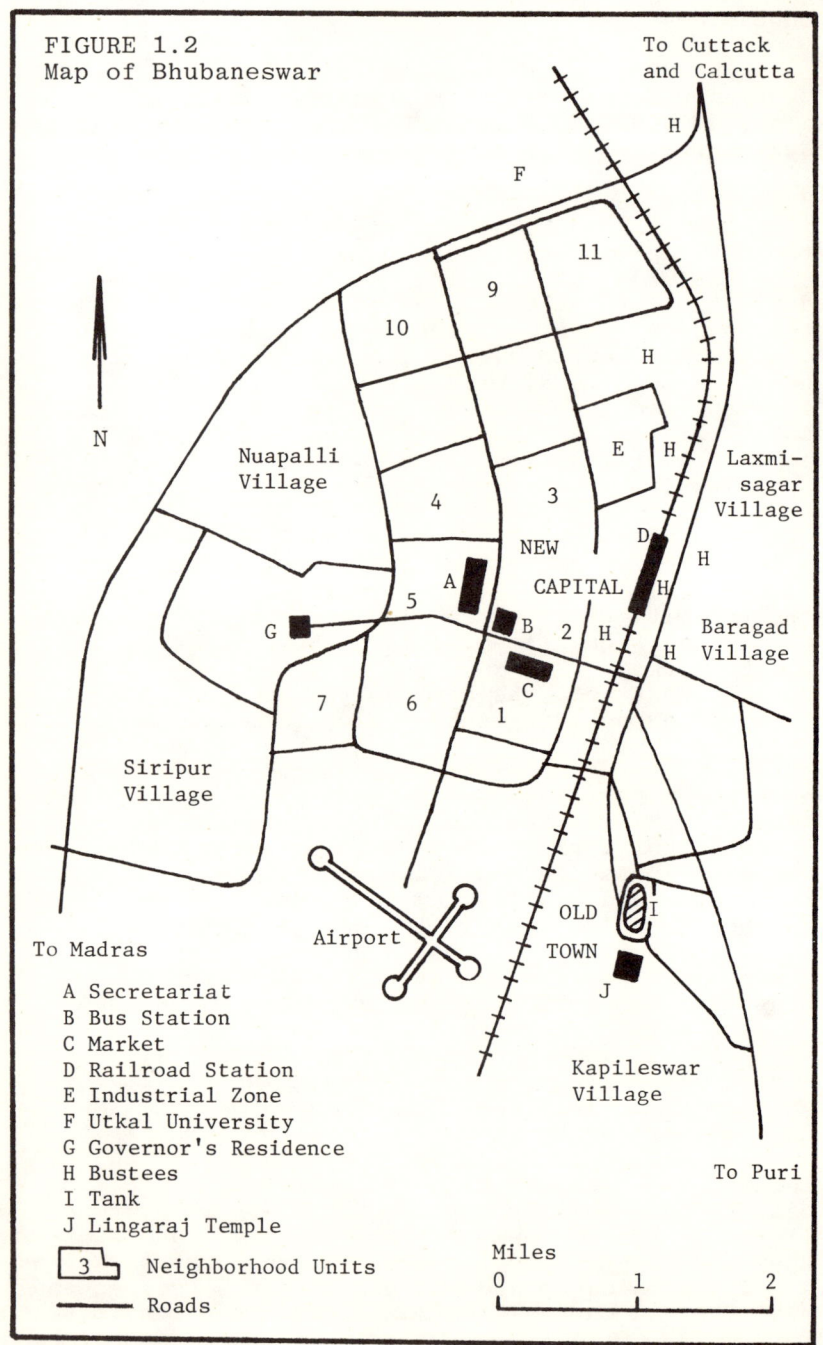

NEW CAPITAL, 1964
Unit VI in foreground and Kandagiri Hills in background.

OLD TOWN, 1964
Lingaraj Temple compound and Bindu Sagar.

22

Private House.

OLD TOWN

Street and row of houses.

Alley between
houses(left) and
temple(right).

Private house
(rented as offices).

NEW CAPITAL

Private house
(Railway Zone).

Private houses under
construction.

Mukteswar Temple.

OLD TOWN

Soft drink vendor.

Banyan tree in front
of Lingaraj Temple.

Utkal University.

NEW CAPITAL

Street peddlers.

Railway Zone shops.

mostly of government servants and their families, some of whom form a highly educated bureaucratic elite. New Capital residents in government service are assigned houses on the basis of their rank in the civil service hierarchy (see Appendix B). Because official housing was built in response to the needs of government departments locating there, people live in neighborhoods that are not organized on caste or kinship principles but that contain a mixture of civil servant levels.

The five neighboring villages vary in size, wealth, caste, and economic composition. The construction of the New Capital in the late 1940s offered new economic opportunities which left the villagers less completely at the mercy of an environment that gave them alternatively abundance and disaster. Through 1965 Bhubaneswar experienced rapid growth, some of which benefited certain of the villagers. After that year, however, the pace of development slackened and employment opportunities increased.[3] A number of villagers either sold their land or had it taken from them by the government for the construction of the New Capital in exchange for compensation. These people, later faced with considerable economic hardship, had nothing to fall back on (see Chapter 8).

Finally, squatter colonies and other slum habitations *(bustees)* cropped up between the New Capital and the Old Town, on the capital's outskirts, and in adjacent villages (see Figure 1.2). These settlements house much of the New Capital's service population: washermen, rickshaw-pullers, cowherds, sweepers, small tradesmen, manual laborers, and others who cannot find housing in the New Capital, the Old Town, or the villages. The squatter colonies closest to the New Capital are periodically obliterated by the government by means of slum clearance operations, but they usually reappear soon afterward because the services of their residents are still needed by the New Capital's populace.

Cuttack did not experience the same type or degree of development as Bhubaneswar, but it did increase its population by more than 30 percent during the 1960s (*Census of India*, 1961 and 1971). It also maintained its pre-eminence as Orissa's commercial and industrial center in spite of the development of new centers such as Bhubaneswar, Rourkela, and Paradip.

APPENDIX A

The Caste Hierarchy in Bhubaneswar

The caste hierarchy in Bhubaneswar, as in most other parts of India, is extremely difficult to specify. Inter-village variations, immigration, attempts by castes to upgrade their status, and the confounding influence of temple servant hierarchies all act to undermine efforts to clarify inter-caste hierarchies. In addition, many caste members no longer follow their traditional ritual occupations: for example, Khandaits, who were formerly warriors, are now for the most part cultivators. The following list is suggestive of the caste order in the Bhubaneswar area: the New Capital, the Old Town, and the surrounding five villages.

Caste Name	*Caste Occupation*
High	
Kyetravasi Brahman	Priest
Sasani Brahman	Priest
Suar Brahman	Priest
Halua Brahman	Priest
Khuntia Brahman	Priest
Misra Brahman	Priest
Other Brahman	Priest
Karan	Scribe
Middle	
Khandait	Militia, warrior
Gudia	Confectioner
Sunar Bania	Goldsmith
Potoli Bania	Betel seller
Teli	Oil presser
Chasa	Cultivator
Gauda	Herdsman
Kamar	Blacksmith
Badhei	Carpenter
Low	
Kumbhar	Potter
Keuta	Inland fisherman
Nolia	Sea fisherman
Barik	Barber
Jyotish	Astrologer
Untouchable	
Dhoba	Washerman
Bauri	Laborer
Mali	Gardener
Hadi	Sweeper

The above list does not include tribal names or castes foreign to the Bhubaneswar area. Many such people have come to the New Capital, and may have similar ritual occupations but are called by other names. Karans and Kayasthas are both scribes, for example, but the latter are from Bengal.

The Government of India uses the terms "scheduled castes" and "scheduled tribes" to identify untouchables and tribal people respectively. According to the 1971 Census, approximately 9 percent of the Bhubaneswar Notified Area's (NAC) population of 105,491 consisted of scheduled castes and tribes. Scheduled castes comprised 7 percent of that total, or 7,648 people. In 1961 about 80 percent of the scheduled caste population lived in the Old Town. Slightly more than half of the scheduled tribe population at that time resided in and around the village of Siripur, near the Agricultural University, and near the rickshaw colony in the railway zone. The new Capital was thus inhabited predominantly by caste Hindus who relied upon the people living on the outskirts of the city for menial services and the labor required to construct their houses.

APPENDIX B

The Structure of the Orissa Government

The Orissa Government can be viewed as consisting of three interrelated hierarchies (see Figure 1.3). There is the political and policy-making hierarchy, headed by the Chief Minister and subordinate ministers, and two administrative hierarchies. One administrative hierarchy, headed by the Chief Secretary, is primarily concerned with development, administration, and law and order; the other is mainly concerned with revenue collection. (See Taub 1969, pages 39-47, for a fuller description of these administrative hierarchies and their respective responsibilities.)

FIGURE 1.3
The Three Governmental Hierarchies and Their Lines of Responsibility
(Reprinted by permission from Taub, 1969, p.43.)

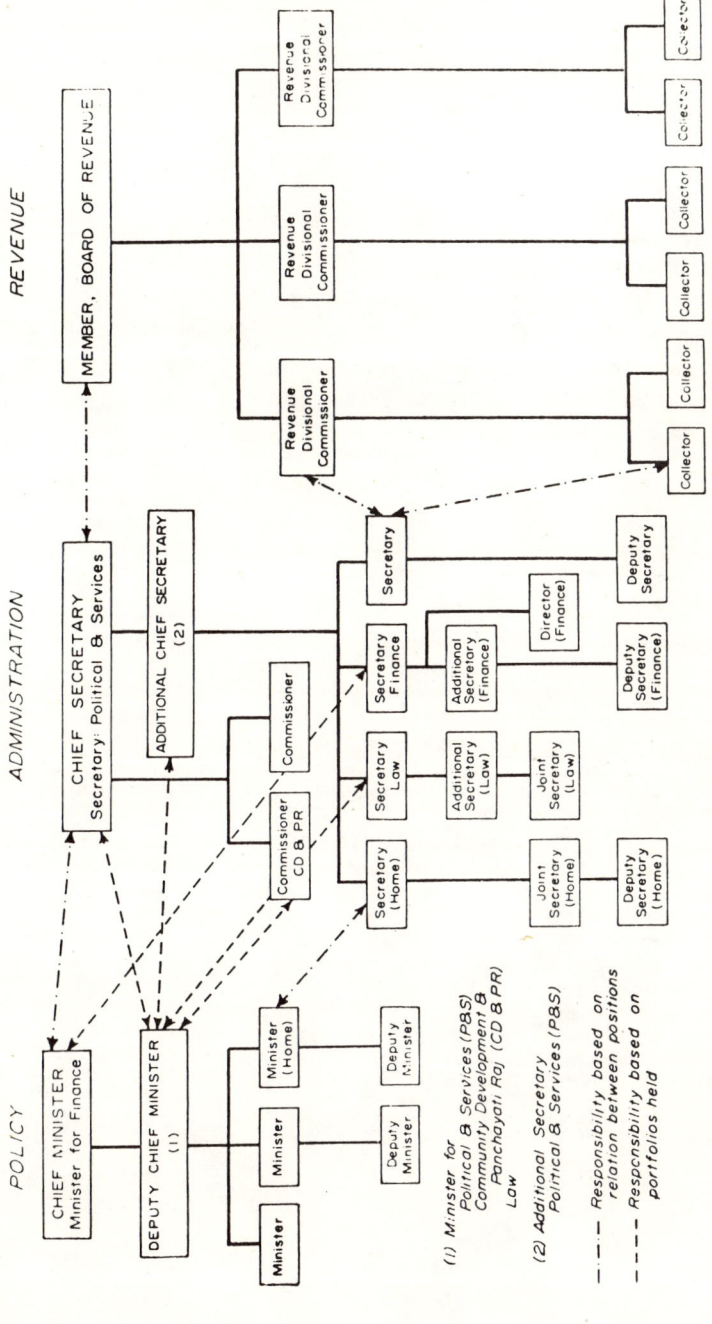

NOTES

1. All provinces, including Orissa, became states after Independence.
2. A Notified Area is an administrative jurisdiction established under the provisions of the Orissa Municipal Act and governed by a nominated or elected body with the power to exercise some or all functions of municipal government as set out in the Act. The extent of these functions is determined at the time of the body's establishment.
3. In recent years there has been another increase in the pace of development in Bhubaneswar. Since 1965 the population has tripled, reaching an estimated 150,000 in 1978, and a new phase of building is underway. Construction work, together with the need for shops and services by a rapidly expanding population, has produced an improved job market.

REFERENCES

Bailey, Fred G. 1963. *Politics and Social Change: Orissa in 1959*. Berkeley: University of California Press.
Census of India, 1961. Orissa District Census Handbook, Puri. Cuttack, India: Orissa Government Press.
Census of India, 1971. 1972. Final Population. New Delhi, India: Government of India Press.
Orissa Legislative Assembly. Proceedings. II, 22 (September 30, 1946):964.
Panigrahi, K. C. 1961. *Archaeological Remains at Bhubaneswar*. Bombay, India: Orient Longmans.
Taub, Richard P. 1969. *Bureaucrats under Stress: Administrators and Administration in an Indian State*. Berkeley: University of California Press.

2

Planning the New Capital of Bhubaneswar

Peter Grenell

This book gathers together several inquiries into how a mainly rural population is adapting to change in a context of rapid urbanization due to the construction of a new capital city in Bhubaneswar, Orissa. What makes the New Capital especially interesting is the fact that it was a deliberate effort at planned change. It was planned and built as a symbol of both Indian Independence and the determination to build a better life. The city itself, in its evolving physical manifestation and in the process by which it came into being, thus provided an unusual research opportunity: the opportunity to explore how urban planning activity influenced and was influenced by the behavioral adaptations required for survival in rapidly changing postindependence India.

As problems of human survival and the attainment of a better life become more acute, planning is becoming more widely accepted as a legitimate and necessary form of decision making. It is important to know, therefore, what planning is capable of achieving, and what it is not; which planning decisions and which outcomes are culture-specific and which are more readily transferable from one culture to another; and what kinds of planned change are, in terms of a human lifetime, unavoidable or irreversible.

In exploring these questions, this chapter first examines the overall chronology of planning for Bhubaneswar, including the different concepts of the New Capital which guided the principal actors involved in the capital's conception, and some of the major planning decisions and their consequences. Second, the planning process itself is reviewed in order to see how these decisions were reached. Third, three important factors in planning decisions are examined: the role of crisis, and the effects of an expanding bureaucracy and of increasing political pressure.

THE CHRONOLOGY OF PLANNING FOR BHUBANESWAR

There were, in effect, two distinct planning periods for the New Capital. They span twenty years and are separated by a period of construction based on the outline of the original plan drawn up by Otto H. Koenigsberger. The initial planning phase (1944-1951), which includes the site selection process, was characterized by the activity of a small number of highly placed decision makers in the Orissa Government, together with a distinguished foreign planner who was accorded high status and a free hand in the new town's design, and by the urgent necessity of establishing as quickly as possible the facilities minimally necessary for running the administration.

Fifteen years later there was no such urgency. The city's growth was thought to require a planned development program, but more important matters took priority. With the expansion of governmental activities, the loci of decision-making power had multiplied and diffused. In many instances, this made decision making more difficult and cumbersome. The town planners were now Indians employed as full-time government servants in a newly constituted, temporary town planning agency. And, finally, the apparent scope of planning activity was narrower than it had been in 1948.

This chapter draws upon material from both periods in order to highlight the evolution of planning decisions, their consequences, and the similarities and differences in the social, economic, and political contexts of planning at the outset and after the new city had become a reality.

Differing Concepts of the New Capital

The idea of a New Capital for Orissa meant different things to different people. During the middle and late 1940s, when the New Capital site was selected and planning started, these differences surfaced and the Orissa Government was faced with a series of controversial decisions. These concerned, first of all, where the New Capital should be, and second, what kind of place it should become.

Bhubaneswar was first thought of as a possible site in 1945 by B. K. Gokhale, then Advisor to

Governor Sir Hawthorne Lewis's caretaker government.[1] Pursuing the site selection question informally, Gokhale ultimately hit upon Bhubaneswar "as a flash...of...intuition" (Gokhale 1966:3). As his plan evolved, Gokhale saw Bhubaneswar as one-third of a Greater Cuttack scheme. This ambitious project was one of the government's many postwar reconstruction and development efforts. According to Gokhale's plan, Cuttack, Orissa's largest city and at that time the seat of provincial government, would remain as the principal commercial center; Chowdwar, a Cuttack suburb on the north bank of the Mahanadi River, would be developed as an industrial area; and Bhubaneswar, roughly twenty miles south of Cuttack, would become the New Capital as well as the chief educational and cultural center.

Advisor Gokhale visited Orissa's foremost citizen and political leader, Harekrushna Mahtab while Mahtab was still in prison for his Independence Movement activities. Gokhale realized that Mahtab would lead Orissa's first elected postwar ministry and eventually convinced him of the merits of Bhubaneswar as a site superior to crowded and riverbound Cuttack.

Mahtab was able to gain enough political support by late in 1946 to get Bhubaneswar chosen as the capital site. Those interested in the growth and development of Cuttack truncated Gokhale's vision for the new town, however. Under strong pressure from those interests, the new government decided that the High Court and Utkal University should remain at Cuttack, thus assuring that the foci of legal, educational, and cultural activity would remain there as well.

The Orissa Government felt an increasing urgency to establish itself in more spacious accomodations so that it could move ahead quickly with provincial development and handle the coming incorporation of Orissa's twenty-six princely states into the province. Thus, from the beginning, the government's concept of the New Capital was of an administrative colony, patterned roughly on the model of New Delhi. Cuttack was definitely to remain "the premier city of Orissa" (*Orissa Legislative Assembly Proceedings* 1948:50). As one Member of the Orissa Legislative Assembly put it: "...Bhubaneswar will be a sort of Washington of Orissa, but Cuttack will always remain its New York" (*OLA Proceedings* 1949:24). For example, in 1946 the Public Works Department anticipated that about three-fourths of the new city's projected population of 15,000 would be government servants and their families. This modest figure itself is a clue to the government's expectations regarding urban growth.

The limited amount of private development envisioned for Bhubaneswar was to be kept physically separate from government offices and residential quarters so as not to interfere with administrative functioning. Industrial development was also discouraged because, apart from the noise, dirt, and congestion it might entail, it posed the potential threat of labor troubles which might also adversely affect government activity.[2] It was these kinds of considerations that reinforced the idea of developing Chowdwar as an industrial center.

Given the generous amount of government-owned land available, the small projected population, and prevailing living patterns which called for much outdoor living, the government thought that single story construction would be most appropriate for the residences it would build for its employees. As to architectural style, the proximity of the old temple town and the towering Lingaraj Temple inspired Mahtab and the government to propose an architectural blend of "old and new" for the New Capital's main structures.

No development was projected at first for Old Bhubaneswar and the five villages which surrounded the New Capital site. The Old Town and two of the villages were across the railway line over a mile away from the site, and the government's primary aim was to move quickly on land it completely controlled. All that was done during 1946 and 1947, when jungle clearance of the site commenced, was to encourage people to settle near the New Capital site by selling some government-held land at bargain prices. Although there was brisk land speculation in and around the Old Town after the site was announced, this soon declined and did not resume for many years. Bhubaneswar was still known as a "wild" place where bandits and tigers could be found, and few people wanted to move there. As one official who was there from the beginning expressed it: "They [the government] were begging us to buy land there."

The actual town planning was done by several individuals in roughly three stages. In 1945 the government appointed Julius L. Vaz, a Goan from Bombay, Government Architect and assigned him the task of preparing a New Capital plan. Vaz was to remain in Orissa for fifteen years in this capacity and was closely associated with Bhubaneswar's development throughout this period. Vaz drew up an initial sketch of the new town based on population projections and other physical and cost guidelines given him by senior administrators in the Public Works Department, Finance Department, and other departments.

Soon afterward, engineers from the Public Works Department suggested that a town planning expert be brought in to advise on the planning. Vaz concurred. V. C. Mehta, a planner with experience in Kanpur and other cities, was retained. Then, in 1947, over a year after the Assembly had voted to move the capital to Bhubaneswar, a Chief Engineer suggested that Otto H. Koenigsberger be requested to assist in the planning effort. The government, even more pressed for time and still without an approved plan, quickly agreed, and in February 1948 Koenigsberger came to Orissa for the first time.

Koenigsberger was a European who had come to India in the 1930s and whose talent was much sought after there. His work included a development plan for the new steel-manufacturing city of Jamshedpur in the neighboring province of Bihar. At the time of the Orissa Government's invitation, Koenigsberger was in the service of the Maharaja of Mysore and had attained some reknown in governmental and professional circles. His reputation and his status as a distinguished foreigner influenced the government's choice.

Koenigsberger was well aware of the need to give priority to meeting the essential administrative and spatial requirements of the government. However, he viewed the capital in much broader terms than did his clients. He wrote:

> When New Delhi was planned, an administrative capital was a town mainly for Government officers and clerks. In 1948 the term 'administrative capital' means much more. It describes the lively nerve centre of provincial activities where workers and their representatives, manufacturers, businessmen, scientists, officials and last but not the least, politicians meet and collaborate in the development of all aspects of provincial life (Koenigsberger 1960:1).

Koenigsberger feared that a new "administrative caste" might arise from such a rigid occupational and spatial structure, one "as harmful to the country as the old castes we are trying to abolish"

(1960:2). The government had other views, and only Government Architect Vaz supported Koenigsberger's concept of diversified development.

Koenigsberger's recommendation for the form of local government was vetoed as well. He proposed a town council with representatives elected from the New Capital's neighborhood units. The government preferred to maintain direct and complete control over the town's administration through the state-appointed Notified Area Council (NAC), which had been established in 1948 for this purpose. This arrangement continued through 1967, by which time a strong local movement centered in Old Bhubaneswar had developed and was demanding municipal status and calling for municipal elections.

The Old Town was another bone of contention. Koenigsberger's plan was focused on the new administrative headquarters in accordance with the government's wishes. Nevertheless, Koenigsberger consistently urged that Old Bhubaneswar should receive more attention and that the entire Notified Area, which included both Old Town and New Capital, should be placed under strict government control to thwart land speculation and "haphazard" construction. He pressed the government to give priority to integrating the old and new towns and to assume greater authority over the area between the two settlements, particularly the area around the railway station. He warned that future slum problems would arise and suggested the enactment of a town planning act to direct Bhubaneswar's growth and that of other Orissan towns as well. The government eventually had a redevelopment scheme prepared for the transitional area between Old Bhubaneswar and the New Capital and expanded the NAC boundaries. A Town Planning Act was passed in 1956 but not promulgated until years later.

The most effective way of controlling private development proved to be the government's policy of limiting the amount and pace of the administrative relocation from Cuttack to Bhubaneswar. It was the combination of a continuing shortage of development funds and opposition from Cuttack that was responsible for this policy. It also dampened the enthusiasm of nongovernmental people for moving to Bhubaneswar until, in 1957, the government publicly committed itself to completing the capital.

As for the Old Town itself, it was not until Governor Katju toured Old Bhubaneswar in 1949 and expressed concern for the town's condition that the government supported the NAC Secretary's efforts to

provide improvements in the form of a better water
supply, paved drains, street lighting and the removal of encroachments on public roads. After this
spurt of activity, however, little was done to Old
Bhubaneswar for over a decade.

Koenigsberger's view on architectural design
also differed from that of the government. He
thought that the New Capital should be a modern city
which could stand proudly by the side of its famous
medieval sister. Here again, he met with opposition
from the government. Koenigsberger's plan for a
blend of old and new contrasted with Le Corbusier's
bold and widely acclaimed designs for the Punjab's
new capital at Chandigarh.

Koenigsberger's most important and lasting contribution was his basic sketch of the city's layout. It was a simple linear scheme depicting neighborhood units of roughly half a square mile arrayed
on either side of a central traffic artery. This
design made access to the main commercial area, central government complex, and surrounding countryside relatively easy for all and also provided for
future expansion.[3] Although government officials
adopted the main outline of Koenigsberger's plan,
they made some fairly substantial changes in it
which are discussed below.

Some Planning Decisions and Their Consequences

As the new city took shape, several factors intervened to further influence its evolution. Six
important areas about which decisions had to be made
will be discussed to illustrate this process: selection of a site for the New Capital, development of
the city as an administrative colony, adoption and
modification of the linear design, incorporation of
hierarchical principles into the city layout, setting standards for the construction and design of
housing, and treatment of Old Bhubaneswar.

New Capital site selection. The shift of the
government from Cuttack to Bhubaneswar was necessary
for Orissa's expanding administration to function
effectively. It meant a decline in Cuttack's influence as Orissa's first city, although perhaps less
of a decline than some of its businessmen anticipated. The building of the New Capital was the
source of a host of major changes in the lives of
people in Old Bhubaneswar and its nearby villages,
but chief among them were temporary economic booms
during the periods of peak construction from 1948 to

1951 and from 1957 to 1963. These boom periods were followed by declines in construction, however, which brought financial hardship to those families who no longer possessed cultivable land or who had depended on construction activity for income and had no other source of livelihood. The government's importation of labor from outside Orissa in order to expedite construction contributed to the problem because these people often remained in Bhubaneswar in squatter colonies after their employment ceased and competed with local people for scarce jobs.

In addition, the government acquired some land from the surrounding villages for the possible future expansion of the capital, and although they had been compensated, many families whose land had been taken ended up in financial difficulty. In the capital's early years, the government approached these villagers with offers of compensation for land to be taken at some time in the future. They could choose to be compensated in one of two ways: They could accept either a straight cash payment or a plot in a nearby jungle area that was scheduled to be cleared. These new plots would be owned in full by the villagers who agreed to the exchange. Most villagers elected to receive cash payments. Their lands were not actually acquired until several years later, and they continued to farm them. By this time, the villagers had spent most of the compensation money they had received, however, and few had been willing or able to take up new nonagricultural jobs in the capital. These people now suffered acute financial distress but had no legal recourse. Such experiences gave rise to much local anxiety when, in the mid-1960s, the government proposed to promulgate the Orissa Town Planning Act in order to control development in the Greater Bhubaneswar area. This anxiety influenced the pace and direction of planning for the capital's future growth.

The New Capital also brought with it an expansion of government jurisdiction which affected the temple-based power hierarchy of Old Bhubaneswar. For example, the Bhubaneswar NAC administered both the New Capital and Old Town. The NAC was dominated by the government and gradually assumed many of the duties and responsibilities traditionally held by the Lingaraj Temple trustees. As more and more younger residents of Old Bhubaneswar were educated and employed in the New Capital, they became more politically active and posed a further challenge to the old power structure.

The New Capital as administrative colony. After selecting the site for the new city, the government focused almost all its attention on establishing the administration in new accommodations as fast as possible. At this time it became apparent that the consequences of limiting the nongovernmental development of Bhubaneswar would be profound. Strict controls on the type of development permitted had to be enforced; there was a chronic lack of funds for construction; and strong anti-Bhubaneswar feelings from business interests in Cuttack had to be dealt with. These factors led to higher costs later on, lack of commercial and recreational services and facilities, which for many years caused people to "commute" to Cuttack for things they needed, and relatively little attention being paid Old Bhubaneswar and the peripheral villages.

The slow pace and rigid pattern of development resulted in fewer slums than probably would have arisen under other circumstances. However, the inadequate concern about providing space for the service population resulted in the formation of squatter settlements along the railway line between the New Capital and the Old Town and on the capital's outskirts. In later years, when more choice land was needed for commercial activities and for the capital's expansion, the squatters were subject to periodic eviction.

Another consequence of the selection of Bhubaneswar as the site for the new city and its early controlled growth was a spate of land speculation in and around Old Bhubaneswar followed for several years by a drop in such activity. Only after 1957, when Chief Minister Mahtab decided to complete the administration's move from Cuttack and the capital had filled up the first six neighborhood units in Koenigsberger's plan, did private interest in Bhubaneswar reawaken. This came about after Mahtab, in an effort to accelerate construction and obtain more funds for development, decided to lease out government land for the building of private homes. Thereafter, speculation in plot leases and land continued, and demand for space in the capital soared.

The linear plan and modifications. The government's adoption of Koenigsberger's linear layout of the capital was sound. Some substantial changes were made, however, which affected later development considerably. Among these was the conversion of one of the cross-streets into the main thoroughfare

(Rajpath) and the placement on it of the main shopping area. This change was made, apparently, because it ran between the first two neighborhood units to be built. In later years, people living in the northernmost units had to travel great distances to the town center (there was, in 1965, still no public transportation besides bicycle rickshaws), which would have been more centrally located had the original plan been adhered to. Several years after construction had started, new areas were developed to the southwest near the Agricultural College and the Governor's Residence, thereby abandoning the linear pattern until the 1960s. The shift of growth southward resulted in the incorporation of one village, encroachment upon another, and a further extension of the capital.

More important than the above changes was the government's decision to build even less densely than Koenigsberger had recommended. It had been agreed that single story construction was appropriate for residences, but the government did not expect Bhubaneswar to grow as large or as fast as Koenigsberger had projected, and in 1948 there appeared to be a very large supply of free land. Only years later, with the increasing demand for more land and the benefit of hindsight, did officials realize the cost of this extravagant early land policy. Thus, single story dwellings were discontinued in 1961 in favor of multi-story flats. These dwellings were disliked because of their small floor area and minimal outside space (balconies were no real substitute for courtyards and rear yards), high density, limited privacy, and relative lack of storage space, but the administration felt constrained to build them. In any case, officials reasoned that people would adjust to them as they had in Bombay.

Hierarchy and physical design. As in any government administration, the sense and reality of hierarchy in Bhubaneswar were strong and overt. The main government buildings—the Secretariat, the Assembly, the Governor's Residence—dominated the skyline just as Lingaraj Temple dominated the view of Old Bhubaneswar (see photos in Chapter 1). More significant, though, was the physical analogue of the administrative hierarchy that the New Capital became as a consequence of the official approach to residential design, construction, and allocation. The senior officials were provided with accomodations in Bhubaneswar first because they were considered indispensable to the administration's operations

especially during the turbulent period just after
Partition, Independence, and the incorporation of
the princely states. These officials, therefore,
resided close to government offices and the center
of the city. This fact was less important, however,
than the actual process of designing and allocating
quarters for all civil servants.

The government reasoned that the housing allotment process should be public and based on merit.
A series of quarters were designed by the Government
Architect for all levels of service, from Type II
two-room quarters for junior clerks up to Type VIII
six-room quarters for ministers and senior officers.
Accommodations were allocated on the basis of official rank and salary, which were public; rents,
which were subsidized, were commensurate with the
type of dwelling.

In the first neightborhood units to be built,
widely different quarters were erected adjacent to
one another, in accordance with the government's and
Koenigsberger's idea that various levels of civil
servant should live in the same locality. There was
apparently some ill-feeling generated by the very
visible disparities in accommodations, however, and
later units either were composed of more subtly
graded residential types or were more homogeneous.
Thus, the government built a physical representation
of its own social structure, and a new set of status
symbols was adopted as residents became conscious of
the number of rooms, windows, and water taps each
house had and whether flowers or vegetables were
planted in front or rear yards.

This hierarchical analogue was apparent in private development as well. Areas and plots were allocated according to official status or income range.
The largest and most expensive plots were located in
the southern and southwestern fringes of the New
Capital near the original development. Smaller and
cheaper plots, including most of those designated
for nongovernment people, were developed along the
railway line to the east, across the railway on the
Old Bhubaneswar side, and to the north following the
linear pattern.

Housing standards and supply. The Orissa Government was committed from the outset to providing
improved living conditions for its constituents, including the civil servants who were to reside in the
New Capital. To this end, they opted for single
story construction which was consistent with prevailing living styles. This decision was made even

Type VIII Senior
Officer's quarter.

NEW CAPITAL

Government Quarters.

Government flats.

Type IV quarter.

NEW CAPITAL

Government quarter with hut attached.

Rickshaw pullers' huts (Railway Zone).

though in 1948 most of the administration's senior officers were not native Orissans. Moreover, the government sought to maintain relatively high standards of design and construction. This was attested to later when demand was highest for the oldest quarters which were thought to be better designed and better built than later models. The quarters built later on were more spartan than the earlier ones because of rising costs and were less desirable for the reasons already enumerated above. Nevertheless, in spite of some design limitations, the New Capital provided better housing than was available in most urban areas of India. Surprisingly, notwithstanding rising construction costs and recurring criticism of the administration in the Legislative Assembly, by 1965 roughly two-thirds of all civil servants in Bhubaneswar had been allotted government quarters. The private service population had to fend for itself, however.

Development of Old Bhubaneswar. Except for the brief but intense period of ameliorative activity initiated by the NAC Secretary and the Governor in 1949, Old Bhubaneswar received little attention from the government until the early 1960s. At this time a nonpartisan group began agitating for municipal status and elections. Achievement of these goals would insure that Old Bhubaneswar would receive what the group considered its rightful share of development funds and that its residents would participate fully in decisions concerning the Old Town. This movement had its roots in local political struggles which had little to do with the New Capital itself. It did reflect the administration's lack of concern for the Old Town, which was physically on the other side of the tracks from the seat of government and the New Capital status and power hierarchies. The government eventually agreed to hold elections, but these were postponed indefinitely in 1962 because of the national emergency caused by the Indo-China border dispute.

In planning for Greater Bhubaneswar, the Town Planning Organization, the Central Town and Country Planning Organization, and the Orissa Government agreed that the Old Town should be preserved as a national historic and cultural site of major importance, its temples and tanks restored and maintained, and strict controls put on further construction. Having arrived at this decision, official attention turned to more critical matters such as whether the capital should expand to the north or south and where the future center should be located. The immediate concerns of the residents of Old Bhubaneswar were not issues for the town planners at this stage. The Greater Bhubaneswar Master Plan was a general land use plan, and only after it had been approved could the government prepare a city development plan incorporating specific local schemes. This was the planning procedure as outlined and advocated by the Central Town and Country Planning Organization in Delhi. In the meantime, the Bhubaneswar NAC was the appropriate official body to handle Old Town problems.

The recommendation that the Old Town be preserved also provided a partial rationale for maintaining it as an entity separate from the capital, thus avoiding the issue of extending representative local government to Bhubaneswar. This question was raised again in 1964. The government wanted to keep the entire settlement, or at the very least, the New Capital, under its complete control, much as Washington, D.C. is a creature of the United States Government. Again, these were not matters which concerned the Orissa Town Planning Organization. Its mandate was only to prepare the land-use plan for Greater Bhubaneswar.

THE PLANNING PROCESS

The preceding sections have described the most crucial decisions made for Bhubaneswar's planning and construction, the concepts guiding these decisions, and some of their anticipated and unanticipated consequences. This section explores the process by which decisions were made over the twenty year period in question.

To the Government of Orissa in 1948 town planning mainly meant town layout design. For this purpose the government consulted Koenigsberger, whose recommendations actually went beyond the government's expectations. The administration set the financial, physical, and social parameters of the project; Koenigsberger's task was to find a spatial expression for them. The amount of assistance available from the Government of India determined the financial scope and the pace of the project. Decisions concerning which departments would shift and when guided the determination of acreage requirements and housing needs. Project reports containing estimated costs and construction schedules were drawn up and revised by Public Works Department engineers on the basis of the budgets and departmental moving schedules provided by a few senior officials in the Finance Department and other departments. Koenigsberger and Vaz then prepared town and neighborhood designs showing streets and principal land uses, as well as a design for the main administrative complex.

The process by which this happened will be briefly outlined. Periodic meetings were held on various aspects of the project. These meetings were chaired by the Chief Secretary, who was the senior official in the administration. Occasionally ministers attended these meetings, but this was unusual. Regular attendants included the Chief Engineer and the Secretary of the Public Works Department,[4] the Government Architect, and other relevant departmental secretaries and executive heads. Decisions made at these gatherings were sent for approval to the Minister of Works and other relevant ministers. Having met with their approval, cost estimates, if needed, were prepared by the Government Architect and the Superintending Engineer, who was Vaz's immediate superior. These estimates were then submitted for higher level approval. A proposal direct from Koenigsberger was given top priority and was usually forwarded by the Works Secretary to the highest levels for prompt disposition. Most of his recommendations dealing with other than physical aspects of the New Capital were turned down, however, although his less sensitive design suggestions were quickly approved. The administrative approval process outlined above remained the typical way in which decisions were reached during construction and much later when planning for the New Capital's expansion began. There were some important differences between these two phases, however, which will become apparent below.

The high levels of intensity, attention, and dispatch which characterized the New Capital's early planning gradually decreased, especially after Koenigsberger's association with the project ceased in 1951. From that time until 1957, the government's interest in Bhubaneswar focused on three main issues: financing construction, deciding which departments would shift from Cuttack and when, and providing housing for government employees. The availability of funds and shifting political pressure for or against the New Capital led to an uneven development pace and to departures from the Koenigsberger plan. Throughout this period, most decision making had to do with the selection of sites for major structures and the location of additional government housing within the spatial framework of the six neighborhood units outlined in the Koenigsberger plan.

Meanwhile, Bhubaneswar's early champion, Chief Minister Mahtab, had joined the Government of India for a few years and then returned to Orissa in 1956 to resume leadership of the Orissa Government. Upon his return, Mahtab decided to complete the administrative shift from Cuttack to Bhubaneswar. To do this, he had the New Capital project inserted into Orissa's Second Five Year Plan as a priority item and accelerated the construction of both residences and official buildings.

Because the capital had reached the limits of the Koenigsberger layout, a way of coping with further expansion was needed. Mahtab decided to lease out large amounts of government land in and around the New Capital for private residential construction. This had been tried several times before, but with neither determination nor success. Now that the government had clearly chosen to stay in Bhubaneswar, the decision brought prompt results. Cooperative house-building societies were established, and land was allotted to them. A steady demand for house plots became a fact of life in the New Capital from that time on.

Another method of handling expansion was to build more flats. This alternative had been studied during the Second Five Year Plan, but was decided upon only in 1961 when Bijoyananda Patnaik succeeded Mahtab as Chief Minister. The decision was made as part of Patnaik's new policy of conserving scarce land throughout Orissa and of attempting to reduce housing costs. Neither the decision regarding private development nor that regarding the construction of flats was considered a town planning question by the administrators or ministers. Both decisions were based mainly on initiatives taken by Chief Ministers Mahtab and Patnaik; the administrators worked out the details, particularly the cost implications. Government Architect Vaz and his successors had little to do beyond site layout and structural design, and all of their work was carried out within strict administrative guidelines.

Bhubaneswar's expansion led to renewed town planning activity. In 1958 the Orissa Government invited the Ford Foundation's Urban Planning team, then being consulted on the preparation of the Delhi Regional Plan, to advise them on Bhubaneswar's future development. The Ford team met with Orissa officials and particularly with Government Architect Vaz, who was charged with looking after town planning matters. Several planning guidelines were specified: (1) Bhubaneswar's expansion should be northward as suggested by Koenigsberger's linear layout; (2) a distinct separation should nonetheless be maintained between the cities of Bhubaneswar and Cuttack, some twenty miles away; (3) as Koenigsberger had also recommended, Bhubaneswar should accept more diversified economic and social development; (4) higher residential densities should be permitted; (5) multi-story construction should be seriously considered; and (6) development on the capital's periphery should be firmly controlled. These points were to form the basis for immediate expansion as well as for the Greater Bhubaneswar Master Plan, on which work began in 1962.

The planning of Greater Bhubaneswar occurred in roughly two phases. The first, from 1962 to mid-1964, resulted in the preparation of a preliminary plan for an area of about 172 square miles, with expansion to the north, south, and west. This work was initiated at a top priority meeting of senior officials headed by the Works Secretary in August 1962. This group recommended that the Government Architect, Simon Solomon Reuben (Vaz's successor, who was on deputation to the Orissa Government from the Government of India), be provided with a staff by the Local Self-Government Department to undertake the required survey work. The Local Self-Government Department was responsible for municipal affairs and town planning, although the Government Architect was formally part of the Public Works Department. Thus, as in 1945, planning began with a broad sketch done by the Government Architect.

Out of the same meeting came the proposal that the Orissa Town Planning and Improvement Trust Act of 1956 be activated for the New Capital area as soon as possible in order to curb rapid and uncontrolled expansion. The officials concluded that it might be necessary to remove some villages from under the administration of Cuttack District and incorporate them into that of Puri District, in which the New Capital was to be located, for administrative and jurisdictional reasons; the Bhubaneswar Notified Area limits might also have to be extended to include these villages. While this rearrangement appears relatively innocuous, it became a sensitive issue later on.

The high level meeting was a device used by the administration to raise issues, discuss options, and reach decisions. Because of the expansion of governmental activity and the growth of the administrative structure, such meetings became more inclusive; lower echelon officials and technicians were called in.

As a rule, decision making still remained centralized at the highest levels, but other influences began to encroach upon what had been, under the British, the exclusive preserve of senior administrators.

Orissa's Governor, Ajudhia Nath Khosla, became actively interested in planning for Greater Bhubaneswar during this time. He suggested a large planning area and an extended time frame, and his interest gave the planning work somewhat more importance in the minds of the administrators than it might otherwise have had. In fact, Governor Khosla, by virtue of his temperament and technical training, was rather more than the usual figurehead. Both he, particularly because of his position as Governor, and Chief Minister Patnaik symbolized the active, development-oriented stance of the Orissa Government during this time by the construction of several government and government related institutions, the building of flat blocks, and the resurgence of town planning.

The next phase of Greater Bhubaneswar planning began in April 1964 with a meeting at the Governor's Residence to discuss town planning in Orissa. The Governor mentioned that he had invited the Ford Foundation to advise on town and village planning projects in several localities, including Bhubaneswar.[5] This invitation had undoubtedly been discussed previously with Chief Minister Patnaik, who had initiated the planning and construction of a new port and township at Paradip, an iron ore exporting terminal on Orissa's coast.

In July 1964, D. R. K. Patnaik was hired as Town Planner, and other staff members were retained shortly thereafter. The Orissa Town Planning Organization was established as part of the Local Self-Government Department with five offices to cover the state, including one in Bhubaneswar.[6] Once again, town planning expertise was sought by the government after the initial sketch was completed by the architect. This time, however, the planners were not foreigners. (It was decided to retain Ford Foundation aid for towns other than Bhubaneswar.) A town planning process existed with well-defined stages and procedures, and financial and technical assistance was being provided by the Government of India as part of the Third Five Year Plan. As in the first planning period of years earlier, however, after the first burst of interest at the highest levels, the town planning effort came to be viewed as relatively unimportant.

The most pressing issue facing the government was the delimitation of the boundaries of the expanded Bhubaneswar Notified Area and the Greater Bhubaneswar Master Plan area. This was the first step that had to be taken, for administrative control over future growth required extension of the NAC's jurisdiction, while promulgation of the Town Planning Act in new areas required designation of those areas so that a list of villages to be included could be compiled. The Act had not previously been applied to Bhubaneswar; only in 1960 had it been applied elsewhere in Orissa because of public apprehension about the use of land acquisition powers and apparently because of inadequate official assurances that fair compensation would be given. The subject was raised in the Assembly, where Local Self-Government Department Minister Biren Mitra said:

> The necessity of this Act was well felt in 1956. But this was not enforced then pending ensuring the support of the general public for this Act. It would not be proper to enforce any act disregarding the general opinion (*OLA Debates* 1961:7-8).

Extending the NAC limits raised questions regarding the extent to which the provision of urban services and consequent increased taxation should be spread to previously rural areas and whether or not financing would be available to back up a commitment to provide services. The transfer of the Cuttack villages to Puri District was a problem because it would cause villagers the inconvenience of having to travel farther to the new district headquarters in order to transact their business.

Issues surrounding the size of the planning and NAC areas, the direction of expansion, and whether or not the areas of expansion should be coterminous became both technical and political. The controversy involved both the political and administrative hierarchies of government, the Town Planning Organization, the Central Town and Country Planning Organization, and even the military.

The Indian Army entered the picture because of Chief Minister Patnaik's proposal of a couple of years earlier that a military cantonment be located at Bhubaneswar. If the cantonment were located there, the 8,000 acre site north of the capital tentatively set aside for it by the Orissa Government would require shifting the bulk of future urban development, as outlined in the Master Plan, to the south. However, nearly all of the southern area was rural, and many villages did not want to be taxed for urban services they did not need and probably would not get for some time. In addition, the Central Town and Country Planning Organization, which had some influence because it reviewed the Orissa Town Planning Organization's progress reports and budget requests, had recommended that the capital be "redensified," that vacant areas be filled up, and that new development be reduced to a minimum in order to conserve land, especially cultivable land.

The master planning process was held up until the cantonment issue was resolved. Town planner Patnaik proposed that the cantonment site be moved westward to permit urban development to the north. He urged his superior, Local Self-Government Department Secretary Armit Lal Nair, to seek an early decision from the Government of India as to whether or not there would be a cantonment at Bhubaneswar at all. Finally, in 1965 the Central Government decided not to locate a cantonment there for logistical reasons, and planning proceeded once more.

It was also in mid-1965 that an ad hoc committee of senior officials met for the first time under the chairmanship of the Deputy Chief Minister to discuss the Master Plan/NAC boundary issue. The Town Planner had repeatedly urged that such a body meet, but until that time he had not been successful. The committee, which met just before the cantonment issue was finally settled, suggested, among other things, that legal provision be made for expansion in a southerly direction. After the cantonment decision, however, investigations of northward expansion were resumed from the Chief Secretary's level on down.

The Town Planner had little influence on these high level decisions. As a technician, he directed several revisions of the master plan during 1965 and 1966 so that it would conform with the administration's latest position on NAC boundaries. The Plan was a preliminary land-use layout, showing large blocks of land zoned for residential, institutional, commercial, and other uses. Detailed development schemes for these new areas and for existing areas of the capital were to follow in accord with official procedure.

The draft of the Greater Bhubaneswar Master Plan was eventually approved by the Local Self-Government Department and forwarded to the Deputy Chief Minister with a request to convene the ad hoc committee again for formal approval. This meeting occurred in December 1966, but the Deputy Chief Minister then suggested further study of areas south of the capital. This suggestion was one consequence of continued agitation from the Cuttack District villages against being shifted to Puri District and the apparent new interest of some southern villages in being included in the expanded NAC. Eventually, the big decision was postponed until after the Fourth General Election of February 1967. A new coalition government was elected in Orissa, and things were further postponed until a new ad hoc committee could be constituted to resolve the issue. Throughout this entire process, the administration demonstrated relatively little concern for the content of the draft Master Plan. Nearly everyone involved—politicians, administrators, engineers, planners—thought that town planning was of little consequence. This attitude was, first of all, a function of the Indian planning profession's concept of the planning process and its goals, as interpreted by the Government of India and Orissa planners and acquiesced to by ranking administrators. From this point of view, the immediate necessity was to publish a master land-use plan to control all development within an urban area until detailed development plans and projects could be prepared. But as Orissa Local Self-Government Department Secretary and Town Planning Director Nair frequently pointed out, this process had a major weakness in that it was almost impossible to control development during the long and pains-taking process of preparing the master plan. In the case of the Greater Bhubaneswar Master Plan, for instance, work began in 1962, and the plan had still not been approved by the end of July 1967. Meanwhile, construction of more government quarters, offices, private homes, and peripheral squatter shacks continued.

What was needed was a simple interim plan which could be produced and made legally binding in a few months and which could control ongoing government and private construction, while providing an overall structure for the comprehensive plan to follow. Secretary Nair wanted Town Planner Patnaik and his staff to insert this recommendation directly into the revised Town Planning Act on which they were working in addition to their work on the Master Plan. In the absence of such an interim plan, the situation was more or less as a senior architect described it:

> They are doing just paper planning. They are never seeing that one of their plans is executed. They never enforce the Town Planning Act. They never give check [sic] on unauthorized constructions. By the time

> the plan is published, it is too late.
> Why should a fellow wait for your plan?
> Let us put [sic] some plan, some sensi-
> ble plan, and execute it rather than
> wait for the best plan.

This statement mirrors the frustration of the planners themselves, who were quite aware of the limitations within which they labored but who had no power to alter things beyond whatever personal influence they might have with their departmental superiors. The opinion also reflects the tension that existed between the planners and architects, and the Estate Officer's Capital Administrative Branch. The Estate Officer, who was in the Political and Services Department, was responsible for land development and administration in the capital. His job included site selection for new construction, which was done in consultation with the planners, the Public Works Department, and other officials; allocation of government quarters; and distribution of plots for private house building and commercial construction. In short, he held a very important and influential position. In the 1960s, the Estate Officer was under extreme pressure to develop new land for private and institutional construction. The planners preferred to have their plan approved first, but development could not be held in abeyance while this was done. Thus, several conflicts over land use allocation occurred during the course of the planning process, usually resulting in a plan revision.

The limitations of this mainly regulatory view of planning were forcefully criticized by an Indian Administrative Service officer, writing for the 1966 town planning seminar held in Bhubaneswar:

> To expect that controlled land use will
> be anything more than a mere trickle of
> a solution for such overwhelming prob-
> lems, is to demonstrate an unjustifiable
> and excessive concern with abstract
> notions of balance and harmony in physi-
> cal planning (Kutty 1966:26).

The regulatory approach was derived to a great extent from Western planning concepts of the time. Land use controls, slum clearance, and comprehensive planning were considered the chief means of controlling urban growth. This view reinforced some long-standing official attitudes toward the New Capital's planning. In 1948 Koenigsberger's planning proposals were faced with opposition from several fronts: from politicians sensitive to the conservative views of their constituents, from status-conscious officials concerned with retaining the traditional forms of government they had recently inherited from the British, from those same officials seeking to minimize the potential for political and social unrest in the capital, from the architect and others interested in aesthetics, and from engineers eager to complete the construction. In 1965, Town Planner Patnaik and his staff were faced with the frustrating task of formulating a master plan which they, and the administration generally, expected to be out of date by the time it would be approved, but which would be less controversial if formulated in this manner than in a more unconventional way.

FACTORS AFFECTING THE PLANNING PROCESS

The preceding analysis of the Bhubaneswar planning process suggests three important factors that may influence the way in which decisions are made: Crisis may be a catalyst for planning decisions; an expanding bureaucratic structure may affect the planning process; and political pressure may become increasingly influential in determining the direction of growth as construction gets underway. These factors will now be examined.

The Role of Crisis in Planning Decisions

The process of planning and building the New Capital was mainly a series of governmental responses to particular crises as perceived by those who were the key decision makers at the moment.[7] Several examples will illustrate this point.

The great pressure to provide accommodations for governmental activities spurred the search for a New Capital site and accelerated the process of approving the basic layout for the new town. In fact, Prime Minister Nehru's agreement to lay the capital's foundation stone in April 1948 prompted the Orissa Government to ask Koenigsberger to hasten preparation of his layout plan so that it would be ready in time for the foundation ceremony. He was given less than six weeks to devise it.

Once construction was underway, its slow and uneven pace was at least partly caused by the administration's need to handle more urgent problems, such as floods and refugee resettlement. Although

Chief Minister Mahtab was well aware of the necessity of providing adequate work space for the administration, his successor, former Gandhian worker Nabakrushna Chowduri, had a different opinion and channeled funds to the rural areas in preference to Bhubaneswar and Cuttack.

After the political disturbances of 1956 surrounding the reorganization of the states, Mahtab's return to Orissa and his prompt decision to complete the administration's shift to Bhubaneswar created still another crisis situation. This was heightened by increased government activity related to the Second Five Year Plan which was being initiated then and was much larger in scope than the First Plan. Decisions to encourage private residential development and to undertake slum clearance to make land available for it were soon implemented. The building of flats was later also resorted to as yet another means of accommodating the capital's rapidly growing population.

Chief Minister Patnaik's vigorous efforts to bring more public institutions, business establishments, and activities to Bhubaneswar added to the town's growth in the early 1960s and stimulated the planning of Greater Bhubaneswar as well as the construction of flats. It was Patnaik who initiated the proposal for a military cantonment, which also influenced the planning process. The active Patnaik was also instrumental in arranging to have the All India Congress Committee meeting of 1964 held in Bhubaneswar. In order to house all the delegates, an entire neighborhood unit was built in record time, and another wave of slum clearance swept through the railway zone's squatter colonies and other such settlements in the capital.

Finally, the 1967 General Election delayed completion of the Greater Bhubaneswar Master Plan, especially because of two sensitive issues: drawing the master planning and NAC boundaries and transferring the six Cuttack District villages to Puri District. The government chose to defer action on these matters until after the election was over, thus delaying completion of the Master Plan but not further development, which went on as usual without much reference to the draft plan.

The town planners, first Koenigsberger and Government Architect Vaz, and later Patnaik, were aware of the pressing issues of their respective periods. They also were acutely conscious of the need for rapid official action to guide the New

Capital's development, both at the outset and fifteen years later. The senior administrators who actually had day-to-day decision-making power tended to focus their attention on items requiring immediate attention, however, and the New Capital was not one of these except at its very inception. This narrowing of administrative concern became increasingly necessary as the burden of work increased, especially for top level officials. According to one Indian Administrative Service officer:

> If you have a good program...and want it badly enough, you can get it through and implemented properly. This means that one must stay on top of the file, know where it is at any given time, and keep it moving. The minute you lose track of it, all may be lost. By this aggressive behavior, you can have the business expedited. In response to my suggestion that only a small quantity of business would be transacted if so much energy had to be devoted to getting each particular bit passed, most agreed. One must decide, they said, on priorities.[8]

Another reason for the delay in approving the Greater Bhubaneswar Master Plan boundaries, for instance, concerned the relative lack of top official interest. One senior Indian Administrative Service officer put it thusly: "The delay was not due to a search for perfection, rather a lack of interest at certain levels, or the need to realize the importance of it." If the "top men" did not get personally involved, little, if anything, could be accomplished. The problem was summed up by one of the architectural staff:

> After all, what is Government? It is the architect, the chief engineer, the administrator. If one officer is interested, he can get the plan implemented. Officially or personally I'll see the Secretary, the Chief Engineer, or whomever. But no one takes interest.

The Influence of An Expanding Bureaucracy

Between 1945 and 1965 the Orissa Government gradually enlarged its administration to keep up with the demands of development. In 1950 there were only fifty-two Indian Civil Service and Administrative Service officers in the Orissa cadre which was allowed ninety-six officers; in 1963 there were 100 Indian Administrative Service officers out of a sanctioned strength of 144 (*OLA Debates* 1963:22-23). An even more striking indication of growth was the increase in the number of workers involved in planning. From one Chief Engineer and a Government Architect grew a Town Planning Organization which, in 1965, was composed of five planning units. One consequence of this bureaucratic expansion was a partial diffusion of decision making across departmental lines and downward through the hierarchy. The former trend is illustrated by the overlapping activities of the Town Planning Organization, the Estate Officer, and the Public Works Department. The latter trend is exemplified by the many situations in which hard-pressed senior officials limited their concern to top priority matters and left less important questions, such as the New Capital, for subordinates to handle. Thus, while the development of sites for private construction and the allocation of private plots received attention at the highest levels of government, the process of approving flat designs and site plans received perfunctory treatment after the initial decision to build flats had been made. This was the result of both the increase in top-level workloads and the greater complexity of the administrative structure. The former, coupled with the lower priority accorded the capital in the 1960s as compared to 1948, resulted in rather unimaginative site development; the latter, in increasing the elapsed time between approval and completion of construction, thereby heightened the housing shortage. One private building contractor contrasted decision making in the 1960s with that of the capital's early days: "They took decisions quickly in those days." The increasing amount of time needed for decision making particularly affected the usefulness of town planning proposals, which required fairly quick responses in order to be effective: for example, allocating land for future development before it disappeared. It also explains the frustration experienced by the town planners and the lack of attention given by the administration to what was considered to be only "paper planning."

The continued growth of the administration and division of functions had another effect on the New Capital in addition to prolonging decisions. It produced a decline in the influence of town planners relative to that of former town planner Koenisberger and architect Vaz. In 1948 politicians and administrators considered town planning to be mainly a matter of layout design. Nevertheless, the housing crisis, the shortage of technical people in government, Governor Katju's concern for Old Bhubaneswar, and Koenigsberger's status as a distinguished "outside expert" led to his and Vaz's continuous participation in New Capital decision making, with the exception of basic decisions concerning financial issues and the shifting of departments to the New Capital.

By 1965, however, the New Capital already existed as a sizable city. Besides the Town Planning Organization and a much larger Public Works Department, the Estate Officer and his Capital Administration Branch existed to handle what amounted to city government in concert with the NAC, of which the Estate Officer was Secretary *ex-officio*. Even though Town Planner Patnaik and Deputy Government Architect Adikanda Biswal (Reuben's successor in the Public Works Department) sat on the site-selection committee with the Estate Officer to determine where new buildings, such as the bus terminal and proposed stadium, would be located, they had far less influence than the Estate Officer. His importance stemmed from his position in the powerful Political and Services Department whose chief, the Development Commissioner, was one of the three senior officials in the administration; from his involvement in the capital's day-to-day administration, which enabled him to make appeals for immediate action, especially regarding further private residential development (in contrast to the planners' longer-range view and less urgent responsibilities); from his role as NAC Secretary, which gave him great authority over matters relating to the Old Town (with which the Town Planner was not concerned beyond recommending its preservation); and from his role as State Protocol Officer, which gave him better access to ministers and top officials.

Increasing Political Pressure

The roles played by democratically elected representatives, and by the whole political structure which paralleled the administrative machinery, became increasingly influential ones in relation to Bhubaneswar's development. These influences took various forms and had various effects.

The centralization of decision-making power was personified by the chief ministers, who were powerful catalysts for action and who acted as guides for the type, pace, and direction of the New Capital's growth. For example, Mahtab was instrumental in getting Bhubaneswar selected as the site: Advisor Gokhale had to obtain Mahtab's cooperation even though he was still in prison; and Mahtab had to arrange a political compromise with Cuttack's economic and political interests before the Assembly finally ratified the decision. Mahtab also provided the impetus to get construction of the capital underway and pushed successfully for its expansion during his second term. Between Mahtab's two terms, Chief Minister Choudhury lowered the New Capital's priority in the interest of rural development and in response to renewed Cuttack opposition to the administration's move to Bhubaneswar. During his ministry budgets for the construction of the New Capital were reduced, the pace of development was slowed, and the Public Works Department was instructed to explore less expensive housing designs. Attempts to modify the original designs for government quarters to reflect local criticisms (e.g., larger rear yards and verandahs were preferred) occurred during Choudhury's tenure. Chief Minister Biju Patnaik's concern for developing the New Capital as an institutional center, rather than just an administrative colony, his decision to construct flats in preference to single-story dwellings, and his tendency to initiate action without going through normal administrative channels all stimulated a new round of planning and construction activity.

Important members of the Chief Minister's cabinets also had increasing influence over the New Capital's planning and construction. Chief Minister Choudhury's Finance Minister was a Cuttack resident who owned an important Oriya newspaper published in Cuttack; in the early 1950s he supported a reduced level of New Capital construction activity. The Works Minister for many years was also the Member of the Orissa Legislative Assembly representing Bhubaneswar. He was almost always involved in any decision of importance concerning Bhubaneswar, and as Works Minister, he directed the Public Works Department's capital construction activities. After the Town Planning Organization was reconstituted in 1964 the Deputy Chief Minister played an important role in the preparation of the Greater Bhubaneswar Master Plan, particularly in determining the direction of expansion. Villagers in Cuttack District, as well as those south of Bhubaneswar in Puri District, expressed their concerns through the political network.

Both groups received favorable attention at various points in time, although the administration eventually left the whole redistricting issue for a new ministry to resolve. The Orissa Assembly itself was, of course, extremely important because it voted on such matters as the selection of the site for the New Capital and the construction budgets. Usuallly the incumbent ministry gathered support for its position before putting it to a vote, but the Members of the Orissa Legislative Assembly had to be consulted nonetheless. The governors, though not normally active in administrative matters, occasionally influenced particular decisions. The most striking instances of this were Governor Katju's concern for improvements in Old Bhubaneswar in 1949 and Governor Khosla's interest in urban development and planning for Greater Bhubaneswar during the early 1960s.

The administrators' authority was clearly waning; it had been absolute before Independence, except for the brief interregnum of representative government from 1937 to 1939. The shift toward a more representative structure also affected the details of decision making, partly because of particular demands made on ministers and members of the Orissa Legislative Assembly by constituents and partly because of the ministers' own rising self-confidence. As one minister reported:

> In 1948, the ministers were not really conscious of their powers. They were content with laying down broad general policy, and leaving everything else to the administration. Every year this awareness of their importance and power increased. And they are taking increasing interest in every detail of the proposals. They get involved in all kinds of petty details, like who gets assigned to what job, which are best left to the administrators. Among administrators, there is a growing feeling on their part that they must work to maintain peace with politicians. They used to be more of the complete boss (quoted in Taub 1969:109).

The problem for the administration grew because of the increasing presence of technicians, engineers, planners, and others in the now more numerous executive branches of government. For example, the ad hoc committees and working groups convened to work out issues having to do with the construction and expansion of the capital now had increased technical assistance. Rivalry between administrator and technician became acute. According to one technical officer, talking about the New Capital project:

> The opinion of the technical fellow was never taken into consideration by the higher fellows, the political fellows. [The administrators]...are administering the whole capital.... They decide everything; not the architect, the chief engineer, or anybody else is consulted.
> In my opinion, in a new place, like Chandigarh,[9] the architect should build everything, not the administrator....
> As long as development is going on, the architect should be responsible.

The other side of the coin is illustrated by the following anecdote. Three senior administrators were discussing a high-level vacancy. One said that a resolution had been passed by the Orissa Engineers' Association that this post should be kept reserved for a technical man. A second officer commented, "The administration would collapse in a minute." The third officer said, "It would be a waste of a talent. It is not a technical post." With some insight into the nature of intrabureaucratic competition, the second officer then replied, "All it means is that some assistant engineer will be promoted to executive, an executive will be promoted, and so on." All agreed, however, that an administrator should continue to hold the position.

Another obvious indication of the rising influence of the political structure on both administrative and technical functions in Bhubaneswar was the movement for local self-government. In spite of the fact that urban local self-government was the first British effort to expand self-rule in India, after Independence many Indian administrators felt that the people were unaware of their civic responsibilities and, therefore, needed a few more years of "guided democracy." In Orissa, this opinion was partially responsible for the lack of direct participation by the population in the town planning process beyond the legal requirement enabling them to make comments on draft master plans once they had been published by the government. On the other hand, there was little done to interest people in these long-range plans; their only concern, as evidenced by the questions raised during reviews of the plans, was whether or not their land might be taken by the government for some development activity. Of more importance to the people was the issue of local elections, which was not a matter for the planners and other technicians. The government continued to find the status quo more satisfactory than holding local elections, however, at least until 1967.

Meanwhile, the Town Planning Organization, faced with bureaucratic sluggishness, changing political currents and demands, the low priority accorded its work, the insecurity resulting from temporary status, and the knowledge that there were funds for master planning but little or none for implementation, proceeded to prepare alternative master plan after alternative master plan in response to administrative needs. They were able to make their technical views known and to stimulate decision making on the cantonment location issue, but on few other issues. Other spatial planning decisions either did not warrant high level consideration or, as with the planning area NAC boundary question, were sensitive enough to require treatment at the highest levels of government.

CONCLUSION

The intention of the Orissa Government to build a new state capital at Bhubaneswar resulted in the construction of a new city that was different, both from most Indian cities and from the kind of urban development that probably would have evolved without planning activity. The generally higher physical standards, linear town layout and neighborhood units, hierarchical pattern of official and private housing, multi-story flats, comparatively few squatter settlements, shortage of commercial and recreational services, concentration of development activity on the New Capital rather than the existing old temple town, and lack of elected local government were all consequences of deliberate planning decisions.

Planning activity, both explicit in the work of town planners and implicit in administrative decision making, was influenced, in turn, by the social, economic, and political contexts in which it occurred. By and large, after the decision was made to shift the administration to Bhubaneswar and the first increment of construction was completed around 1951, the New Capital was given a relatively low priority by the government. This was primarily a function of initial political opposition to the capital project, chronically insufficient funds for planning and construction, the government's conception of the New Capital as an administrative colony rather than a new city, and, later, more pressing developmental concerns. Koenigsberger's broad and ambitious conception of the New Capital was, for the most part, unacceptable to the political and administrative decision makers of the time; Koenigsberger was planning for change, whereas they were planning mainly for stability. Fifteen years later, the accepted view of town planning as mainly a regulatory activity carried out through master planning limited the role of the town planners in influencing the capital's future development. In addition, the expanding administrative machinery, and the increasing influence of the political structure on the administration, further diffused the government's decision-making ability with regard to Bhubaneswar's growth.

The consequences of town planning activity were significant, nonetheless. Koenigsberger and architect Vaz influenced the capital's basic layout and the pattern of future development. They, the Ford Foundation consultants, and the Orissa Town Planning Organization identified actual and potential development issues that were eventually recognized by the administration, even if they were not immediately acted upon. On the other hand, the decision to limit the advisory role of professional town planners to technical matters, a decision which was largely the planners own, reinforced the views of administrators and politicians and restricted the relevance of much town planning activity and the influence of planners in guiding Bhubaneswar's short-term development. The latter was especially crucial to Bhubaneswar's inhabitants, but it was for all practical purposes outside the scope of town planning as defined by the administration.

The New Capital project affected Old Bhubaneswar, the five neighboring villages, and the New Capital's residents in numerous ways which can be considered irreversible. Some of these are treated elsewhere in this book. It suffices here to mention the economic effects of the New Capital construction activity, including the permanent jobs and markets created by the growth of the new town, the changes brought about by educational opportunities, the immigration of thousands of strangers, many from outside Orissa, the improvements and physical dislocations brought to the existing settlements in the name of economic development and urbanization, and the declining ritual and economic influence of the Lingaraj Temple hierarchy. Those New Capital residents who were government servants and who came to Bhubaneswar early were comparatively fortunate in that their accommodations were most satisfactory, in spite of some design problems and the lack of urban amenities and services; later arrivals were less fortunate because they had to adapt to multi-story living, unless they were able to find space in a private house. In either case, however, the physical setting was not what Orissans were accustomed to, and many people viewed the New Capital as fit only for retired people.

Now, with the benefit of hindsight and thirty years of postwar development experience, the usefulness of cross-cultural comparisons for understanding much of what occurred in Bhubaneswar is more apparent than it was when this investigation was undertaken. Many factors operate in diverse cultural contexts in much the same way and with similar consequences (see, for example, Crozier 1964; Friedman 1966; Gross 1967; Hirschman 1963; and Turner and Fichter 1972). In particular, the pervasiveness of certain characteristics and consequences of bureaucratic decision making,[10] the recurring importance of political influence on administrative and technical deliberations, and the critical importance of crisis as a stimulus to planning and other decisions are apparent. Although the details surrounding the development of this particular site were unique, the planning of the New Capital was unique neither in process nor in outcome.

NOTES

1. The first elected Indian government in Orissa had resigned with other elected provincial governments as part of the Independence Movement's accelerated campaign of a few years earlier.
2. Interview with Harekrushna K. Mahtab, Bhubaneswar, December 22, 1965.
3. This and other Koenigsberger town design concepts are discussed in his survey of new town development in India (Koenigsberger 1952).
4. These two posts were held concurrently by the same man until about the beginning of 1949. After this, the posts were separate ones because of the great increase in workload.
5. Eventually, in 1965, a Ford consultant was attached to the newly reconstituted Orissa Town

Planning Organization to assist in completing master plans for several coastal towns exclusive of Bhubaneswar.

6. The Orissa Government first established a Town Planning Organization in 1954. Its mandate was the preparation of a master plan for the improvement of Cuttack, the state's largest town. V. C. Mehta, who had been consulted on Bhubaneswar's planning before Koenigsberger, was appointed Town Planner. After completing a Civic Survey of the town, Mehta was released and the Organization was absorbed into the Architect's Branch of the Public Works Department under Julius Vaz. The Government Architect remained in charge of town planning until D. R. K. Patnaik was appointed in 1964, and the new Town Planning Organization was relocated in the Local Self-Government Department.

7. See, for example, discussions of crisis-oriented planning in the work of Gross (1964:792-94 and 1967:224-27), Hirschman (1963:261), Crozier (1964:285), and Friedman (1966:30).

8. Taken from Richard Taub's 1962-64 unpublished field notes.

9. See Grenell (1972) for further discussion.

10. See Friedman (1967) for further discussion.

REFERENCES

Crozier, Michel. 1964. *The Bureaucratic Phenomenon*. Chicago: University of Chicago Press.
Friedmann, John R. P. 1966. *Regional Development Policy: A Case Study of Venezuela*. Cambridge: MIT Press.
⎯⎯⎯⎯. 1967. Conceptual Model for the Analysis of Planning Behavior. *Administrative Science Quarterly* 12 (September):225-252.
Gokhale, B. K. 1966. Bhubaneswar New Capital. Mimeo.
Grenell, Peter. 1972. Planning for Invisible People: Some Consequences of Bureaucratic Values and Practices, pp. 95-121 in *Freedom to Build*, edited by John F. C. Turner and Robert Fichter. New York: The Macmillan Company.
Gross, Bertram. 1964. *Managing of Organizations*. Vol II. New York: Free Press.
⎯⎯⎯⎯. 1967. *Action Under Planning: The Guidance of Economic Development*. New York: McGraw-Hill.
Hirschman, Albert O. 1963. *Journeys Toward Progress*. New York: Twentieth Century Fund.

Koenigsberger, Otto H. 1952. New Towns in India. *Town Planning Review* 2 (July):94-131.
────── 1960. *Master Plan for the New Capital at Bhubaneswar*. Cuttack, India: Orissa Government Press.
Kutty, M. G. 1966. The Administrative Vacuum in Indian Planning Law. Paper submitted to the 15th Annual Seminar, Institute of Town Planners, Bhubaneswar, India.
Orissa Legislative Assembly. Debates, I, Part 1, 3 (August 24, 1961):7-8.
Orissa Legislative Assembly. Debates, IV, Part 1, 2 (February 28, 1963):22-23.
Orissa Legislative Assembly. Proceedings, VII, 3 (March 3, 1948):50.
Orissa Legislative Assembly. Proceedings, IX, 3 (March 4, 1949):24.
Taub, Richard P. 1969. *Bureaucrats under Stress: Administrators and Administration in an Indian State*. Berkeley: University of California Press.
Turner, John F. C. & Robert Fichter, eds. 1972. *Freedom to Build*. New York: The Macmillan Company.

Part 2
Religious Adaptations

Dr. Manamohan Mahapatra received his M.A. in anthropology from the University of Utkal in 1963 under Professor A. Aiyappan. He then entered upon a study of Lingaraj Temple in the Old Town of Bhubaneswar as a collaborator in the Harvard-Bhubaneswar Project. His Ph.D. thesis, "Lingaraj Temple: Its Structure and Change, ca. 1900-1962," was submitted to Utkal University in 1971 under the final guidance of Professor Laxman Mahapatra who had replaced Professor A. Aiyappan as chairman of the Department of Anthropology. The present chapter is an edited version of the summary and conclusions of his unpublished Ph.D. thesis that has been updated to 1976.

Dr. Mahapatra is a member of a Temple Cook (Suar) family that still maintains its perquisites and services in Lingaraj Temple. His data derive primarily from interviews with temple servants (sevak) and particularly from interviews with members of the three leading Brahman groups of that institution.

The absence of precise dates will trouble historians. But the virtue of Chapter 3 lies precisely in its reflection of oral traditions purveyed by the writer's respected elders. Historical precision is not at issue here. Dr. Mahapatra is a man interstitial to contemporary westernized schooling and that which can be learned from the purveyors of oral traditions. He chose the course of oral traditions for his dissertation research. Therefore, this chapter emphasizes primarily the changes that occurred from 1803, when the British took over control of Orissa to the present. Readers who wish a more carefully documented chronology of the historic past are referred to a few English language sources appended in Note 1.

3 | Lingaraj Temple: Its Structure and Change, ca. 1900-1976

Manamohan Mahapatra

The present chapter aims at discussing the traditional structure and change of a mid-eleventh century Shiva temple in Bhubaneswar, Orissa, built by the Kesaris. The study is not an historical one as I have not focused on the inscriptions and copper plates available on the Lingaraj Temple. I chose essentially to study that generation in which extensive changes occurred and which can be recaptured from the memories of the elderly people still living. I have utilized the oldest persons associated with the temple and publications relating to the study to determine the base line of 1900 and to assess changes that have occurred up to 1976.[1]

The year 1900 is taken as the base line in the study for the following reasons.

1. Orissa became a separate province in 1936.
2. The Orissa Hindu Religious Endowment Act (O.H.R.E.A.) was passed in 1939.
3. The new state capital was built close to the old sacred town beginning in 1948.
4. After 1948, other general changes, such as urbanization, the growth of communication, and the development of an educational system, occurred in the town mainly with the establishment of the New Capital.
5. The earliest date at which changes could still be recalled with some precision by living informants was 1900.

One of the four sacred places *(kshetra)* still existing in Orissa, according to sacred texts, Bhubaneswar is famous for Lord Lingaraj. It has never occupied as outstanding a position as the Jagannath Temple complex in Puri. Nevertheless, it has a long cultural and political history. As a sacred place, Bhubaneswar is otherwise called the *Ekamra Kshetra*. It has also been referred to as the *Sambhava Bana* ("Forest of Shiva")in the sacred literature of the third century B. C. Bhubaneswar has served as a seat of cultural activity intermittently and as the political capital of important dynasties for centuries. The Dhauli, Khandagiri and the Udayagiri Hills, and the site of Sisupalgarh, situated in the vicinity of the sacred town, are extant reminders of its past greatness.

In 1900 Bhubaneswar was a multicaste village with a population of about 3,000, most of whom were temple functionaries. Outsiders visited the place primarily as pilgrims to see Lord Lingaraj on their way to Puri. The local residents, and especially the temple functionaries, earned their livelihood mainly from the Temple and its allied enterprises. Outside of the state this place was famous for Lingaraj and its temples. The importance of the town increased after it was selected as a site for the new state capital in 1947. The construction of this new urban center for administration was accompanied by a growth of population. Its importance and population increased to the point that it was declared a subdivision with headquarters at Bhubaneswar on January 26, 1950.

The sacred town of Bhubaneswar covers an area of ten square miles. The actual settlement clustered around the Lingaraj Temple is constricted, whereas the sacred zone covers a far more extensive area. The new town, built two miles north of the old temple town, lies within the original kshetra. The boundary of the sacred area still remains unaltered in spite of changes in the township. In 1900, the sacred area consisted of the densely clustered temple town and sixteen villages interspersed among paddy fields and tracts of scrub jungle and connected, if at all, by bullock tracts. In 1962 the paddy fields were still largely undisturbed, but patches of jungle had been cleared and a growing network of motorable roads had been built to connect the modern town and the adjacent villages. The physical appearance of the traditional kshetra had altered from a rural landscape to a burgeoning township.

The Kesari kings, who originally built and endowed the Lingaraj, invested the direct administration of the Endowment in a corps of hereditary officials. Thus, both temple functionaries and outsiders were appointed to look after the internal affairs of the Lingaraj Temple. Six such officers constituted the Panchayat. This Panchayat system of administration of the Endowment reflected the traditional secular administration of village comunities. This delegated administration continued until 1803.

When the British occupied the coastal districts of Orissa in 1803, the intrusion of external authority into the internal management of the Lingaraj Temple, and more particularly of the Jagannath Temple in Puri, began to be felt. Even before the accession of the British, mismanagement of both the secular and sacred affairs of the temples occurred. These irregularities were not confined to Lingaraj Temple but occurred in many religious endowments. For example, the Potter servants of Lingaraj Temple sold their endowed temple lands and stopped supplying new earthen pots on their service days. When such examples of mismanagement were brought to the attention of the British, it became obvious that they preferred not to interfere in these religious institutions directly; they had a general policy of noninterference in such matters.

The first formal legislation passed for the proper management of the religious endowments was in the year 1810. According to Regulation XIX of the Code of Civil Procedure, the public Hindu religious endowments were placed under the direct control of the Board of Revenue. This Board appointed a *parichha* ("superintendent") to act as an intermediary between the Board and the endowments. The administration of the Board was no more effective than the traditional system, however, as most of the members of the Board were foreigners and knew nothing about the institution. Furthermore, they lived in areas other than that in which the temples were located and were unable to supervise the management either closely or knowledgeably. Therefore, the Act of 1810 was replaced by the Code of Civil Procedure Act II of 1863, which placed the religious institutions under the direct control of the District Judge. The Lingaraj Endowment, being situated in the district of Puri, was placed under the direct control of the District Judge of Puri.

With changes in the administrative organization of the temples, a new group of secular officials was appointed in accord with the Orissa Hindu Religious Endowment Act of 1863 and the traditional hereditary functionaries (e.g., Panchayat, Parakaran) became defunct. They retained their titles and the prerequisites associated with such offices, however. In addition, a corps of persons was appointed to look after the secular administration of the temples. The Hindu Religious Endowment Act of 1863 was provincialized in 1939 when it was found inadequate for the management of the religious institutions. This revision also underwent similar changes in subsequent years when several amendments were added.

Many administrative changes occurred in the Lingaraj Temple as a result of these amendments to the O.H.R.E.A. of 1939. The "Committee of Management" appointed by the District Judge was renamed the "Board of Trustees," and alterations were made in the body's powers, functions, activities, and also in the terms of service of its members. Furthermore, when the general provisions of the O.H.R.E.A. of 1939 were found ineffective in the management of the institution, a "Scheme" was framed by the state government. This Scheme specified the powers, functions, terms of office, etc., of the members of the Board of Trustees and the Executive Officer. It also mentioned the methods of framing and approving the annual budget and different items of receipts and expenditures. This Scheme came into force in 1952.

Up to 1957 the maintenance and repair of the Temple were looked after by the Endowment itself, and the funds for such work were collected mainly from public donations. When the Endowment and public gifts failed to finance the maintenance of the Temple, this responsibility was given over to the Archaeological Survey of India in February of 1958. With this shift in responsibility, another secular organization entered into the affairs of the Temple.

According to tradition, 360 households were required to perform the different services of the Deity in the daily and annual ritual rounds. In the daily rituals thirty-six different persons were engaged who were reinbursed in cash, kind, or some combination of both by the Endowment (see Table 3.1). They constituted the twenty-five categories of temple servants, twenty of which were called *sevakas* ("servants"), while the others were known as *kalabethias* (literally, "black free laborers"). These twenty-five different caste categories lived in separate hamlets *(sahi)* in the vicinity of the Temple and were related to each other both in the sacred and social spheres. For instance, the Kshyatrabasis acted as priests to the other functionaries, with the exception of the scheduled castes; the Great Cooks supplied cooked food to the sevakas according to their need; Washermen cleaned the clothes of the clean caste functionaries; and Barbers shaved their heads and beards.[2] Thus, a jajmani relationship existed among them. The Temple sevakas were given tax-free house plots, paddy lands, etc., as emolument in addition to their daily or annual payment in cash or kind. They were also permitted to peddle their goods in the Old Town free of charge. Some services also entailed free paddy lands. The three main groups of sevakas, the Priests (Kshyatrabasi), the Offerends (Pujapandas), and the Great Cooks (Suar or Mahasuar), in addition to their Temple duties also served as sacred pandas to the pilgrims of their jajmani estates who visited the Temple. This occupation provided a lucrative source of income.

In 1900 caste solidarity was very strong among different categories of temple servants, and traditional rules and regulations were strictly observed in the Temple community. Caste rivalries, mainly based on the Temple, existed among the three leading priestly specialists. All the caste categories serving the Deity had their respective caste associations called *nijoga* and *jatiana sabha*. The former referred to the caste associations of the Brahman functionaries, whereas the latter referred to the non-Brahman sevakas. However, the caste association of the Badus (a group of non-Brahman functionaries) was also called a nijoga as they were considered one of the principal sevakas of the Deity. Officers of the nijoga were elected every year, and their terms of office were for specific periods of time, whereas in the jatiana sabha the position of the officials was hereditary. The nijoga officials were consulted by the Temple administration in serious matters pertaining to the internal governing of the Temple. These caste associations, whether nijoga or jatiana sabha, functioned not only to enforce internal discipline but also to settle intercaste and intracaste quarrels. Intermarriage and commensality were frowned upon and were often severely dealt with by the caste elders.

When the princely states merged to form the present state of Orissa in 1947, the rajas became mere pensioners. They were no longer able to endow the Temple with land, cash, and treasures as they did in the past. The monastery heads, like the rajas, had also supported the Temple and presented food offerings in large quantity on festive as well as on ordinary days. But with the introduction of the O.H.R.E.A. of 1939, the monasteries lost their autonomy as well. Monastery heads were granted a

TABLE 3.1
Traditional Roles of Temple Servants

Name of Service	Duty
Palia Budu	Dresser of the Deity and commander of the Temple
Faraka	Guard
Khataseja	Decorator of the Deity's bed
Pochha	Cleans the Deity
Pahada	Screens the cella
Pujapanda	Offers the food to the Deity
Mahasuar	Cooks the food of the Deity
Patri	Arranges the puja materials
Pantibadu	Decorator of the place of food offerings
Garabadu	Supplier of flowers, water, etc., to the Pujapanda
Hadapnaik	Prepares the betal of the Deity
Bhitar Khuntia	Guards the cella during food offerings
Dhopakhal	Cleans the Temple kitchen
Changada	Supplier of the clothes at the time of the dressing of the Deity
Chhata	Holds the parasol of the Deity
Trasa	Holds the fan of the Deity
Puspalaka	Bathes the deputies of the Deity
Parvati	Worshipper of Goddess Parvati

specified sum of money for their maintenance. The monasteries were put on a budget, and, as a result, the food offerings to Lingaraj on different occasions were reduced as of 1962 and in some instances discontinued altogether. Thus, there was a steady deterioration in gifts and services to the Deity. With the abolition of the zamindari system in the state, even the Garland Makers and the Weavers residing on the landed estate of the Deity stopped their supply of garlands and threads to be used for the Deity on different auspicious occasions.

TABLE 3. 1 (cont'd)

Name of Service	Duty
Gopalini	Worshipper of Godden
Mekap	Temple storekeeper
Characheita	Temple supervisor
Akhanda	Lamp burner in the cella
Puspanjali	Offers handful of petals to the Deity
Kothabhoga Bisoyi	Supplier of the daily ration of the Deity to the kitchen
Gudia	Supplier of sweet dishes of the Deity
Masala	Supplier of spices for the prepared betel
Rosa Paika	Supplier of water to the Temple kitchen
Ghanta	Gong beater
Samartha	Supplier of powdered rice, etc., for the preparation of cake
Madala	Drum beater
Astrologer	Astrological forecasting for the Deity
Telenga	Orchestral musician
Kahalia	Trumpeteer
Dhoba	Washes the clothes of the Deity
Masalachi	Torch bearer
Kumbhar	Supplier of new earthen cooking pots to the Temple kitchen

After the establishment of the New Capital three miles northwest of the traditional sacred town in 1947, many new opportunities became available. The new jobs in the capital offered increased income as well at a time when the general inflationary trend of the economy had reduced the real value of traditional Temple renumerations. The tax-free house plots were an exception since the need for housing was acute, and sky-rocketing land values accompanied the growth of the new town. Secular employment yielded more income than that of the Temple.

For those members of the younger generation who were educated and could enter the civil service, prestige as well as increased income accrued to them from such secular occupations. In other respects also the basic economy of the temple servants changed with the establishment of the New Capital. The opening of roads and other means of communication furthered the process. In the case of the non-Brahman servants, the traditional occupations such as cloth washing, milk selling, barbering, and even wage labor were in high demand in the new town as compared with the old Temple town. It should also be noted here that the traditional remuneration for such services was much less in the Old Town. Therefore, Washermen, Barbers, and the like paid more attention to their customers in the New Capital than to their hereditary patrons. Hence, there was a breakdown in the traditional jajmani relationships which existed as part of the social system of the Temple community. These relationships broke down in favor of commercialized ones that were more profitable. As the younger generations of priestly specialists were gradually attracted by the secular occupations in the New Capital, there was a shortage of priests in the Temple. As a result, the number of proxies[3] increased in the ritual round of the Deity. The chief incentive to maintain one's duties in the Temple was to retain one's rent-free house plots, agricultural lands, and other privileges. Many hereditary officials have slighted their duties and in some cases have even stopped performing services in the sacred complex since the Endowment authorities have been lax in dispossessing servants who neglect their hereditary duties. The new secular engagements of the Temple priests have also reduced the time available for the worship of the deities. As a result, ritual performances have been neglected.

    The rise in the cost of living has forced the Temple servants to seek alternative secular sources of income. Moreover, money has increasingly become a measure of prestige, status, and power. Simultaneously, the rapacity of those who remained as pilgrim guides[4] and tried to meet the new economic necessities by means of their traditional occupations has resulted in a loss of esteem by pilgrims and devotees for their guides or pandas. Pandas began to be seen as exploitative. As a consequence, visitors to the Temple felt free to dispense with their secular services, such as providing lodging and food. The status of the priests, therefore, declined not only because of competing statuses provided by the

New Capital but also because of a withdrawal of esteem on the part of their traditional clients. The priestly class was caught between the Scylla of the new alternative economic and social opportunities and the Charybdis of declining traditional earnings and prestige. Thus, the retreat from sacred services has had not only economic but also status implications.

With the changes in the Temple organization, the physical assets of the Endowment have not increased and, in fact, may even have decreased due to the illegal alienation of hereditary landholdings. However, the financial value of the Temple lands has increased considerably over time as a result of the pressing demand for land that has accompanied the growth of the New Capital.

During the years under discussion there have been changes in the number of temple servants and in the number of officers of the Endowment establishment. For example, the position of Astrologer Sevak has been filled only irregularly since 1955; the position of the Telenga Musician has fallen vacant for the lack of a suitable replacement; and the post of Torch Bearer has been abolished due to the installation of electricity in the Temple in 1957. The Washerman Sevak performs his duties only occasionally.

All of these factors have resulted in new orientations among the Temple priests. For example, a Samartha Sevak has become a mason; Brahmans have become civil servants; and Bauris have taken to rickshaw pulling, shopkeeping, and performing in musical orchestras. Table 3.2 compares traditional religious and new secular occupations for a sample of the three principal priestly groups in 1976. At present nearly 90 percent of the Kshyatrabasis, formerly the highest ranking caste group in the Old Town, do not pursue their traditional occupations. A Kshyatrabasi serving in his sacred capacity has an uncertain income at best, whereas a civil servant or businessman is assured of a fixed monthly income. An informant once jokingly remarked that, "During Kaliyuga salt and Brahmans are cheap." The Mahasuar, the most numerous of the priestly groups, have also experienced a defection of younger members who feel that work in the New Capital has more status than priestly service. On the other hand, the very growth of the New Capital has generated a large and wealthy clientele desirous of the Food of Grace which only the Great Cooks can prepare and sell.

Finally, in matters of status most of the categories of temple servants have experienced a curious

TABLE 3.2
Main Occupations of Priestly Groups in 1976

	RELIGIOUS		SECULAR			
Priests	Temple Service	Pilgrim Service	Civil Service	Private Service	Shop-keeping	Gov't & contracting
Kshyatrabasi	2	2	8	2	3	1
Pujapanda	6	6	3	0	2	0
Mahasuar	50	50	60	8	15	5
Totals	58	58	71	10	20	6

anomaly. For example, the Badus have struggled during the last decade to prove themselves equal to Brahmans. Intermarriage and interdining are no longer frowned upon. Furthermore, involvement in the secular occupations of the New Capital has loosened caste solidarity. The caste associations have become lax in doling out punishments to their erring members. Such modern amenities and facilities as barber saloons and laundries have undermined certain punishments in any case. Because of them, the traditional punishment *(eka gharikia)* has little effect. The All-India move to ameliorate the stringencies of caste structure have been felt particularly strongly in the Lingaraj complex because of the compounding influence of the new township. In addition, varied economic opportunities have contributed to members' loss of interest in their caste associations. As a result the nijogas have become paralyzed and fail to perform their duties properly. Intercaste rivalries, formerly exemplified by the nijogas, have collapsed organizationally, if not interpersonally, and have been replaced by a new consolidation of the sevakas in the Lingaraj Sevayat Samiti, an expression of the union of self-interested traditional groups in opposition to new alternatives. Thus, change has resulted not only in a gradual defection from traditional caste occupations and associations, but also in a consolidation of traditional interests in the face of modern erosions.

NOTES

    1. Some annotated English language references that provide an historic background to the Lingaraj Temple in the context of Orissan history:

>Mahtab, Harekrushna, ed. 1957. *The History of the Freedom Movement in Orissa*. Vol. 1 (1757-1856); Vol. 2 (1857-1911); Vol. 3 (1911-1930); Vol. 4 (1930-1947). Cuttack, India: State Committee for Compilation of History of Freedom Movement in Orissa.
>
>>These volumes cover, more or less accurately, much of the period portrayed in Dr. Mahapatra's article.
>
>Mitra, Rajendralala. 1961. *The Antiquities of Orissa*. Vol. I and II. "Indian Studies Past and Present." Calcutta, India: Firma K. L. Mukhopadhyaya.
>
>>The most relevant portion is in Vol. II, Chap. 2.
>
>Mukherjee, Prabhat. 1953. *The History of the Gajapati Kings of Orissa and Their Successors*. Calcutta, India: S. Mukherjee, General Trading Company.
>
>>A somewhat disorderly compilation of information and its sources on Orissa kings and customs from the mid-fourteenth century to the end of the nineteenth century.
>
>Panigrahi, Krishna Chandra. 1961. *Archaeological Remains at Bhubaneswar*. Bombay, India: Orient Longmans.
>
>>Chapter IX, "Chronology of the Temple," and Chapter X, "A Short Political and Cultural History of Bhubaneswar," will prove especially helpful.
>
>Sahu, N. K. 1956. *A History of Orissa*. 2 vols. Calcutta, India: Susil Gupta. Ltd.
>
>>A series of articles by British officials—W. W. Hunter, Andrew Stirling, John Beans—with notes and comments by the editor. A useful overview from the British standpoint.

    2. The origin of the priestly castes of the Lingaraj Temple is obscure. According to oral tradition, non-Brahman functionaries, called "Badu," were the original and only servants of the Deity. As the only servants of the Deity, they bathed,

dressed, and decorated it. In the absence of Brahman priests, they also cooked the food and presented it to the Deity. This practice continued until a group of orthodox Brahmans, called "Kama," were brought to what is now the Old Town to perform the priestly functions within the sacred complex. The Raja granted tax-free house plots northeast of the Temple to the Kama Brahmans. With the recruitment of the Kama to the Temple establishment, the Badu servants ceased to cook and to offer food to the Deity within the sacred complex. However, the Kama Brahmans did not perform these ritual functions for very long. Each of them met with an untimely death. No one took over these functions after the demise of the Kama Brahmans, and the religious activity in the Temple deteriorated. In response to this situation the Raja of Khurda (popularly known as the Gajapati Raja of Puri), who claimed descent from the Kesaris who built the Temple, appointed Offerends (pujapanda) from the Krishna Temple at Sakshigopal to perform daily the sacred duties in the Temple. Although Sakshigopal was about thirty miles from Bhubaneswar, the Offerends walked back and forth to the Temple each day. The Raja, seeking to relieve the Offerends of this undue hardship, finally sent for two families to take up permanent residence in Bhubaneswar. They were known as "Pujapanda Mahapatra." At a later date, according to a Temple record, the local Raja decided to establish the "Chhatisa Nijoga System" in the Temple to insure the performance of the daily rituals. This system divided the tasks among thirty-six persons drawn from different castes ranging from high caste Brahmans to low ranking Hadi Sweepers.

 3. By "proxies" the author means that a service-holder who did not wish, or was not able, to perform his duties on a given day would ask a fellow priest of proper rank to serve as his surrogate.

 4. The "guides" referred to in this context were the recruiters who went out to the countryside to bring pilgrims to the Temple and who attended to their mundane needs during their visit. The priests were temple servants who kept benological records of their patrons and who performed for them such rites as they requested. These had been lucrative activities in the past. Many pilgrims on their way to or from the great car festival of Jagannath in Puri stopped briefly to worship at the temple complex of Bhubaneswar. With the improvement of roads and the establishment of the railroad in the nineteenth century, the number of pilgrims and tourists is reported

to have increased markedly. As late as the 1920s a hostel was built by a rich Bengali donor in the Old Town to accommodate less wealthy pilgrims. Although rough estimates of the number of pilgrims to the Jagannath Car Festival are provided by the Police, no reliable figures can be provided for the Bhubaneswar temple complex. Informants state that pilgrims usually stay two or three days and that the New Capital's administrative buildings are often included in their "sightseeing" tours.

David Miller received a Ph.D. in comparative religion from Harvard University in 1968 and is currently an associate professor of religion at Concordia University in Montreal. In 1963-64 he studied the monastic institutions of the Old Town. Together with Dorothy Wertz, he has published a book, HINDU MONASTIC LIFE: THE MONKS AND MONASTERIES OF BHUBANESWAR, McGill-Queen's University Press, 1976, based upon that research. In 1977-78 he returned to India as a Shastri Indo-Canadian Institute Senior Fellow.

Chapter 4 is based upon Dr. Miller's 1963-64 research and his follow-up study in 1977-78. In the chapter he demonstrates that monastic life in Bhubaneswar is thriving and argues that the **guru-shisya** relationship is an adaptive core of Hinduism.

4 Religious Institutions and Political Elites in Bhubaneswar

David Miller

One of the oldest roles in India is that of the "ascetic" or the "holy man," and one of the oldest existing Hindu religious institutions is the monastery. The heads of monasteries have been, for many Hindus, the bearers of a cultural tradition that goes back to Vedic times. The holy man and the monastery provide a center of sacredness and learning available to anyone who wishes to approach it. Despite the influence of modernization and change occurring in all parts of India, the lives of holy men still represent ideals relevant to contemporary people regardless of rural or urban residence. Bhubaneswar is no exception.

In 1963-64 there were twenty-two monastic establishments in Bhubaneswar, all located in the Old Town, with some forty-one ascetics residing in them.[1] They varied greatly in terms of physical dimensions, income, and number of resident ascetics and servants. The largest compound belonged to the Ramakrishna Matha and covered an area larger than the Lingaraj Temple complex. In 1964 it consisted of a three-story main residence, an equally large guest house for special dignitaries, a library of 2,232 books, a charitable dispensary that treated 23,000 cases a year, a primary school for 250 students, and a high school under construction. By contrast, the smallest establishment was an abandoned temple in which a solitary ascetic lived and worshipped a popular eight-by-ten inch print of the goddess Durga.

The Gopala Tirtha Matha, one of the five oldest monasteries located in the center of the Old Town, was the wealthiest institution with an annual cash income of over Rs. 35,000, of which Rs. 22,000 derived from landholdings. Six monasteries owned substantial amounts of land, four having been endowed by medieval kings and two others founded in the twentieth century. Although the Ramakrishna Matha expended the most money for welfare activities, it ranked below four older institutions in income. The poorest monasteries were the residences of solitary ascetics who depended on daily donations of food for their hand-to-mouth existence.

Despite the number of monastic establishments in the Old Town, there has been some question regarding the viability of religious traditions in Bhubaneswar since the establishment of the New Capital. For example, Taub's (1969:176) study of the New Capital bureaucratic elite indicated that a majority of high level government officials held unfavorable attitudes toward religion. The work of Mahapatra (1971) in the Old Town and Freeman (1977) in Kapileswar village support Taub's inference that interest in ritualistic Hinduism *(Karma Kanda)* is declining because "those who are traditionally priests will give up that traditional job in order to enter secular occupations if the secular occupations pay well (1969:180)."[2] In Bhubaneswar this problem has created a minor crisis; more and more temple priests, especially of the younger generations, are leaving their traditional occupations and are seeking employment in the New Capital. The result is a major decline in temple ritual, especially in the daily round of temple services. Because Taub's (1969:178) informants thought of themselves as "men who are committed to modernization," they sought to dissociate themselves from ritualistic Hinduism and from temple worship. The temple, although the most prominent religious institution, has never been the core of Hindu faith, which remains centered around the family and its relationship to a guru and to other religious specialists who serve the family.

One of the key organizing principles upon which philosophic Hinduism *(Jnana Kanda)* is based, as distinct from ritualistic, caste-associated Hinduism, is the *guru-shisya* (teacher-disciple) relationship. The *guru-shisya* relationship is as old as Hindu tradition itself, finding its first concrete expression in the earliest Upanishads. In the Upanishads the *guru-shisya* relationship was not limited to the formal tie between an ascetic-guru, living in a forest hermitage, and the student who came to study under him. The Chandogya Upanishad, for example, tells the famous story of Uddalaka Aruni, the father, who leads his son, Shvetaketu, to a realization of Brahman the Absolute through a series of pratical exercises that take place in the informal setting of his home. In medieval India the guru often remained a householder who functioned solely as a teacher, but more commonly he was an ascetic *(sadhu)* who lived in total detachment in a forest hermitage *(ashrama)* or who resided in a large monastery *(matha)* located near a temple in an urban area. During this period the *guru-shisya* relationship became concretely expressed in the Sanskrit concept, *sampradaya* (teaching order).

A teaching order or *sampradaya* can be traced back to one of five historical teachers or Acharyas who expounded a philosophical system and who established a monastic order to carry out the teaching of the philosophical tradition. The five Acharyas were: Shankara (788-820 AD); Ramanuja (ca. 1017); Nimbarka (CA. 1162); Madhva (1199-1278); and Vallabha (ca. 1500). In time, due to the almost limitless flexibility of Hinduism, other gurus created an endless number of sub-teaching traditions, often synthesizing the philosophical systems of two or more founder Acharyas. The *guru-shisya* relationship remained the basic unit of organization of philosophic Hinduism.

There has been a tendency, when examining Hinduism as a total system that includes both ritualistic and philosophic aspects, to understand it in "sectarian" terms analogous to the "belief" structures of Christian sectarianism. The focus, then, has been upon the chosen deity *(ishtadevata)* selected by one group or another rather than upon the *sampradaya* and the *guru-shisya* relationship. The latter are dynamic systems that must be examined separately. For example, it may be possible to document a decline in temple rituals associated with specific deities, and it may be the case that Hindu sectarianism is declining under the impact of "modernization." However, the *guru-shisya* relationship, as the basis for ever-evolving *sampradayas*, may provide a conceptual structure for understanding the adaptive core of living Hinduism—a core that will remain long after many temples in India have become national museums, state monuments, or tourist attractions.

In this chapter I wish to illustrate and to analyze the involvement of New Capital lay elites in the life of the monastic institutions of the Old Town in order to demonstrate the viability of this one component of Hinduism—namely, the *guru-shisya* relationship. Upon my first observations, there appeared to be little or no interaction between the two parts of town. The Old Town seemed like a

survival of the past, encapsulated by the growing
New Capital. Gradually, however, a complex and subtle pattern of interrelationships became apparent.
I learned that numerous civil servants, including
some engineers, scientists, and university professors all living in the New Capital, provided the
main source of financial support for some monasteries in the Old Town and attended ceremonies held
within them. I also learned that a few leading ascetics gave advice to some government officials who
were their patrons and that officials sometimes used
their contracts with those ascetics considered religious leaders to gather information about the political climate in the Old Town. It turned out that
even seven of Taub's (1969) elite government informants were recorded on the lists of donors maintained
by the Old Town monasteries. The actual number of
politicians, civil servants, businessmen, and other
New Capital lay elites associated in some way with
monasteries and with ascetic-gurus probably numbered
in the hundreds. Of more significance than the number, however, is the amount or depth of their involvement, which can best be illustrated by describing several case studies.

The case studies that follow have been selected
as typical examples of the involvement of Bhubaneswar elites in the life of the monastic institutions
of the Old Town. The extent of the involvement represents a variety of *guru-shisya* relationships from
a *patron*, who seldom visits a monastery but provides
financial assistance, to a *disciple*, who has taken
a lay initiation ceremony and who, therefore, shares
a more intimate relationship with his guru. Other
case studies could have been chosen without significantly altering the analysis.

THE LAY FOLLOWER AS A PATRON

I have defined a patron as one who financially
supports a monastery, but who visits it infrequently.
One such patron was an Oriya politician who earlier
in his political career had been Chief Minister of
Orissa, India's Minister of Industry and Commerce,
and Governor of Bombay. During the time of my first
field work in Bhubaneswar, he had been elected to
the Lok Sabha and consequently spent much of his
time away from Bhubaneswar. He was a member of the
Congress Party, but politically he was opposed to
the Chief Minister of Orissa, also of the Congress
Party. In addition to being a leading politician,
he was a patron of Oriya culture. He had written a

history of Orissa in English and was acknowledged by some as "the most versatile writer in modern Oriya." His Bhubaneswar residence was located in the Old Town near the Arya Rishikula Bhubaneswar Ashrama, which was founded in 1945 by a Shankara Dashanami Samnyasin named Jagadananda Bhakti Sastri Tirtha.

Jagadananda was the most influential Bengali ascetic, with the exception of the Ramakrishna Matha ascetics, lving in the Old Town. About one half of the forty-one ascetics resident in the Old Town were of Bengali origin; the other half were Oriya. The backgrounds of Jagadananda and of the Arya Rishikula Bhubaneswar Ashrama represent a good illustration of the flexibility and eclectic nature of the *sampradaya*, which is not bound by either tradition or sectarian limitations. Translated freely, Arya Rishikula means "descendants of a Vedic seer." The first guru of the Arya Rishikula movement was a semi-legendary figure named Gangadhara Tirtha, a Shankara Dashanami Samnyasin, who is believed to have been an incarnation of the Vedic seer, Vasishtha. Gangadhara was succeeded by Nityananda Chaitanyaghana (1862-1931), who was a Bengali contemporary of Ramakrishna. Nityananda was deeply influenced by the Chaitanya movement, although he remained a Shankara ascetic. In 1928 Jagadananda was initiated into monastic orders by Nityananda, and after Nityananda's death, he became head of a small monastic institution with its headquarters in West Bengal. In 1945 Jagadananda moved his headquarters to Bhubaneswar, where with the financial support of the Minister of Education, another prominent Oriya politician, he purchased 30,000 square feet of land and began construction of the main residential hall. The altar within the main building honors a print of Krishna as well as photographs and drawings of the two previous gurus. In his philosophy and in his practice Jagadananda continues the synthesis of the Shankara and Chaitanya Sampradayas that was begun by Nityananda.

During the monsoon season of 1958 the roof of the main residence collapsed, and the former Chief Minister of Orissa provided the financial support for the repairs. In the same year, the politician laid the cornerstone for the construction of a "temple and religio-cultural hall," but funds were exhausted before the building was completed. By the beginning of 1964 only the outer shell of the structure had been erected, although the annual festival celebrating the living guru was held in the hall in March of that year. Over the years the former Chief Minister has been listed occasionally as the main speaker for the festival, but in 1964 he was not present. His secretary, however, visited the monastery during the politician's absence to pay his respects to Jagadananda. In 1964 Jagadananda had expectations that the former Chief Minister would make an annual contribution of Rs. 1,000.00.[3]

    The patron, typified by the former Chief Minister, functions primarily as a benefactor who makes an annual or monthly subscription of money to be used for the general maintenance of the monastery. Occasionally, the money is utilized for a specific project, such as the repair of a roof or the construction of a new building. The patron may also attend a festival as the principal guest or honored speaker. Otherwise, his visits to a monastery are infrequent, although he maintains contact with the guru through his secretary or other employee who pays respect to the guru on behalf of the patron. From time to time, a patron might request a private audience with the guru. Furthermore, a patron, unlike a disciple, need not commit his loyalties to one particular monastery; often his name appears on the patronage lists of other monasteries. If the monastery were as large as the Ramakrishna Matha, the patron might gain some political or social advantage in having his name on the list of contributors. In the case of the former Chief Minister, he gained little political benefit from belonging to a Bengali monastery since most of his constituency were Oriyas. Nevertheless, to be a patron of a few Old Town monasteries helped to promote his image as a benefactor of Oriya culture and tradition.

THE LAY FOLLOWER AS A DISCIPLE

    A disciple, as distinguished from a patron whose relationship to a guru or gurus is informal and casual, often undergoes a formal ceremony of initiation *(diksa)* by which he is taken into the Sampradaya as a lay member. The guru, who performs the initiation rite, becomes *his* guru to the exclusion of other gurus. I did not witness a lay initiation, although from descriptions of it recorded elsewhere I can outline the principal features. The lay follower must make a formal request, and the guru then sets the date for the ceremony. The rite itself may be very elaborate, but usually contains three elements: 1) the guru touches various parts of the initiate's body and may give him a set of religious beads or a new cloth garment as an outward sign of his initiation; 2) the guru then recites several sacred chants and gives the initiate his own personal *mantra* or sacred utterance as an inward sign of his initiation; and 3) the guru gives the initiate instruction in the proper way to perform the religious duties of his order. The point is that the lay follower who becomes a disciple maintains a deeper, more intimate relationship with his guru than does the patron.

Since in 1964 I did not have the opportunity to interview lay followers who were listed by heads of monasteries as their disciples, I cannot describe in any detail the intimacy of that relationship. I was assured by my guru informants, however, that their disciples frequently seek private audiences with them. In two cases that I was aware of disciples were instrumental in establishing religious or monastic institutions at Bhubaneswar in response to requests from their gurus.

The first case centers around an Oriya Dashanami Samnyasin ascetic named Saccidananda Sarasvati Svami, of the Shankarananda Matha. In my estimation, he was the most reknown and highly respected monastic head *(mahanta)* in Bhubaneswar. Saccidananda had about him the largest number of lay followers of any monastery except for the Ramakrishna Matha. Most of his followers were Oriyas representing a wide range of vocations and backgrounds. In 1964, over three hundred followers attended Guru Purnima, an annual festival honoring the guru. Among those attending were heads of other monasteries, mostly from Puri, Sanskrit pandits and teachers, as well as well-known politicians and businessmen. Saccidananda was learned in Sanskrit, and in 1939, after soliciting patronage throughout Orissa, he opened a Sanskrit school *(tol)*, which in 1964 the Orissa Government subsidized, recognizing its important contribution to the advancement of Oriya culture.

The Shankarananda Matha is one of the oldest monastic institutions at Bhubaneswar, founded by the Oriya king, Bhanudevo IV in the fifteenth century A.D. From the time of its founding to the present day, the Mahanta of the Shankarananda Matha functions, in addition to his traditional duties, as the administrator of lands endowed for the maintenance of the main temple at Bhubaneswar. Saccidananda, therefore, was not only a highly respected guru, but an efficient administrator as well.

One of Saccidananda's closest disciples was the editor of the Oriya daily newspaper, *The Samaj*, which was published in Cuttack. The editor was a former Minister of Finance in Orissa and as such proved to be a valuable disciple. He assisted Saccidananda as President of the Managing Committee for the Sanskrit school. More importantly, in 1961 at Saccindananda's request, his disciple called together a group of influential residents of the Bhubaneswar area to discuss what might be done to avert "a disaster of unthinkable proportions." In 1961 Indian astrologers had predicted that an extremely rare alignment of the planets would occur on February 3, 1962, and create utter chaos throughout the world, especially in India. The editor's friends organized a Managing Committee composed of:

  Chief Patron: Saccidananda Sarasvati Svami
  President: Speaker of the Orissa Legislative
    Assembly
  Co-Vice President: Editor of *The Samaj*
  Co-Vice President: Minister of Public Works for
    Orissa
  Secretary-Treasurer: A retired district judge

The Managing Committee quickly organized a large sacrificial fire ceremony *(yajna)* "to combat the evil influence of the planets" and invited a renowned sacrificial priest *(hotr)* to perform the ceremony that was to begin in December and last for fourteen months and eighteen days. Land was purchased, three stone buildings were built, and all other necessary items were secured. According to the editor's article, which appeared in *The Samaj* on December 18, 1961, the priest, assisted by twenty-six other priests, began a ceremony that consisted of "the taraka Mahavishu sacrifice, day and night recitation of the Bhagavad Gita, unending burning of the wick in the ghi lamp, recitation of the Candi Mahatmya near the Bhubaneswar temple and an elaborate worship of Lord Lingaraja." During the critical period, February 3-4, the priest kindled a sacrificial fire *(homa)*, which in time consumed three truckloads of wood. Although later a dispute arose between members of the Managing Committee and the priest, Saccidananda was very pleased with the role that his disciple had played in successfully accomplishing the Yajna under the pressures of a limited amount of time. The priest remained at the Bhubaneswar site after the Yajna had been completed, establishing a forest retreat for the aged who wished to retire from active life, and the disaster that had been predicted never came.

    The second case concerns two disciples whose guru moved from Bengal to Orissa, making Bhubaneswar his monastic headquarters. The Assistant Secretary of the Orissa Planning Department and the Development Commissioner of Orissa provided the funds, secured the land, and supervised the construction of the main residence for their guru, Svami Prajnananda Sarasvati, an elderly Dashanami Samnyasin, who was head of five branch monasteries in Bengal. During the building of the residential quarters Prajnananda remained as a guest at the home of the Development Commissioner. The monastery was named Nigamananda Ashrama, after the Nigamanda Sarasvati, the guru of Prajnananda. The September 27, 1964, issue of *The Samaj* announced that the opening day festivities were attended by "a large number of distinguished personalities," including his two distinguished disciples and, it was rumored, the Deputy Chief Minister of Orissa. As the monastery was within a short distance of my residence, I was often informed by neighbors that Prajnananda's two civil servant disciples had come to the monastery for a private audience with their guru.

The contact that a disciple shares with his guru is more constant and intimate than the relationship of a patron to a guru. The disciple seeks spiritual advice and guidance from his guru, who is for him the principal embodiment of the sacred and the most important living transmitter of Hindu philosophical traditions. He believes that only through the immediate presence of his guru can he realize *moksha*, the final goal of his religious tradition.

It is, therefore, significant that seven of the twenty-two monasteries in the Old Town were founded during the period when the New Capital was being constructed. My field research was confined to the Old Town, but it is likely that the situation of the Old Town was repeated elsewhere in the Bhubaneswar area as prominent disciples, resident in Bhubaneswar but from other parts of India, established branch monasteries in order to achieve a closeness to their gurus or to the ascetic disciples assigned by the head gurus to live in Bhubaneswar.

CONCLUSION

In 1977, I returned to India to study the Sivananda Ashram at Rishikesh, Uttar Pradesh, and its branches throughout India. Although my visit to Orissa was brief, I felt that many of my previous assumptions were verified.

The Sivananda organization, known as the Divine Life Society, is a good example of the type of "modernistic" *sampradaya* that appeals to more educated elites throughout India. Much smaller in size and in number of adherents than the Ramakrishna Matha and Mission, the Divine Life Society is similar to reformist-revivalist movements that I have described elsewhere (Miller and Wertz 1976:33, 185-186, 196). With the noted exception of Orissa, all of the branches that I visited were run by laity in much the same way that voluntary associations have functioned in Protestant Christianity. Each branch was committed to "the betterment of society": some branches had established schools for the poor or underprivileged; others ran dispensaries and medical camps; still others stressed publication of religious journals. The larger branches engaged in all of these activities.

The Divine Life Society in Orissa, which numbered more branches (65) than in any other state, had been organized by the laity but an ascetic disciple had been assigned by the head ashram at Rishikesh to look after philosophical and religious matters. He traveled from one town to another, holding religious meetings and arranging for disciples to be initiated at Rishikesh. In October 1977, I attended the All-Orissa Conference of Divine Life Societies at Bolangir (in western Orissa), which attracted a crowd of nearly 30,000 people each day for four consecutive days. On the first day the Governor of Orissa, the Chief Minister of Orissa, and the Oriya Minister of Finance spoke to the enthusiastic crowd.

The role of the Finance Minister is of particular interest. Although he was not an initiated disciple, as a resident of Bolangir he had worked closely with the Divine Life Society Managing Committee. The Chairman of the Managing Committee, a high school teacher, looked upon the Finance Minister's role as absolutely essential for the success of the conference. The Finance Minister had secured funds to support the conference and as its chief patron persuaded the Governor and the Chief Minister to be the principal speakers.

Two years before, the head of the Bhubaneswar branch of the Divine Life Society, who was a member of the faculty of education at Ravenshaw College in Cuttack, had organized an equally successful All-India Conference of Divine Life Societies which was attended by many of Bhubaneswar's elites as well as other elites from outside Orissa. The number of elites in attendance at a large annual conference says nothing, however, about their commitment to religious organizations and to the gurus who head them.

In part, I would agree with Taub's generalization regarding the Bhubaneswar elite associated with the Ramakrishna Matha and Mission: "Many are supporters, although few are really followers of the Ramakrishna Mission, a reform Hindu group whose spiritual beliefs are more consonant with Western ones...(1969:181-182)." But Taub's remarks do not take into account the distinctions between patrons and disciples that I have made. During my recent trip to India I interviewed laymen associated with the Divine Life Society branches in New Delhi, Calcutta, Bhubaneswar, Madras, Bangalore and Bombay. For each organization the list of patrons included many members of the political and business elite of the area, but the hard work of running the branches fell upon those more dedicated disciples who, like the editor of *The Samaj*, were called upon by their guru, Svami Chidananda, the President of the Divine Life Society, to perform tasks that took considerable time, energy, and in some cases, money. Taub's statement, therefore, tells only part of the story. We must look more closely at the few who are really followers in order to discern the importance of institutions like the Ramakrishna Matha.

The *sampradaya* with the *guru-shisya* relationship at the center is an extremely adaptive religious institution, capable of almost infinite change and capable of meeting the religious needs of Hindus at all social and economic levels. As I pointed out earlier, this has been true since Vedic times. The basic Neo-Vedantic philosophical position that underlies groups such as those begun by Ramakrishna and by Sivananda is as open-ended and eclectic as the institution it supports. This is attested to in our own society by the impact of such "modernistic" gurus as Maharishi Mahesh Yogi, Svami Satchidananda, and Bhagwan Shree Rajneesh, to name only a few whose Western disciples number in the thousands. Elsewhere I have argued that:

> ...in the varieties of North American Hinduism that we see about us, the guru is at the centre of sacredness. Sacred texts and the worship of deities are secondary matters compared with the centrality of the guru whose interpretations of the texts are often looked upon as more sacred than the texts themselves. I believe that this has always been true of Hindu tradition.... We have too often and too long understood

Hinduism in terms of sacred scriptures and ritualistic systems, perhaps reflecting the centrality of doctrinal and ritualistic debates in the history of Christianity (Miller 1976-77:528).

Religionists have invariably understood Hinduism in terms of sacred texts, whereas sociologists and anthropologists have generally focused upon Hindu ritualistic structures and functions, perhaps relating them to the caste system. Neither set of scholars has concerned itself with the *sampradaya* as one of the most central and hence most important religious institutions of Hindu tradition. If we do so, a different picture of Hinduism is disclosed. The gurus of Hindu tradition have continually established religious and monastic institutions in an attempt to bring about practical applications of their teachings, adopting and changing both their institutions and teachings to better fit the times in which they were living. The guru, and the *sampradaya* established by the guru, therefore represent and function as the dynamic center of Hinduism, contributing significantly to the difficult process of shaping and creating contemporary India. Even Agehananda Bharati (1970:277), as critical as he is of "the gurus of the Hindu Renaissance," admits that they are "at the helm of things." In the process of social and religious change, the guru in turn depends upon his disciples to carry out and support the ideals that he wishes to communicate. At Bhubaneswar many of the disciples are the New Capital political elite whose commitment to religious values may be obscured by the very questions that we Western observers tend to ask.

NOTES

1. See Miller and Wertz (1976) for a more extensive description and analysis of these monastic establishments and ascetics.
2. Also see Chapter 3 by Mahapatra and Chapter 5 by Freeman and Preston in this volume.
3. This figure seems high. For example, at the Ramakrishna Matha, which is a much larger organization and which draws its patrons from a prestigious clientele, the largest contribution in 1959 to the monastery's school and dispensary fund was Rs. 1,000.00, but most donations ranged from Rs. 25-50 (*The Ramakrishna Mission, Bhubaneswar Report, 1957-*

59, Calcutta, India: Modern Indian Press, 1959, pp. 12-13).

REFERENCES

Bharati, Agehananda. 1970. The Hindu Renaissance and its Apologetic Patterns. *Journal of Asian Studies* 29 (2):267-287.

Freeman, James M. 1977. *Scarcity and Opportunity in an Indian Village*. Menlo Park, California: Cummings Publishing Company.

Mahapatra, Manamohan. 1971. *Lingaraj Temple: Its Structure and Change*. Unpublished Ph.D. dissertation, Utkal University, Orissa, India.

Miller, David. 1976-77. The Guru as the Centre of Sacredness. *Studies in Religion* SR 6/5:527-533.

Miller, David M. and Dorothy C. Wertz. 1976. *Hindu Monastic Life: The Monks and Monasteries of Bhubaneswar*. Montreal: McGill-Queen's University Press.

Taub, Richard P. 1969. *Bureaucrats Under Stress: Administrators and Administration in an Indian State*. Berkeley: University of California Press.

James M. Freeman received a Ph.D. in anthropology from Harvard University in 1968. He is currently a professor of anthropology at San Jose State University, San Jose, California. His research interests in South Asia are religion, urbanization, life histories, untouchables, and humanistic aspects of change and adaptation. He has conducted two field research projects in India: (1) a sixteen-month study of an urbanizing Hindu temple village in 1962-1963; and (2) a twenty-two month follow-up study of the same village in 1970-1972. He has published several articles on India as well as two books: SCARCITY AND OPPORTUNITY IN AN INDIAN VILLAGE, Cummings, Menlo Park, 1977; and UNTOUCHABLE: AN INDIAN LIFE HISTORY, Stanford University Press, 1979. His post-doctoral research and writing on India have been supported by fellowships from the American Institute of Indian Studies (1970-1972), the Social Science Research Council (1976-1977), and the Center for Advanced Study in the Behavioral Sciences (1976-1977).

James Preston received a Ph.D. in anthropology from the Hartford Seminary Foundation in 1974. He is currently an assistant professor and chairman of the Department of Anthropology at the State University of New York, Oneonta. In 1972-1973 he conducted fieldwork in Cuttack under the guidance of Dr. Bhabagrahi Misra in Orissa. Dr. Preston has published several articles on India and a book based upon his research there, CULT OF THE GODDESS: RELIGIOUS CHANGE IN A HINDU TEMPLE, Vikas Publishers (in press). In 1968 he returned to India to participate in the Xth International Congress on Anthropological and Ethnological Sciences held in New Delhi.

Chapter 5 is based upon Dr. Freeman's long-term research in Kapileswar, a village that has been incorporated into the Bhubaneswar municipality, and Dr. Preston's research in the nearby city of Cuttack. In it they explain why during the same period of time Kapileswar Temple has declined while Chandi Temple in Cuttack has flourished. The chapter raises important questions about the relationship of religious institutions to other facets of socioeconomic change.

5

Two Urbanizing Orissan Temples

James M. Freeman and James Preston

Chandi and Kapileswar Temples, located in the towns of Cuttack and Bhubaneswar respectively, are both undergoing changes brought about by urbanization, but their directions of change are quite different. Kapileswar Temple is declining in income, patrons, and performance of services, while Chandi Temple has greatly increased its income and patronage over the past two decades. This chapter focuses on the contrasting developments in these two temples and the implications they have for understanding processes of change and adaptation in Orissa and India.[1]

Although less than twenty miles from each other, Cuttack and Bhubaneswar differ considerably in their urban environments. While Bhubaneswar is comprised of an old religious center and a new administrative section, Cuttack, the preindustrial capital, has been a cultural and commercial center of Orissa for the past ten centuries. With a 1971 population of nearly 200,000 persons, Cuttack is nearly twice the size of Bhubaneswar. The differing characters of the two towns account in part for the different patterns of change at Kapileswar and Chandi Temples.

CHANDI TEMPLE

As the largest city in Orissa, Cuttack is located on a rich rice-producing delta some thirty miles from the coast where the Mahanadi River bifurcates before it empties into the Bay of Bengal. It became a major center of trade as merchants and pilgrims traveled from various parts of India to the famous pilgrimage sites at Bhubaneswar, Konarak, and Puri. In addition, Cuttack housed the offices of the Government of Orissa until they were moved to

Gateway to the temple.

CHANDI TEMPLE

Entrance to the temple.

Chief priest worships Chandi in her Kali aspect.

KAPILESWAR TEMPLE
Above: Full view of the temple.
Below: Selling sacred food to pilgrims in front of the temple.

Bhubaneswar (see Chapter 2).

Despite its history as the political headquarters of Orissa, the city of Cuttack continues to have a small-town atmosphere. It is not an industrial center, nor are there any large imposing temples like those in Bhubaneswar and Puri. Instead, Cuttack is a collection of small to medium size businesses located along meandering streets. A brief tour through Cuttack's neighborhoods impresses the visitor with life styles reminiscent of Orissan villages. These neighborhoods vary greatly in caste, composition, house type, and distribution of wealth; yet all have in common the familiarity one would expect among people who have recently migrated to the city and continue to maintain strong rural ties.

It is impossible to know why Cuttack never developed an important pilgrimage site as did other Orissan cities. The temples of Cuttack can be classified for the most part as neighborhood shrines, some of which attracted city-wide attendance on special religious holidays. One of the smallest of these temples has had an unusual burst of popularity in recent years. This is Chandi Temple, located at an intersection between an older commercial part of the city and a quiet residential area formerly occupied by British colonial officials and wealthy members of the merchant class.

Chandi Temple was established over a hundred years ago with the assistance of a raja. At first the image of Chandi was housed in a small mud shrine with one Brahman priest assigned by the raja's family to perform sacred rites for members of the neighborhood. The ceremonies were simple and oriented to the personal needs of the raja and a few local attendants. Most of the usual rites for goddess worship in the Hindu calendar were performed at Chandi Temple, but these were secondary to the special ceremonies conducted at the request of local families who turned to the goddess with personal problems and rites associated with the routine life cycle events.

Until Independence in 1947, attendance was sparce but relatively steady at the small neighborhood shrine. As more people were gradually attracted to it, the mud shrine was torn down and a new stone temple built in its place. By the early 1970s Chandi Temple was experiencing a meteoric rise in popularity among the people of Cuttack and surrounding regions. Rapid change in the popularity of a temple is often related to miracles attributed to a specific deity, but the growth of the Chandi Temple is not associated with a miracle tradition. The change that has occurred here has broader implications and deeper roots, reflecting transformations at work in the social structure of Cuttack.

Other studies of Orissan religious institutions (Mahapatra 1971, Freeman 1975, and Miller and Wertz 1976) have noted a general trend toward the decline of priestly functions, attenuation of rituals, and loss of morale. This pattern seems to be characteristic of some large pilgrimage shrines. However, Chandi Temple is different because of its small size, relatively recent history, lack of complex interlocking caste duties, and close articulation with a new set of urban patrons.

Chandi Temple's growth is not as surprising as it first appears if one notes the series of social changes that have led to present conditions in Cuttack. These changes can be attributed to four key events which have taken place during the last thirty years. They include 1) the decline of the old pattern of temple patronage, 2) the establishment of the Orissa Hindu Religious Endowments Commission, 3) the rise of a strong mercantile class, and 4) increasing stylistic borrowing through cultural diffusion from Calcutta in West Bengal. These four variables are interlocking elements in a broad pattern of change that has affected the religious sphere. The temples of Cuttack have been challenged to respond to a new social order, with an associated power structure and symbolic component. These changes will be examined below.

Independence from the British in 1947 sent a wave of new political consciousness throughout the subcontinent. In 1948 the twenty-six princely states of Orissa were officially dissolved, and the Orissan rajas, who had been a source of patronage for many temples, experienced a gradual decline in their wealth, prestige, and influence. This resulted in a crisis of patronage among temples that relied heavily on large contributions in cash and land from the rajas. Chandi Temple was an excellent example of such a temple. The raja who had supported the temple was unable to contribute as consistently as he had in earlier times and gradually lost his power as manager over the institution. By 1968 he lost all legal control as the result of a court case which challenged his authority and transferred management of the temple to an agency of the Orissan government. The new patrons at Chandi Temple became the local merchants, government officials, and other members of a rising urban elite.

This change in patronage could never have occurred if it had not been for the Orissa Hindu Religious Endowments Commission which intervened in a dispute between the raja and priests who were competing for control over the temple's treasury. Although the Endowment Commission had roots that reach back into the British period, its influence over the internal affairs of religious insitutions was previously minimal. Today, however, it wields enormous power over 12,000 (approximately one-third) of Orissa's temples. In most cases when the Endowment Commission enters into a temple dispute, it tries to preserve the existing power structure, acting as a mediating influence wherever conflicts over temple management occur. At Chandi Temple, however, this government agency effected a break with the old patterm of royal patronage so that the new order of wealthy merchants and upper-class citizens could gain a position of strategic control over ritual performances and the expenditure of temple funds.[2] As a result the earlier personal orientation of temple ceremonies, often performed at the whim of the raja, were replaced by a predictable schedule of rites devoted to the goddess Chandi. In addition, the Endowment Commission has regulated prices for commodities purchased at shops located in the temple and standardized fees for sacred services performed by the priests. It has also been instrumental in establishing the lucrative yearly auctions of licenses for concessions which sell flowers, sweetmeats, incense, and other religious items to devotees who attend daily services. These auctions account for more than a third of the temple's yearly income.

Since Independence there has been a steady growth in the commercial sector of Cuttack. Merchants from outside Orissa (Bengalis and Marwaris) have invested in many new businesses. Cuttack's population doubled between 1951 and 1971. New bridges across the Mahanadi River, along with improved roads and train service, have forged a closer link between Cuttack and Calcutta. All of these conditions have helped to develop the city's commercial sector, and a powerful class of merchants has emerged as a result of this economic growth. They have gained community respect by making large donations to local temples. Most merchants traditionally worshipped some form of the mother goddess as their tutelary deity. With the declining influence of the raja, they began to channel a portion of their profits into Chandi Temple and to modernize it by installing tile floors, new silver plated doors, loud speakers, and toilet facilities.

Chandi Temple's rise to prominence in the ritual cycle of Cuttack is also related to a long tradition of cultural exchange between Orissa and West Bengal. Although Orissa has remained somewhat isolated from the mainstream of Indian civilization, it has always maintained important connections with both north and south India. The relationship with West Bengal has been particularly close because the two states were part of a larger political unit under British rule. Many Bengali customs were also carried to Cuttack by Orissans who had lived in Calcutta. However, during the British period large portions of Orissan land were sold at auctions in Calcutta because of the failure of landlords to pay taxes. Much of this land was purchased by Bengalis who eventually settled in Orissa. As a consequence, while some urbanized Orissans look toward Calcutta for models upon which to pattern their lives, some degree of ambivalence toward things Bengali persists among them.

Although goddesses are ubiquitous in both states, there are clear differences in styles of worship. Until recently Orissan goddess worship was tied to a complex balance of power among local rajas (Kulke 1976; Mahapatra 1978). Each princely state had its tutelary goddess whose shrine was located somewhere near the raja's palace. For example, the fall Durga festival was connected to the establishment of the raja's authority over a particular territory. She was his tutelary deity and protectress of the kingdom. Thus, the annual ceremony in honor of Durga was characterized by elaborate pageants and military rites displaying the royal symbols of power (see Preston, *Cult of the Goddess*, in press). At another level mother worship permeated Orissan folk religion in the form of fertility deities, earth mothers, and disease goddesses. For the most part, however, these lower level goddesses were secondary to Lord Jagannath and other male deities. Rarely were they worshipped with the same pomp and ceremony associated with other deities. Except for a few goddesses thought to possess miraculous powers, only the tutelary goddesses of the rajas were given special attention or raised to pilgrimage status.

Until the late 1960s the fall Durga Puja in Cuttack was a minor festival celebrated mostly in homes or small neighborhood temples. Today Durga Puja is the biggest event of the year. No longer is it a quiet domestic ceremony, but it has become instead a popular and boistrous street festival with all the components of a full-scale carnival. This popular version of Durga Puja has appeared in Orissa's largest cities (Freeman 1975:129) and seems to have been borrowed from a similar event which takes place in Calcutta. The new style of worshipping the goddess seems to be most evident in urban areas and represents the democratization of a symbol which was previously bound to a feudal social structure.

Today Durga Puja in Cuttack is celebrated with hundreds of clay statues of the goddess which are constructed by wealthy merchants, neighborhood associations, and student groups. These are paraded through the city streets and finally submerged in the Mahanadi River on the last day of the festival. For three days the streets of Cuttack are crowded with thousands of people who exchange gifts, visit relatives, participate in religious rites, and enjoy the many performances of religious stories conducted along the streets.

Chandi Temple plays an important role in this new form of goddess worship. The expansion of the popular city-wide Durga Puja has been an important factor in the rise of the goddess Chandi to the position of tutelary deity of Cuttack. Thousands of people crowd into the temple during the festival. Over 400 goats are sacrificed in honor of the goddess. It has become customary as well for the parade of mud Durga images to stop in front of the temple and pay respects to Chandi. In addition, Durga Puja is the time for both Bengali and Orissan merchants to make special offerings at the temple in the form of cash, gold, or saris.

The changes at Chandi Temple cannot simply be attributed to external events in Cuttack alone. We have noted the crucial relationship of the growth of Chandi temple to changes in patronage, government influence, and cultural diffusion, but this temple's adaptation to these broader changes is also linked to unusual internal characteristics of the institution.

Most of Orissa's temples have several families of priests who compete for a share in the offerings. Only one family of Brahmans presides as priests at Chandi Temple, and they have deliberately opposed attempts to bring in others. This has resulted in a strong sense of unity among the priests, attracting many devotees who are fed up with the bickering among priests at other temples. Also, the head priest at Chandi Temple is a young, charismatic figure who inspires great admiration. He has spent

time in West Bengal learning elaborate details of
the tantric rites performed in honor of the goddess.
This special training has given him a degree of le-
gitimacy among both Orissan and Bengali worshippers.
Perhaps the most important contributing factor to
Chandi Temple's growth can be traced to the "modern"
outlook of this priest who welcomes religious and
social change. He is keenly aware of the needs of
people who are recently urbanized and encourages the
elaboration of dramatic rites which captivate the
participants. Although the head priest may be considered unscrupulous by a few orthodox members of
the community, he is a source of inspiration and a
model of holiness for most people.

Today Chandi Temple continues to flourish. Over
1,500 people attend on a typical day. During the
Durga Festival as many as 60,000 devotees may visit
Chandi Temple. Its income has increased to over
250,000 rupees per year. This amount is on a par
with some of the largest temples in India and is
more than sufficient to cover operating expenses.
Although the temple still relies on some economic
support from individual donors, most of its income
is derived from the auction of concessions introduced by the Endowment Commission. The present condition of economic independence from the raja has
thrust the temple irreversibly into the commercial
economy of Cuttack.

Religious institutions caught up in the vortex
of rapid change may adapt, decline, or cling to the
old traditions. Many temples can be found in the
last category. They somehow manage to operate without being seriously affected by changes around them.
This is particularly true of neighborhood shrines
located on side streets in quiet enclaves of Cuttack.
Most of these temples maintain stable attendance
and do not have the problems associated with larger
pilgrimage centers. Chandi Temple was once one of
these, but has come to hold a key position in the
religious life of Cuttack. Its economic infrastruc-
ture articulates well with the commercial economy
of the city. Thus, it is a prime example of the
adaptability of Hinduism's institutional base. The
exiting religious atmosphere at Chandi Temple adds
to its popularity and may be seen as a response to
the growing demand for religious institutions which
can appeal to needs of newly urbanized people.

This popularism, however, has its price. Temples that depart from more traditional patterns of
piety develop a reputation in conservative circles
for being shallow and disloyal to the spiritual

tradition of Hinduism. Remnants of the past do not die easily. Many conservative Hindus are suspicious of sudden popularity; too often they have seen the results of insincere religious specialists who have taken advantage of an innocent public. Although their caution is often well founded, sometimes it is taken too far and masks a deeper conservatism that sees any hint of modernity or change as a corruption of some bygone era when Hinduism was pure. When a religious institution adapts to a new social order, it becomes vulnerable to attacks from conservative quarters. This has happened in the case of Chandi Temple.

Fortunately, in most quarters Chandi Temple has managed to sustain a good reputation. If it continues to strike a balance between modernity and tradition, its role of prominence in Cuttack will most likely be sustained. However, fame and fortune may become burdensome. Already there are signs of internal dissention about how to spend the large profits of the temple. There is also the possibility that further growth could bring about problems similar to those found among Orissa's larger pilgrimage shrines. Whatever the outcome, the case of Chandi Temple suggests that future studies of religious change in India need to address themselves to the unique combination of variables which influence the institutional base of Hinduism.

KAPILESWAR TEMPLE

Kapileswar is a small, multicaste village of about 2,800 inhabitants. It lies adjacent to Old Bhubaneswar, famous for its ancient temples (Panigrahi 1961). Although Bhubaneswar is a secondary pilgrimage center with predominantly local patronage, Lingaraj Temple with its satellite temple in Kapileswar, like the great Indian temples, once provided a livelihood for many castes devoted to the care of the deities and properties of the temples and had many social and educational functions as well. (Aiyer 1946; Bhardwaj 1973; Mishra 1971; Ramesan 1962; Stein 1960; Vidyarthi 1961).

Until the mid-twentieth century, Kapileswar Temple and its endowed properties and paddy lands were controlled by a hereditary trustee from a temple servant caste called Mallia. This trustee distributed the temple lands to Mallias and to other castes in return for their performance of obligatory, specialized, interdependent, hereditary services in the

temple.
There were three types of services: first, daily rituals at which the deity of the temple was bathed, clothed, fed its four meals, entertained, and put to bed at night; second, annual festivals which focused on life-cycle rituals for the deity, including birthday, sacred thread, marriage, and ritual bathing; finally, rituals for pilgrims who visited the deity and bought sacred food cooked in the temple. In all, three-quarters of the villagers received some economic benefit from the temple.

As late as the last quarter of the nineteenth century, Kapileswar was a flourishing, if small, temple complex (Mitra 1880:58). Like other religious institutions in British-held Orissa, the lands of Kapileswar Temple remained by law nontaxable and nonsalable. This provided Kapileswar with greater stability than Orissan villages without temple land grants (Hunter 1872:264-267, 273-274; O'Malley 1929: 233-234, 227-228; Sahu 1956:395-396). During this period the Mallias directed extensive temple repairs and new construction. They also expanded existing rituals by bringing additional Brahmans into the service of Kapileswar Temple.

Decline of the Temple

Since the early twentieth century, six major changes have affected Kapileswar Temple. First, many obligatory rituals and offerings have been abandoned. The most critical loss is that of the obligatory daily temple rituals of a caste called Khuntia Brahman. Only two young Khuntias of Kapileswar have received any ritual training, and they do not know or perform these rituals accurately. When the older generation dies, these rituals will die with them.

Second, since 1920 attendance at daily services at Kapileswar Temple has declined from nineteen to ten persons.

Third, public participation in annual temple festivals has declined. Even at the deity's birthday, Shivaratri, formerly Kapileswar's most important and widely attended festival, the only attendants are those who have obligatory services that day. The decline of this festival occurred between 1966 and 1972.

Fourth, daily services since 1957 have frequently been suspended, sometimes for months on end. Since Kapileswar does not attract many pilgrims, some Mallias and most Khuntia Brahmans supplement their incomes by working at the Lingaraj Temple, the main shrine of Bhubaneswar, which draws many pilgrims. The Mallias have no hereditary privileges at Lingaraj, but the Lingaraj priests hire them to take pilgrims on tours and find them food and lodging. The Khuntias have the hereditary right to cook and sell sacred food to Lingaraj pilgrims. Consequently, most Khuntias have virtually abandoned services at Kapileswar in favor of working at the larger and more remunerative shrine. Since the Mallias depend on the Khuntias to cook their sacred food, the Khuntia absence has led to disputes and work stoppages at Kapileswar.

Fifth, in 1946 the Orissa Hindu Religious Endowments Commission removed the hereditary Mallia manager of Kapileswar Temple because Mallias complained that he mismanaged the services. The Commission appointed a Brahman outsider as the trustee of the temple. The Mallias realized too late that they had lost all administrative control of their temple. Their activities led to court cases, frequent work stoppages, disputes, and violence, culminating in the year-long Mallia take-over of the Khuntia Brahman temple kitchens. Finally, in 1969 a well-known state political leader who lived near Kapileswar proposed an acceptable compromise. The Mallias handed back the kitchens to the Khuntia Brahmans and, in return, the Commission restored the management of Kapileswar Temple to the Mallias. Nevertheless, the Commission retains the power to remove the present Mallia manager.

Sixth, by 1971 fewer than 22 percent of the Mallia males depended on the temple for their main source of income, and 52 percent of the 252 working Mallia males had abandoned temple service altogether. Mallia businesses increased from four in 1950 to thirty in 1971. In 1953 only three Mallias worked as government servants. By 1971 sixty-three Mallias, or 25 percent of the work force, held government jobs. Over the same period there was a similar spectacular increase in the formal schooling of young Mallias, with a corresponding increase in the number and percentage of Mallias who secured higher level government appointments as clerks. By 1971 half of the Mallias who held government positions were clerks (Freeman 1971:5-7; 1974b). The age difference between these high school and college educated clerks (average age twenty-nine) and the illiterate and semi-literate Mallias whose main occupation is temple work (average age twenty-nine) and the illiterate and semi-literate Mallias whose main occupation is temple work (average age fifty-four) provides the most striking indication of recent shifts in Mallia occupations.

Since working in a government office conflicts with being able to do pilgrim work, not a single Mallia government servant relies on pilgrims as an important source of income. But they do have time to do occasional pilgrim work as well as obligatory services and personal worship at the temple. Nevertheless, the Mallia government servants have largely abandoned services and prayers at Kapileswar Temple, their ancestral caste temple.

Flourishing Popular Religious Movements

The foregoing changes do not necessarily mean that the villagers of Kapileswar are secularizing or abandoning religion. They appear rather to be turning to other forms of religious expression. Many villagers consult kalasis, or shamanistic faith curers, for help in crises. Kalasis are said to become possessed by the goddess Kali and thus gain her curative powers. Kalasis may be either men or women, but they usually come from low or untouchable castes. Many of the curers participate in an annual firewalking and physical ordeal ceremony, or Jhammu, held in mid-April (Das 1953:49, 83-84; O'Malley 1929:84; Freeman 1974a:54-63). In 1971, although seven kalasis lived in Kapileswar, only one, an untouchable, did firewalking.

The Jhammu is widely attended by Kapileswar villagers. Many of them go to the ceremonies held at a village located a mile away. With the kalasis leading the way, people of all castes walk over hot coals as a testimony to their faith that the goddess Kali can cure them or help them out of difficulties. Permission to walk over the coals comes from the kalasis who remain in trance throughout the day. In this condition they are said to be the goddess Kali herself. After walking over the coals, the kalasis drink the blood of sacrificed animals and then offer advice and cure their followers, who include high-caste educated government servants as well as illiterate low caste peasants.

Within Kapileswar, kalasis as well as other villagers of all castes worship at twenty small mother goddess shrines. These popular religious activities represent a vitality which is lacking in the reluctantly performed obligatory services of Kapileswar Temple.

One of the most interesting new developments is the rise of the Trinath Mela, an intercaste devotional songfest at which devotees share sacred food and ganja, or hemp. The ceremony is considered a form of diversion as well as a religious ritual. Although previously worshipped inside the house, since 1950 the worship of Trinath has become a public spectacle performed at shrines and front-house verandas throughout the Bhubaneswar area. This ritual is widely attended by government clerks.

Another new development for Bhubaneswar, as in Cuttack, is the dramatic rise of Durga Puja activities. In 1950 and in 1962 Durga Puja was a small festival in Bhubaneswar celebrated primarily by a few Bengali residents. The villagers of Kapileswar did not celebrate the festival because they believed that Kali, their patron goddess, would resent it and punish them. By 1971 Durga Puja had become one of the big events of the festival year in Bhubaneswar. Throughout the Old Town and the New Capital, residents built large cement pandals—roofed structures of three walls and one open side—in which images depicting events in the life of the goddess were constructed. Over twenty neighborhoods in the Old Town built displays and entered them in a competition which was judged by a leading resident of the Old Town. Kapileswar's Fisherman ward, which is adjacent to the Old Town and lies outside the traditional boundaries of the village, was the only ward of Kapileswar that competed.

The festivities lasted for three days and nights and included chanting by priests, personal offerings and prayers, feasts, musical performances, and a final celebration in which a singing, dancing crowd gathered all of the images and threw them into a small river near Bhubaneswar. After immersion, the images are no longer considered to have the spirit of the deity inside them.

Reasons for Religious Changes

There are four reasons why Kapileswar Temple is declining while popular religion is flourishing. First, economic fluctuations have profoundly affected the temple. Kapileswar Temple owns over 300 acres of tax-free, non-salable paddy lands. These lands, which were distributed to various castes that served the temple, were supposed to yield an income that would (1) provide economic security for the priests so that they could devote their time to service for the deity and (2) pay for daily services and offerings to the deity of the temple.

During the past century, due to population increases, temple landholdings were subdivided through inheritance into parcels of land that were so small that most landowning families had barely enough to live on. Over half of the families of Kapileswar became landless, including half of the Mallias, who sold or lost their rights to temple-endowed lands. Thus, the temple did not have enough land to provide even minimum incomes for those who were qualified to pursue their hereditary occupations.

Furthermore, the people of Kapileswar were frequently hit for several successive years by major disasters, including cyclones, droughts, floods, and epidemics, causing widespread loss of life, massive destruction of crops, and property. (*Census of India* 1961:11-12; Government of Orissa 1972:22-24, 63-68; Freeman 1977:20-23). Consequently, Mallias and other temple workers sought occupations outside the temple. Those who remained at the temple fought over rights to serve pilgrims or prepare sacred food. Priests simplified or abandoned temple services when the cost of offerings exceeded the income they received from their miniscule parcels of temple land. The morale of temple servants declined.

The construction of the New Capital provided new occupations for the hard pressed villagers of Kapileswar and thus reduced their dependence on the temple. The rise of the new city did not cause the decline of the temple but rather hastened a deterioration that was already well under way. As the Capital expanded, some of its new residents patronized Kapileswar Temple but not sufficiently to offset its economic decline.

In contrast, popular religion benefited from the growth of the urban center. Many patrons from the Capital attended firewalking and other popular festivals and consulted shamanistic curers when they were beset with crises. These curers were individually more easily supported by patrons than were temple priests since donations to priests had to be used to support both the priests and their temple. The Durga Puja celebrations in the Old Town and New Capital were sponsored by businessmen without whose support the festival would not have expanded as rapidly and widely as it did.

A second reason for the decline of the temple was government interference in its management.

Nineteenth century British laws provided the basis for contemporary post-Independence legislation in several Indian states regulating the management of Hindu religious endowments (Derrett 1966:311-336; and O'Malley 1929:233-234). Because temples were frequently plagued by mismanagement and caste factionalism, government officials were understandably often unsympathetic to their plight. In contrast, popular religious activities such as firewalking, the Trinath Mela, and Durga Puja were not subject to the same official scrutiny and control from government officials.

Third, the temple traditionally was associated with elaborate ritualism and caste restrictions that were appropriate for village life but did not fit the ideology of postindependence India and the lifestyle of contemporary cities. The temple service epitomized rigid caste restrictions and separation. Furthermore, the proper performance of temple rituals was complex and time consuming. In contrast, the rituals of popular performances were more flexible and the barriers of caste were loosened. In the Trinath Mela individuals of different castes sang together and shared offerings of food. At Durga Puja multicaste neighborhoods that often were comprised of virtual strangers organized the festival and competed together as a group. Such intercaste festivals are not new to the Hindu tradition, but they have received greater emphasis in urbanizing and modernizing settings. Mallia civil servants did not have time to perform the day-long temple rituals, but in the evenings they had time to sing at the Trinath Mela.

Finally, faced with limited funds Kapileswar Temple could not sponsor large spectacles and spectator attendance declined. Patrons turned instead to popular festivals. Temple rituals did not have the immediacy and personal involvement of popular festivals. Pilgrims who visited the temple had rituals performed for them by hereditary priests. These rituals focused primarily on what Mandelbaum calls the long-term transcendental needs of clients (Maundelbaum 1964:5-20). In contrast, popular rituals like the Trinath Mela involved the direct participation of devotees and usually focused on their immediate, practical needs or desires.

CONCLUSION

The studies of Chandi and Kapileswar Temples describe two cases of change and modernization that have occurred without religious disintegration or secularization, that is, without the loss of a religious outlook or world view. Our conclusions agree with those of Milton Singer (1972:140-144, 246, 385, 398-399) who contends that religion is neither disintegrating nor secularizing in the modern south Indian city of Madras; new expressions of religion have developed that creatively utilize traditional elements and represent an adaptation from a rural to an urban environment. The shift Singer noted is essentially similar to those in Cuttack and Bhubaneswar: away from ritualism and towards devotionalism. In Bhubaneswar, temple rituals have given way to devotional celebrations such as the Trinath Mela; in Cuttack, the worship of Chandi includes devotional worship. In both Cuttack and Bhubaneswar, Durga Puja celebrations have expanded, since they meet the social and psychological needs of burgeoning urban populations.

Some studies of Indian temples purport to show that temples are declining, priestly communities are demoralized, temples are incapable of adapting to modern influences, and the forces of secularization are overwhelming temple communities (Vidyarthi 1961: Jindel 1976). Chandi Temple, located in a bustling commercial city, presents the opposite picture, a temple that is expanding and flourishing precisely because it has both adapted to and is benefiting from modern urban life. Even in Kapileswar, where the temple has declined in the face of urbanization, the modernizing priests, who are now civil servants and businessmen, display no evidence of crises of faith or of viewing their traditional religious lifestyle as incompatible with the modernizing life styles of the town. The crises of the Kapileswar priests are economic and political, not religious. The differing conclusions of temple studies throughout India reflect different assumptions by their authors, but they also suggest that regional variations and types of urban centers affect directions of change.

Max Weber (1958), Gunnar Myrdal (1968), and Marion Levy, Jr. (1966; 1972), as well as many other authors, claim that other-worldly religions such as Hinduism, and life-styles such as the Hindu lifestyle, are incompatible with modernization, since such religious life-styles will either hinder or be destroyed by modernization (Weber 1958:11, 122-123, 325-328; Myrdal 1968:1081, 1148, 1692; Levy 1966: 513-615; 1972:3-10). The events both at Kapileswar and Chandi Temples contradict these views.

The priestly community of Kapileswar finds no difficulty in accommodating modern urbanization to their traditional religious life-styles. They view the changes that have occurred, not as bringing a wholly new life-style, but as an extension of their old one. They consider the roles of government clerk and temple priest to be similar because both are prestigious, embedded in a clear-cut hierarchy, and involve ritualized behaviors. Moreover, the Mallia priests-turned-civil servants, although no longer serving the deity of their temple, remain proud of their caste and their hereditary position as representatives of the deity of Kapileswar, in whom they retain strong faith. They are proud to live within the sacred boundaries of Kapileswar and often speak of themselves as part of a religious tradition and community. Each day they recite prayers and perform personal rituals. Although working in a modern urban setting, they have neither lost nor even questioned the basic symbols of their religious world view. They reveal no loss of religious faith or anguish over religious change. They have separated their secular work from their personal religion, a process of adaptation to modernization that Singer terms "compartmentalization" (1972: 320-325).

Events at Chandi Temple are even harder to explain for theorists who predict the demise of traditional religious institutions. Chandi Temple is an important agent of modernization in Cuttack city. The temple attracts rich, devout merchants who give it large donations and support. The priests of the temple have adapted to the needs of an emerging urban elite, and the temple is tied to the popular city-wide Durga Puja celebrations. The worship of Chandi fits the psychological needs of individuals trying to cope with the new stresses, competition, dislocations, and alienation in the city.

These studies of Chandi and Kapileswar Temples, like those of Singer (1966:55-67; 1972:245-414), question the assumptions that traditional world views are necessarily incompatible with rapidly changing and modernizing social environments and that modernization necessarily produces secularization. Many writers, including Mandelbaum (1972: 638-654 and Lloyd and Susanne Rudolph (1967:6) have observed that tradition and modernity in India are compatible. Chandi and Kapileswar Temples provide additional evidence amply supporting these views.

NOTES

1. Portions of Freeman's part of this chapter first appeared in "Religious Change in a Hindu Pilgrimage Center," *Review of Religious Research*, copyrighted by the Religious Research Association and used here with its permission.
2. The deep conflict over the management of Chandi Temple became so bitter and intense that the Endowment Commission departed from its usual policy of protecting the existing power structure.

REFERENCES

Aiyer, V. G. Ramakrishna. 1946. *The Economy of a South Indian Temple*. Annamalainager, India: Annamalai University Press.

Bhardwaj, Surinder Mohan. 1973. *Hindu Places of Pilgrimage in India*. Berkeley, California: University of California Press.

Census of India. 1961. Orissa District Census Handbook, Puri. Cuttack, India: Orissa Government Press.

⸻⸻⸻. 1963. Orissa: General Report, XII: I-A, Cuttack: Government of India Press.

⸻⸻⸻. 1963. Orissa: General Population Tables, XII: II-A, Cuttack: Government of India Press.

Census of India. 1971.

⸻⸻⸻. 1972. Final Population. New Delhi, India: Government of India Press.

Das, Kunjabehari. 1953. *Orissan Folklore*. Santiniketin, India: Santiniketin Press.

Derrett, J. Duncan. 1966. The Reform of Hindu Religious Endowments, pp. 311-336 in *South Asian Politics and Religion*, edited by Donald E. Smith. Princeton, New Jersey: Princeton University Press.

Freeman, James M. 1971. Occupational Changes Among Hindu Temple Servants. *Indian Anthropologist* 1 (November):1-13.

⸻⸻⸻. 1974a. Trial by Fire. *Natural History* 83 (January):54-63.

⸻⸻⸻. 1974b. Occupational Changes in an Urbanizing Hindu Temple Village. *Man in India* 54 (January):1-20.

⸻⸻⸻. 1975. Religious Change in a Hindu Pilgrimage Center. *Review of Religious Research* 16 (2):124-133.

1977. *Scarcity and Opportunity in an Indian Village*. Menlo Park, California: Cummings Publishing Company.

Government of Orissa, Bureau of Statistics and Economics. 1972. *Report on the Sample Survey for Estimation of Loss in Yield Rates of Khariff Crops Due to the Flood and Cyclone of 1971 in Orissa*. Cuttack, India: Orissa Government Press.

Hunter, W. W. 1872. Orissa: Or the Vicissitudes of an Indian Province Under Native and British Rule. Vol. 2 of *A History of Orissa*, edited by N. K. Sahu. Calcutta, India: Susil Gupta, Ltd.

Jindel, Rajendra. 1976. *Culture of a Sacred Town: A Sociological Study of Nathadwara*. Bombay, India: Popular Prakashan.

Kulke, Hermann. 1976. *Kshatriyaization and Social Change: A Study in Orissa Setting*. Reprint 177. Heidelberg, Germany: South Asia Institute of Heidelberg University.

Levy, Marion J., Jr. 1966. *Modernization and the Structure of Societies*. Princeton, New Jersey: Princeton University Press.

1972. *Modernization: Latecomers and Survivors*. New York, New York: Basic Books.

Mahapatra, L. K. 1978. Gods, Kings and the Caste System in India, pp. 7-26 in *Community, Self, and Identity*, edited by B. Misra and J. Preston. The Hague: Mouton Publishers.

Mahapatra, Manamohan. 1971. "Lingaraj Temple: Its Structure and Change." Doctoral dissertation, Utkal University, Orissa, India.

Mandelbaum, David. 1964. Introduction: Process and Structure in South Asian Religion. *Journal of Asian Studies* 23 (June):5-20.

1972. *Society in India*. Berkeley, California: University of California Press.

Miller, David, and Dorothy Wertz. 1976. *Hindu Monastic Life*. Montreal: McGill-Queen's University Press.

Mishra, Kanhu Charan. 1971. *The Cult of Jagannatha*. Calcutta, India: Firma K. L. Mukhopadhyay.

Mitra, Rajendralala. 1880. *The Antiquities of Orissa*. Vol. 2 Calcutta, India: Wyman and Company. (1963 reprint: *Indian Studies Past and Present*.)

Myrdal, Gunnar. 1968. *Asian Drama: An Inquiry into the Poverty of Nations*. New York: Pantheon.

O'Malley, L. 1929. *Puri District Gazeteer*. Patna, India: Superintendent, Government Printing, Bihar and Orissa.

Panigrahi, Krishna Chandra. 1961. *Archaeological Remains at Bhubaneswar*. Bombay, India: Orient Longmans.

Preston, James J. *Cult of the Goddess*. New Delhi, India: Vikas Publishers (in press).

⎯⎯⎯⎯ 1978. Commercial Economy of an Urban Temple, pp. 27-35 in *Community, Self, and Identity*, edited by B. Misra and James Preston. The Hague: Mouton Publishers.

Ramesan, N. 1962. *Temples and Legends of Andhra Pradesh*. Bombay, India: Bharatiya Vidya Bhavan.

Rudolph, Lloyd and Susanne Rudolph. 1967. *The Modernity of Tradition*. Chicago, Illinois: University of Chicago Press.

Sahu, N. K., editor. 1956. *A History of Orissa*. Calcutta, India: Susil Gupta, Ltd.

Singer, Milton. 1966. The Modernization of Religious Beliefs, pp. 55-67 in *Modernization*, edited by Myron Weiner. New York, New York: Basic Books.

⎯⎯⎯⎯ 1972. *When A Great Tradition Modernizes*. New York, New York: Praeger.

Stein, Burton. 1960. The Economic Function of a Medieval South Indian Temple. *Journal of Asian Studies* 19 (2):163-176.

Vidyarthi, L. 1961. *The Sacred Complex of Hindu Gaya*. Bombay, India: Asia Publishing House.

Weber, Max. 1958. *The Religion of India*. Glencoe, Illinois: The Free Press.

Part 3
Educational Adaptations

Susan Seymour received a Ph.D. in anthropology from Harvard University in 1971 and is currently an associate professor of anthropology at Pitzer College, Claremont, California. She conducted a two-year research project in Bhubaneswar, Orissa, India, from 1965-67, comparing family organization and child-rearing practices in the old and the new parts of town. Her Ph.D. thesis, "Childrearing in a Changing Indian Town: Sources and Expressions of Dependence and Independence," and a number of articles in professional anthropology journals are based on that research. In 1978 she returned to India to participate in the Xth International Congress on Anthropological and Ethnological Sciences in New Delhi and to do follow-up research in Bhubaneswar.

Chapter 6 summarizes some of the more important differences Dr. Seymour noted in her investigation of childrearing practices in the Old Town and the New Capital, their relationship to differences in family organization and socioeconomic status, and some of their implications for dependent and self-reliant behavior.

6

Patterns of Childrearing in a Changing Indian Town

Susan Seymour

Bhubaneswar with its two different parts of town and its two different populations offered an excellent setting for a comparative study of family organization and childrearing practices. For example, in the Old Town people lived in houses of varying sizes and shapes, densely clustered around a set of medieval temples. Households were frequently joint in structure, and neighborhoods were organized by caste and kinship. Thus, Old Town residents generally lived surrounded by relatives. By contrast, New Capital houses were built in similar styles and were well dispersed along neatly organized rows of intersecting avenues and lanes. Because New Capital residents were assigned houses according to their status in the government service hierarchy, their neighborhoods were not organized by caste or kinship. In addition, most New Capital households were nuclear in structure since residents had recently moved there, leaving their extended kin behind.

Not only were Old Town and New Capital households strikingly different in physical setting and structure, but their membership was also very different with regard to educational attainment and occupation. In the Old Town most adults had a low level of formal education and pursued traditional caste occupations, such as temple service, carpentry, and barbering, for which formal schooling was not necessary. By contrast, the occupational structure of the New Capital was dominated by the state government's civil service system for which various levels of formal education were required. As a result, two different systems of social stratification operated in Bhubaneswar. In the Old Town a system of ascribed status based upon caste membership prevailed, whereas in the New Capital a class system based upon such achieved criteria as level of education, occupation, and income was emerging.

My original research problem, therefore, was to determine whether or not these kinds of differences between life in the Old Town and the New Capital would result in significant differences in the handling of children and hence in children's behavior. I chose as a focus the behavioral domain of dependence/self-reliance because of the numerous remarks and hypotheses which have been offered over the years suggesting that certain elements of the Indian social structure tend to produce a passive and dependent personality. For example, it has been suggested that the caste system puts a premium on fatalistic acceptance, conformity, and dependence at the expense of personal initiative, individual decision making, and ambition (Carstairs 1967; Murphy 1953; Taylor 1948). Similarly, the joint family has been characterized as emphasizing passive and dependent qualities to the exclusion of individuality and independence because, presumably, the child is taught to submit to the authority of others, to rely on others for help and support rather than learning to handle his own problems, and to be cooperative rather than assertive (Murphy 1953; Nimkoff 1960; Taylor 1943). Accordingly, Taylor (1948) has concluded that the basic personality in orthodox Hindu culture is one that seeks "security in dependence" and is not ambitious. Finally, two observational studies of Indian mothers and children found that the mothers tolerated a great deal of dependence in their children and did not train for self-reliance (Ames and Randeri 1965; Minturn and Hitchcock 1966). The children, in turn, tended to demand help from others rather than attempting to do things by themselves and to learn primarily through passive observation and imitation rather than by deliberate instruction or experimentation.

Taking these kinds of remarks and observations regarding the handling of dependence and self-reliance among Indian children as a point of departure, I then set forth some propositions concerning Old Town versus New Capital childrearing practices which in a more formalistic study might have been stated in the form of hypotheses. For example, I reasoned that if the child's initial physical dependence were generally indulged and prolonged in India, this tendency would be more characteristic of the Old Town where there were large, joint households and hence more potential caretakers than of the New Capital where households were small and nuclear and where mothers alone cared for their children. Similarly, I reasoned that in Old Town households where people lived surrounded by kin more emphasis would be placed upon the interdependence of household members and less upon their self-reliance, whereas in the New Capital where people lived apart from their extended kin more emphasis would be placed upon the child's self-reliance. Thus, I proposed that New Capital parents would be more concerned with modern educational and occupational goals than Old Town parents. This would be yet another factor encouraging them to train for more self-reliance and independent decision-making in their children.

These propositions juxtaposing Old Town and New Capital childrearing practices were qualified by considerations of socioeconomic status. For example, I expected that the protracted physical dependence of children would be less possible in low caste/class households where women as well as men worked outside the home to help support the family. In such families, where women's workloads were heavy, mothers could not afford to prolong their children's dependence upon them, I reasoned, and would have to train for greater self-reliance. Thus, I expected that low caste/class children would be more self-reliant than other children regardless of Old Town or New Capital residence.

THE SAMPLE OF HOUSEHOLDS

In order to investigate these propositions regarding the handling of dependence and self-reliance in Bhubaneswar children, I selected a stratified sample of households from each part of town to observe for a two-year period.[1] Using caste as the diagnostic criterion for the Old Town, twelve households were selected which represented the range of statuses there from Brahmans, who were the traditional landowners and temple servants, to unclean Shudras and untouchables (Table 6.1). In the New Capital I used the household head's position in the civil service hierarchy, which was correlated with income and education, to select twelve households which represented the ranges of statuses there from high government officials to peons and sweepers (Table 6.2).[2] Altogether, I had a total of twenty-four households that could loosely be designated as upper, middle, or lower in socioeconomic status to

TABLE 6.1
Sample of Households: Old Town

Socio-economic Status	Caste	Occupation of Household Head	Income of Household Head per Month	Years of Schooling of Household Head
Upper	Brahman	Temple Servant	Rs. 340	0
	Brahman	Temple Servant	Rs. 150	7
	Brahman	Contractor	Rs. 400	11
	Brahman	Elementary School Teacher	Rs. 200	7
Middle	Barber	Barber	Rs. 200	0
	Cowherder	Selling Milk & Government Telephone Exchange	Rs. 650	11
	Carpenter	Carpenter	Rs. 200	4
	Bricklayer	Cement and Brick Layer	Rs. 200	0
Lower	Bauri*	Laborer	Rs. 35	0
	Bauri*	Laborer	Rs. 35	0
	Washerman	Washerman	Rs. 200	5
	Washerman	Washerman	Rs. 200	5

*A scheduled caste group of tribal origin.

study, each of which had two or more children under the age of ten (Table 6.3).

The twenty-four households selected for intensive study represented a range in size, structure, and organization of interpersonal roles, factors which are both critical to the rearing of children and suggestive of the flexibility and adaptability of Bhubaneswar families. For example, in the Old Town sample nine of the twelve households were joint, whereas in the New Capital all twelve sample households were nuclear. However, the Old Town joint households represented a variety of types. Four were collateral joint in the full sense of the term: Household members cooked their own food on one

TABLE 6.2
Sample of Households: New Capital

Socio-economic Status	Caste	Occupation of Household Head	Income of Household Head per Month	Years of Schooling of Household Head
Upper	Brahman	Superintending Engineer	Rs. 1150	19
	Karan	Deputy Sec. Revenue Dept.	Rs. 1000	17
	Karan	Deputy Sec. Works & Transport Dept.	Rs. 1100	17
	Karan	Town Planner	Rs. 1300	17
Middle	Brahman	Asst. Sec. Finance Dept.	Rs. 600	14
	Bania	Sec. Construction Dept.	Rs. 600	15
	Brahman	Dept. Controller Mining Corp.	Rs. 700	18
	Karan	Community Dev. Dept.	Rs. 700	17
Lower	Sweeper	Govt. sweeper	Rs. 112	7
	Sweeper	Govt. sweeper	Rs. 112	4
	Kayastha	Govt. peon	Rs. 70	5
	Weaver	Govt. night watchman	Rs. 60	5

hearth, held property in common, shared all of their resources, and participated in common family worship. Three more were partially collateral joint in that sets of brothers, their wives, and children resided together but did not always cook together, share all material goods, or hold property in common. These were lower caste families who were landless but who lived in contiguous quarters, sharing a central yard and caring for one another's children. Thus, for the purposes of childrearing, they operated as joint households. Two other Old Town households were lineal and lineal-collateral joint respectively. Of the three Old Town households which were nuclear, one had only recently become so when two brothers divided up the family property, and all three had extended kin living nearby.

TABLE 6.3
Sample of Children (Birth to Ten Years)

Socioeconomic Status	Old Town	New Capital	Total
Upper	23	11	34
Middle	17	19	36
Lower	23	10	33
Total	63	40	103

Although all twelve New Capital sample households were technically nuclear in structure, nine were "supplemented nuclear" in that an unmarried or widowed relative resided with the family. In three instances these relatives were grandmothers who could help out with the care of the children. Several other families had nieces or nephews residing with them who had been sent to attend Bhubaneswar schools. One young married woman resided in Bhubaneswar with her parents so that her mother could look after her children while she attended graduate school. Her husband, who was an engineer in the government service but posted elsewhere, visited his family on weekends. Thus, even in the New Capital extended family ideals prevailed and, as in the instance just mentioned, the pursuit of a modern goal sometimes resulted in the establishment of an extended household. In addition, all the upper- and middle-class New Capital families depended upon their extended kin living in villages to supply them with rice. These families did not live surrounded by their kin, but they still maintained their extended kin ties.

Household size was, of course, generally correlated with household structure: Most of the large households (ten or more members) were Old Town joint ones, whereas all but two of the New Capital households were small (fewer than ten members).[3] Two of the large Old Town households had as many as twenty-five members, and two of the New Capital households had as few as five members, whereas all the rest ranged from six to fifteen. Actual size probably was not as critical a factor, however, as composition of the household. My concern with child care made *who* resided in a given household of particular interest: Were there other adults to share in the care of children, and how many children had to share the attention of a given adult? In this regard, the preponderance of large, joint households in the Old Town is important because it meant that few women there were alone to care for children and perform other household chores, whereas in the New Capital nuclear households most mothers did not have other women with whom to share housework and child care (See Table 6.7 for a breakdown of child care by different household members for the Old Town and the New Capital.)

Household structure is also important in terms of its effects upon interpersonal roles and relationships. Among upper and middle status households in the Old Town, relationships were governed by traditional rules of respect and avoidance. For example, women prepared food and served their husbands first; they themselves ate only after everyone else had been served. Young daughters-in-law were under the authority of their mothers-in-law and avoided contact with the men of the household, including their husbands. They expressed respect for others by keeping their sarees draped over their heads and their eyes lowered so that their faces were only minimally exposed. In addition, most Old Town women observed traditional rules of ritual pollution by not handling food or touching others during their menstrual periods and after giving birth. Married women of childbearing age in the Old Town also observed purdah and rarely left their houses and interior courtyards. There was a great deal of sexual segregation and emphasis upon relative age and status in these households.

Interpersonal relationships among upper and middle status families in the New Capital were considerably different. Freed from the supervision of in-laws, these New Capital women moved about their homes as they liked and rarely kept their heads covered and bowed. They also tended not to observe rules of ritual pollution. More importantly, New Capital husbands and wives observed fewer restrictions on their interaction together. For example, most had begun dining together rather than separately and rarely observed the rules of sexual segregation in their social lives. Two New Capital couples even shared a bedroom separate from their children, something unheard of in most Bhubaneswar households. Ordinarily, women slept with their children, separate from their husbands. In general, a more intimate conjugal relationship between spouses seemed to have emerged in the New Capital where people lived apart from extended kin.

There were fewer contrasts between Old Town and New Capital lower status households. In these poor families where both men and women worked outside the home, there was far less sexual segregation. Women could not observe purdah, and in general male and female roles were far more equalitarian. For example, husbands and wives took turns performing household chores and caring for children. In this instance, economic considerations outweighed those of etiquette.

SOME PATTERNS OF CHILDREARING

The object of my research was to determine how such factors as those outlined in the previous section might affect the care of children and, hence, the child's development in the behavioral domain of dependence/self-reliance. In order to do this I systematically observed adult-child behavior for a period of eighteen months, using a modified version of the techniques developed by J. Whiting, Child, and Lambert (1966) to record and code behavior for the Six Culture Study.[4] Altogether, after an initial period of learning Oriya and establishing rapport with each family, I collected some sixteen hours of behavior protocols per household. The time spent observing was equally divided among four different periods of the day when behavior was somewhat standardized from household to household. Observations focused upon mothers and their surrogates as they interacted with children under the age of ten. The following observations are based upon some 9,301 such interactions coded from the behavior protocols.

In general, the care of infants and young children in Bhubaneswar was casual and impersonal. Although children were greatly desired, once born, they were taken for granted and received little attention. In fact, there were taboos against praising or focusing attention upon an infant for fear of attracting the Evil Eye or other maloccurences. Thus, the care extended to infants and young children was largely of an instrumental kind, consisting primarily of feedings and the daily bath. The latter was a highly ritualized event during which the child was manipulated while massaged with turmeric and oil and then rinsed with water. The bath might occupy half an hour; most infants cried throughout it but were ignored.

> Mrs. M. (K.'s mother) sat on the floor with her legs stretched out in front of her. She had K. (male, three months) draped along her legs with his stomach down. He was crying. Mrs. M. was busy rubbing his back, buttocks, and legs with oil. K. cried steadily. Mrs. M. did nothing to comfort him. When she finished massaging him with mustard oil, she rubbed turmeric paste all over his body. She put it on thickly and then let it dry on K.'s body for ten minutes. K. continued to whimper. Mrs. M. paid no attention to him. Once she turned her head away from me and seemed to be muttering to herself. She did not talk to or comfort K. After the turmeric paste had dried sufficiently, Mrs. M. rubbed it off K.'s body with her right hand. She massaged K.'s back, buttocks, and legs again in the process. K. continued to complain. When the turmeric paste was removed, Mrs. M. sat K. up on her legs. K. continued to cry. When I asked about the purpose of the turmeric paste, she said that it was good for the body *(deha bhola)* in the sense of making it healthy (an Old Town upper status household, unpublished field notes).

Although nursing constituted the basis of most early mother-child contact, it, too, was handled in a routine and impersonal manner. In due time, mothers responded to their children's demands, but nursing was rarely an occasion when a mother sat quietly with her child, focusing on or enjoying him. Frequently, she continued her household chores while setting the child on her lap or balancing him on her hip with one arm, leaving her other arm free for work, and letting him reach up to her breast.

> Meanwhile Grandmother had come in carrying T. (male, two years). She deposited

130

MASSAGING
AND
BATHING
INFANTS

> T. with his mother and went out. For
> the next twenty minutes T. sat shyly
> near his mother, sucking her left breast
> as he wanted. At first he sat behind
> her left shoulder and leaned forward
> with his mouth on her breast. This was
> while his mother was still cutting vege-
> tables. When she finished cutting vege-
> tables, she stood up holding T. on her
> left hip. She moved to the side of the
> room with T. Then she sat down on the
> floor with him. T. now sat on her lap
> and sucked some more from her left
> breast (an Old Town middle status house-
> hold, unpublished field notes).

When she did sit down to nurse her child, it was usually for just a few minutes. Children were rarely nursed until satisfied; feedings consisted of one to five-minute periods after which a mother would abruptly remove the child from the breast and only continue the feeding when the child complained persistently. Thus, children learned early on that they had to make repeated demands for food and other attention.

> Mrs. S. returned to the back verandah with
> G. (female, one year) and nursed her for
> a moment on her left breast. (This was
> for the third time that morning during a
> one-hour period.) Then she stopped G.
> from sucking and made her sit up on her
> lap. G. sat on her mother's lap, crying
> intermittently, and reaching for her mo-
> ther's breast. Mrs. S. held her saree
> over the breast so that G. could not get
> to it. She laughed and tried to get G.
> to smile. Finally, G. broke into a smile.
> A few minutes later Mrs. S. pulled her
> saree back and let G. nurse some more.
> She let G. suck for a few minutes and
> then sat her up again (a New Capital mid-
> dle status household, unpublished field
> notes).

Although infants and young children were not the focus of special attention, they did experience extensive physical contact with others. While awake, they were often carried about on the left hip of their mothers or other caretakers. At night, during the nursing stage, a child always slept next to his

OLD TOWN CHILDREN
AND CARETAKERS

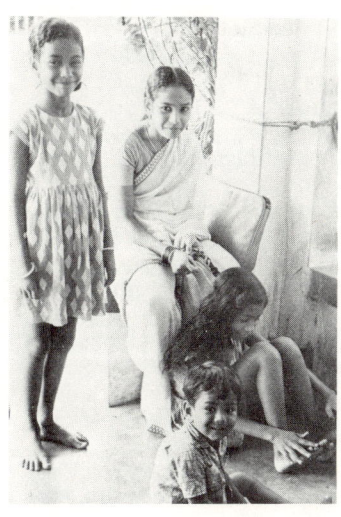

NEW CAPITAL CHILDREN
AND CARETAKERS

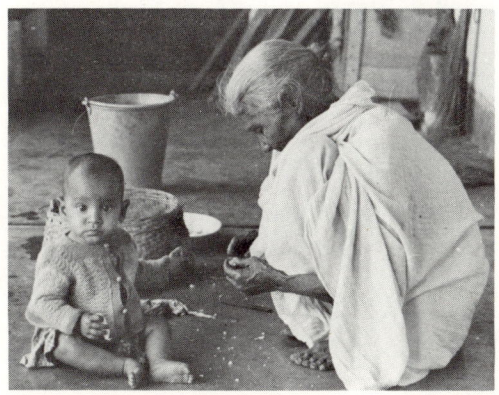

mother and either continued to sleep with her or some other adult throughout childhood. In addition, since there was little or no segregation of activities by age in Bhubaneswar households, children participated in all events. For example, during such long and important ceremonies as weddings, children were always present but usually unsupervised. They ran about freely, simply curling up on the floor and going to sleep when they grew tired. Thus, to a Western observer, Bhubaneswar children were strikingly present at all times but given little guidance or attention.

The child's physical and emotional development also received little or no focused attention. For example, people rarely remarked on a child's efforts to crawl or sit up, and when he walked for the first time, it went unnoticed. Similarly, the child's verbal efforts were not considered noteworthy. The situation was similar to that in Khalapur, India, as described by Minturn and Hitchcock: "The life of the Rajput baby is, aside from the daily bath, bland and free from stress, but it is also free from deliberate creative stimulation" (1966:316). The young child was viewed more as a member of a group than as a growing and developing individual. There was little of the Western notion that the child's development could or should be encouraged and molded. The difference is well captured by the following remark made by an Indian observer to a Westerner: "You bring up your children—we live with ours" (quoted by Murphy 1953:51).

One might correctly infer from the above discussion that the dependence of Bhubaneswar children was not deliberately encouraged. It was just assumed that young children would require routine instrumental care, and children soon learned to make persistent demands for such care and attention. In fact, these children were not passively dependent, simply awaiting the attention of others, but rather by necessity they became active seekers of care and attention.

My proposition that the child's dependence would be more prolonged in the Old Town than in the New Capital received some confirmation. For example, in both parts of Bhubaneswar people said that the appropriate age for a child to be weaned was two years. However, in the New Capital that was viewed as an upper limit, and in several instances children were weaned as early as three or four months and then bottle fed. New Capital mothers seemed embarrassed if their children were still nursing by one and one-half or two years. In the Old Town, on the other hand, children continued to be nursed beyond two years if their mothers did not become pregnant. Thus, I observed three- and four-year-olds still being breast fed. Similarly, it was in the Old Town that I observed mothers hand-feeding, bathing, and dressing their children of up to eight and nine years of age.

Feeding is particularly illustrative of this situation. Around the age of one year when solid foods were first introduced, mothers necessarily handfed their children. However, in many Old Town households mothers continued to handfeed their children well beyond the age at which a child could feed himself. In fact, in many instances a mother forced her attention on the child by not allowing him to feed himself.

> Third Wife put about six cups of rice on a brass plate, some dhal in one bowl, and some fried vegetables in another, and took the things to her room. She set them on the verandah floor. The food was for D. (male, five years) and B. (female, seven years). Third Wife sat down with the two children and proceeded to feed them by hand. B. cried because she did not want to be fed; she wanted to feed herself. Third Wife slapped her and went on feeding her. For half an hour Third Wife stuffed the food down the two children's reluctant throats. She mixed dhal with the rice, formed it into balls, and popped them into their mouths. The children began to refuse the food. Third Wife yelled at them, grabbed hold of their heads, shoved the heads back with her left hand and shoved the food into their mouths with her right hand (an Old Town upper status household, unpublished field notes).

By contrast, in the New Capital, where mothers were alone to care for their children, they allowed them to feed, bathe, and dress themselves. These mothers did not deliberately train their children to perform these actions, but they were more tolerant of their children's efforts to care for themselves.

Mrs. P. rubbed some coconut oil on D.'s

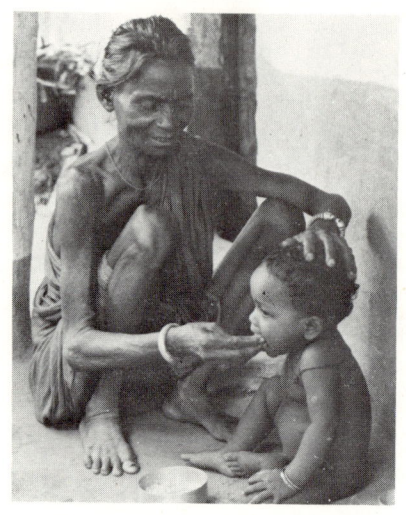

OLD TOWN CHILDREN
BEING FED AND BATHED

NEW CAPITAL CHILDREN
EATING AND BATHING

(male, two-and-one-half years) hair. Then she began to bathe him under a water tap in the courtyard. D. insisted upon pouring the water over himself. He stood up during the entire bath. When his mother tried to soap him, D. insisted on taking the bar of soap and soaping himself. Mrs. P. did not object. Then while Mrs. P. finished the soaping, D. took a cloth and began rubbing his body with it. When it was time to rinse off the soap, D. again insisted on doing it himself. He seemed to be enjoying himself. The only thing that he did not like was having his face washed. He made a face and only allowed his mother to wash it with water, not soap. Mrs. P finished rinsing him and dried him with a towel. D. kept grabbing one end of the towel and trying to dry himself. He also grabbed his mother's saree. She did not object (a New Capital middle status household, unpublished field notes).

The proposition that dependence is more prolonged in the Old Town than in the New Capital also received some statistical confirmation. Table 6.4 demonstrates that Old Town mothers and their surrogates directed a higher proportion of such nurturant acts as feeding, bathing, dressing, comforting, helping, and carrying children to older children (six- to ten-year olds) than did New Capital mothers

TABLE 6.4
Maternal Nurturance: Age-Grade of Child by Location of Residence

Age of Child	Old Town (N=100)		New Capital (N=55)	
	# of Acts	%	# of Acts	%
0-2	577	68.7	521	72.3
3-5	171	20.3	151	21.0
6-10	92	11.0	48	6.7
Total	840	100.0	720	100.0

$x^2 = 8.72$, $p < .014$

and mother-surrogates. Reciprocally, a higher proportion of Old Town children's efforts to seek care from others occurred during that later period than for New Capital children (Table 6.5). However, this relationship of age to nurturance-seeking or dependence is far more statistically significant when analyzed by household size (Table 6.6), which suggests that the critical factor is not simply location of residence but the availability of other persons to whom the child can direct his dependent requests.

TABLE 6.5
Seeking Nurturance: Age of Child by Location of Residence

Age of Child	Old Town (N=63)		New Capital (N=40)	
	# of Acts	%	# of Acts	%
0-2	413	67.4	442	66.3
3-5	127	20.7	163	24.4
6-10	73	11.9	62	9.3
Total	613	100.0	667	100.0

$X^2 = 4.06$, $p<.15$

TABLE 6.6
Seeking Nurturance: Age of Child by Household Size

Age of Child	Large (N=54)		Small (N=49)	
	# of Acts	%	# of Acts	%
0-2	391	65.8	464	67.6
3-5	118	19.9	172	25.1
6-10	85	14.3	50	7.3
Total	594	100.0	686	100.0

$X^2 = 18.9$, $p<.001$

Table 6.7 lists these different categories of people and compares the proportion of nurturant acts for the Old Town and New Capital accordingly. It can be seen that in the smaller, nuclear households of the New Capital, mothers and fathers account for a greater proportion (69 percent) of such acts than in the Old Town (58 percent). In the Old Town child care is both shared by more persons and extended over a longer period of the child's development.

TABLE 6.7
Proportion of Nurturant Acts Performed by Mothers and Mother-Surrogates by Location of Residence

Mother/ Mother-Surrogate	Old Town (N=100)	New Capital (N=55)
Mother	53	58
Father	5	11
Grandmother	10	12
Older Sibling, Female	17	5
Older Sibling, Male	4	3
Mother's Sister	1	2
Father's Sister	4	0
Father's Brother's Wife	2	0
Neighbor or Servant	4	9
Total	100	100

This relationship of dependence and nurturance to the age of the child is even more striking when analyzed by the socioeconomic status of households. Lower status mothers and their surrogates, most of whom had jobs away from the house, had limited time to care for children and thus focused their attention on infants and young children up to the age of three. Beyond that age lower status children were left to fend for themselves. Unlike other socioeconomic groups, lower status mothers in both the Old Town and New Capital directed ninety-three percent of their nurturant acts to children under the age of three (Table 6.8). Correlatively, lower status children beyond three years of age made fewer dependent requests than other children. These differences have a high degree of statistical significance (Table 6.9).

TABLE 6.8
Proportion of Nurturant Acts
  Directed to Different Age-Grades
  of Children by Socioeconomic Status

Age of Child	Old Town			New Capital		
	Upper %	Middle %	Lower %	Upper %	Middle %	Lower %
0-3 (N=28)	65	48	93	54	70	93
3-6 (N=26)	18	38	5	38	20	5
6-10 (N=49)	17	14	2	8	10	2
Total	100	100	100	100	100	100

TABLE 6.9
Seeking Nurturance: Age of Child
  by Socioeconomic Status

Age of Child	Upper (N=34)		Middle (N=36)		Lower (N=33)	
	# of Acts	%	# of Acts	%	# of Acts	%
0-2	146	47.9	310	67.5	399	77.3
3-5	105	34.4	103	22.4	82	15.9
6-10	54	17.7	46	10.1	35	6.8
Total	305	100.0	459	100.0	516	100.0

$x^2 = 75.8$, $p<.001$

Thus, my hunch that the workloads of mothers would affect the extent to which children's dependence was indulged and prolonged was confirmed. In small, nuclear New Capital households where mothers had few, if any, other women to share the workload and the care of children, less nurturance was extended to older children, and these older children made fewer dependent requests. In lower status households where women were busier and frequently absent, children were expected to be self-reliant and responsible members of their households at an early age. Table 6.10 demonstrates the extent to which lower status children performed chores as compared with middle and upper status children. By three or four years of age these children were left to care for themselves much of the time, and by six or seven years they were taking care of younger siblings, running errands, hauling water, and preparing and cooking meals.

> M. (female, ten years) and A. (female, ten years) were in the house working when I arrived. Both of their mothers were out. A. had rice on the fire cooking. She got up and down to watch the fire and to add wood to it. The rest of the time she spent cutting vegetables for a curry. She said that she had not eaten anything that morning. She put some nuts on the fire to roast and she soaked some dried fish in water. Fifteen minutes later A. was still inside cooking and now tending to R. (male, ten months). She set him down on the floor while she put more wood on the fire. Then she took the rice off the fire and put some dhal and vegetables on to cook. R. sat quietly on the floor. Later he began to fuss.

TABLE 6.10
Responsible Acts Performed by Older Children (Six to Ten Years) by Socioeconomic Status

Responsible Acts	Upper (N=17) # of Acts	%	Middle (N=16) # of Acts	%	Lower (N=16) # of Acts	%	Total
Errand	2	8.3	6	25.0	16	66.7	100.0
Household Chore	6	6.3	30	31.6	59	62.1	100.0
Outdoor Chore	0	0.0	2	16.7	10	83.3	100.0
Child care	8	9.9	4	4.9	69	85.2	100.0
Other	2	5.7	5	14.3	28	80.0	100.0
Total	18	7.3	47	19.0	182	73.7	100.0

$X^2 = 22.8$, $p < .005$

> A. was busy with the cooking and sweeping of the house. When she finished these chores, she went to R. and picked him up. She held him and fed him some rice flakes mixed with sugar and water (an Old Town lower status household, unpublished field notes)

This finding confirms other cross-cultural analyses (e.g., B. Whiting and Whiting 1975) which suggest that mother's workload is positively correlated with the assignment of chores to children.

Lower status children were clearly the least dependent and the most self-reliant and responsible children in my sample. However, in general, Old Town children expressed more prolonged dependence than New Capital children and performed fewer self-reliant acts. For middle and upper status children the childrearing factors leading to more self-reliance in the New Capital were subtle because none of these parents clearly trained for it. There were, however, several characteristics of the more educated New Capital parents which may have contributed to their children's greater expression of self-reliance.

Although I have pointed out that most Bhubaneswar parents showed little concern with their children's individual development, the more highly educated New Capital parents did take more of an interest. For example, one father was sufficiently concerned about his one-and-one-half-year-old daughter's inability to walk that he bought her a Western-style walker in New Delhi since children's toys and equipment were not available in Bhubaneswar. Other New Capital parents were delighted with the toys I brought their children from Calcutta when they discovered that such things as simple wooden jigsaw puzzles could keep their children interested for extended periods of time. Old Town parents, on the other hand, took no interest in such toys. In addition, it was only the more educated New Capital mothers whom I observed deliberately trying to teach and stimulate their children by actions such as pointing to objects and naming them and encouraging their children to solve problems by themselves.

> B. (male, five years) intermittently pointed out things in the room to me, reciting their names in English. Mrs. P. encouraged him. Then she told him to recite the ABCs for me. At first

144

LOWER STATUS CHILDREN
PERFORMING CHORES

he would not but later did on his own initiative. He also counted in English up to 100. Mrs. P. recited the English terms for different parts of the body to M. (male, one-and-one-half years), and M. pointed to the appropriate parts of his body. If M. hesitated or pointed to the wrong part, Mrs. P. repeated the term over and over in both English and Oriya until he got it right. Twice she had to help M. by taking his hand and pointing to the correct part of his body. Occasionally, B. chimed in (a New Capital middle status household, unpublished field notes).

New Capital upper and middle status parents were also very concerned that their children do well in school and publicly discussed their performances. They even hired tutors, who came in the evening and went over the day's lessons with their children, to insure that they passed their exams.

In these New Capital households there was, then, less of the laissez faire atmosphere that characterized Old Town households where children's activities were generally undirected and where it was assumed that, given time, children would absorb the appropriate values and learn the appropriate roles. In the New Capital, perhaps because traditional roles were less well entrenched and educational goals were changing, parents gave their children somewhat more direction and stimulation. (These differences were statistically significant at the .005 level.) In turn, New Capital children became better at entertaining and caring for themselves than Old Town children and can be characterized as more self-reliant.

DISCUSSION AND CONCLUSIONS

My several hunches or propositions about childrearing practices as they affected the handling and expression of dependence and self-reliance in Bhubaneswar children have been confirmed, but they need to be put into some kind of broader perspective regarding change and adaptation in Bhubaneswar. What made Bhubaneswar such an interesting site for this study was the fact that it had grown so rapidly from an ancient temple town to a modern capital city and thus represented a particularly dynamic and changing part of India. Given Bhubaneswar's two parts of town and two different populations, it would be easy to conclude that what was observed in the Old Town represents the "old" or the "traditional" of India and what was observed in the New Capital the "new" or the "modern." However, this kind of dichotomous thinking has generally been discarded in the social sciences and replaced by the view that change and modernization is a complex, nonlinear process of adaptation (Ames 1969; Geertz 1963; Poggie and Lynch 1974; Rudolph and Rudolph 1967; Singer 1972). Given this latter approach, how can we best characterize these findings concerning family organization and childrearing patterns in Bhubaneswar?

First of all, the relationship between socioeconomic status and child care underscores the necessity of examining the dynamic interaction of specific variables rather than simply contrasting the Old Town and the New Capital. There were striking differences between the Old Town and the New Capital with regard to physical setting and the organization of households, but when lower status families were examined, these differences were not the most relevant ones. Despite the fact that Old Town lower status families were large and joint in structure and New Capital ones small and nuclear, their childrearing practices were similar. What was critical to the care of and expectations for children in these families was women's work patterns. Lower status mothers, unlike both Old Town and New Capital higher status ones, had to work outside the home, and this had a direct impact upon the handling of dependence and self-reliance in their children.

These lower status families were alike in other respects as well. Although they were all at least partially oriented to job opportunities in the New Capital, most of them were not taking advantage of the educational opportunities provided there. Whereas all the middle and upper status children in my sample of households were attending school by five years of age, 62.5 percent of the eligible lower status children in my sample were not.[5] By not sending their children to school, these families were reinforcing their lower status, ensuring that their children would be unable to compete successfully with middle and upper status children for higher positions in the New Capital. Although one reason so many lower status children were not in school was parental disregard for formal education, the primary reason was that school-age children were needed at home to care for younger siblings and to perform other chores. For example, one New Capital Sweeper father regularly apologized to me for not sending his eight-year-old son to school but explained that the child was needed at home to look after his younger brother and sister.

Only two of the eight lower status families were seriously concerned with upward mobility and were sending their children to school for this purpose. One was the family of a New Capital night watchman. He was literate, hardworking, and totally committed to ensuring that his son and daughter would have an improved lifestyle. The other was an Old Town Washerman family in which the older brother had successfully expanded his business into the New Capital and had sent his younger brother through college so that he could get a government job. With the cash he and his brother were earning they were able to acquire land and raise some of their own rice. In this instance, again, Old Town or New Capital residence was unrelated to these particular individuals' ambitions. In both cases these families were investing in new educational and occupational opportunities for their children while also investing in such traditional goods as land and gold.[6]

For middle and upper status families there were some significant differences between the Old Town and the New Capital with regard to childrearing. Again, however, it is important to try to identify what factors accounted for these differences. Household size and composition are, I believe, the critical factors. Although New Capital families did not necessarily choose to live separate from their extended kin, the fact is that they were, for the most part, residing in small, isolated households. This resulted in changes and adaptations in role behavior which, in turn, affected the care that children received. In general, the behavior of both caretakers and children became more active, as measured by rates of mother/mother-surrogate—child interactions per standardized period of time, than in Old Town households. For example, rates of maternal nurturance were higher in the New Capital (17.9 acts per child) than in the Old Town (13.3 acts per child). Similarly, rates of maternal stimulation, although low, were substantially higher in the New Capital (3.9 acts per child) than in the Old Town (1.5 acts per child). In addition, New Capital mothers and their surrogates were more responsive to their children's requests for nurturance and attention than Old Town mothers and their surrogates. They responded positively 51.1 percent of the time, whereas Old Town caretakers responded positively only 42.8 percent of the time.

What leads me to believe that it is household size and composition that are critical is that when maternal nurturance and stimulation are analyzed by household size, the rates for large households are even lower than for Old Town ones. In addition, caretakers in large households are even less responsive to their children's dependent demands than Old Town ones. They responded positively only 39.2 percent of the time, whereas caretakers in small households are the most responsive, complying with their children's requests 54.2 percent of the time.

These findings suggest that life in large, joint (the two are highly intercorrelated in this sample) households has an inhibiting effect upon adult-child interaction, leading to more passive child care by adults and more passive behavior by children. A partial explanation of this is the greater segregation of the sexes that characterize these households and that results in minimal child care by male members of the household. Another factor is that in such households young mothers are frequently under the authority of a mother-in-law or the wife of an older brother-in-law and are not free to interact openly with their children. They tend to be preoccupied with other household chores as well. Given the presence of more potential caretakers in these large, joint households, one would still expect high levels of adult-child interaction. However, it seems that when child care is handled communally and no one person takes full responsibility for it, it becomes less focused and less reliable. For example:

> K. (female, two years) came out of the house crying. She cried steadily for three minutes. No one did anything. Finally, Older Wife (not K.'s mother) pulled her down and directed A. (female, ten years; a cousin) to take her and hold her. When Middle Wife (K.'s mother) stopped turning rice paddy in the sun, she came over and took K. from A. K., who had been crying all the while, stopped immediately. Middle Wife carried her around for two minutes. Then she returned to the paddy, still holding K. K. pulled at her mother's breast and sucked on it

> for fifteen minutes while Middle Wife
> was busy working (an Old Town lower
> status household; unpublished field
> notes).

In fact, it seemed to result in the kind of laissez faire situation that characterized most Old Town households where children were left to run about and occupy themselves as long as they did not seriously disturb the adults present. In these large, crowded households interpersonal relationships were muted while at the same time there was considerable tolerance for noise and confusion.

In the smaller, nuclear households of the New Capital, by contrast, parent-child relationships were far more intense. Fathers participated more in child care, and children, with fewer adults with whom to interact, focused on their mothers and fathers. Thus, it was in these households where relationships were less diffuse that I observed most instances of sibling rivalry and children's temper tantrums. For example, in one upper status household where there was a three-year-old boy and a one-year-old girl, the children regularly competed for their father's attention, something which I never observed in the Old Town.

> At 9:30 a.m. Mr. P. came in freshly
> bathed and dressed. He sat down. Mrs.
> P. set A. (female, one year) on the
> floor. She crawled towards her father
> (Mr. P.). B. (male, three years) saw
> her, and before she could get there, ran
> to his father and climbed into his lap.
> A. saw this and just sat down on the floor
> where she was and cried. Mrs. P., while
> holding B., motioned to A. to come on.
> She came, and he stood her up next to him,
> letting her rest against his chair. (She
> does not yet stand or walk by herself.)
> Mrs. P. went into bathe. B. sat on her
> father's lap, babbling. A few minutes
> later Mr. P. picked up A. and held both
> children on his lap. Then B. climbed down
> and began playing with some newspapers.
> Meanwhile, Mr. P. continued to hold A.,
> who climbed around his lap, happily bab-
> bling to herself (a New Capital upper
> status household; unpublished field notes).

In addition, in these smaller households where

children received more care from fewer persons, they also initiated more actions of all kinds: i.e., rates for both dependent and self-reliant behavior were far higher for New Capital children than for Old Town children.

The more passive childrearing which characterized Old Town households was congruent with the ideology associated with joint family living there. Where roles are clearly defined, marriages arranged, and occupational goals determined largely by family and caste, it is assumed that children require little conscious guidance. Thus, the more passive, laissez faire atmosphere of such households was suitable to a situation in which children were not expected to acquire skills early on, to be responsible individuals (with the exception of the lower caste children), or to make their own decisions. Adults assumed that with time children would learn what was necessary to participate in adult life, and being surrounded by numerous relatives, children were provided with ample role models. In addition, since the solidarity and interdependence of the group was valued over the vagaries of personal intimacy and individuality, it is not surprising that parent-child relationships were less intense here than in the New Capital.

In fact, the value placed upon family cohesiveness and interdependence in these Old Town families usually outweighed other considerations such as occupational mobility and achievement. Several young men in my Old Town sample had been sent on to college in the New Capital and had acquired government posts. It was considered a worthwhile investment to educate some sons for nontraditional jobs as long as they continued to live at home. However, I observed several instances in which a son was posted elsewhere than in Bhubaneswar, but his family objected and would not let him go. New occupations were deemed good as long as they did not interfere with joint family life.

By contrast, the New Capital families in my sample had already made a break from joint family living. Although they continued to value extended kin ties, the ideology associated with kinship and caste was less pervasive. Separated from extended kin and caste members, New Capital parents could not assume that their children would simply absorb appropriate forms of behavior in due time. In addition, New Capital parents' own expectations for their children were not clearly defined. They had been attracted to the New Capital because of new occupational and educational opportunities there, and they tended to be personally ambitious for their children. Hence, there was more of an emphasis upon formal education and training for professional non-caste-oriented careers. As a consequence, perhaps, New Capital parents exhibited a greater awareness of the socialization process than Old Town parents and a greater concern with their children's development and achievements. These attitudes, combined with smaller households and greater intimacy among husbands and wives, led to more intense and focused parent-child behavior.

These Old Town-New Capital contrasts are similar to those described by others as part of a more widespread modernization process. Two other studies of India (Kennedy 1954; Mencher 1963) have characterized more modern households as small, with more equalitarian relationships between husband and wife, with fathers participating more in child care, and with childrearing less concerned with obedience, respect, and passivity and more with encouraging individual initiative and self-reliance. Similar observations have been made in Lebanon (Prothro 1961) and Nigeria (LeVine, Klein, and Owen 1967). In their comparison of more traditional fathers with more modern fathers in Ibadan, Nigeria, LeVine and his associates found that childrearing ideology had shifted away from a traditional pattern of authoritarian constraint to a more equalitarian fostering of self-direction. The more modern fathers were open and affectionate with their children and treated them more as small adults whose individual tendencies required expression and encouragement. A similar shift in ideology has been described for the Soviet Union (Inkeles 1963) and the United States (Bronfenbrenner 1963) as well. Thus, some of the contrasts observed in Old Town-New Capital family organization and childrearing practices exemplify a more general cross-cultural set of trends.

In conclusion, however, I want to reemphasize the danger of thinking in dichotomous terms and stress the need for examining specific environmental and socioeconomic factors and their effects. Only then can we begin to determine what accounts for differences and changes in peoples' behavior and how people adapt to new circumstances by combining old and new patterns of behavior.

NOTES:

1. Research in Bhubaneswar from 1965 to 1967 was supported by a NIMH Research Training Grant, N.H. 11480.
2. See Seymour (1976) for a more complete account of the selection of stratified samples in Bhubaneswar.
3. Although large, joint households have probably never been that common in village life in India, they do seem to have been characteristic of towns, especially among the higher castes (Shah 1974).
4. For the purposes of this study dependent behavior was defined as the child's efforts to elicit responses of help, care, and nurturance from others, to remain near or in physical contact with mothers and mother-surrogates, and to look to others for attention. Self-reliance was defined as the child's efforts to undertake activities on his own, to entertain himself rather than look to others for attention, and to try to satisfy his own instrumental needs.
5. These findings regarding the relationship of schooling to socioeconomic status fit those of a more comprehensive study of schools and student attrition in Bhubaneswar (Sable 1973). Sable (100-02) found that primary school attrition rates for low caste children in Bhubaneswar were three to four times those of high caste children and averaged 69.4 percent. If analyzed according to father's occupation, they averaged 64.9 percent for children with fathers who had low level occupations. Also see Chapter 7 in this volume, "Indian Education: A View from the Bottom Up."
6. During my return to Bhubaneswar in December 1978, I was able to contact both of these families. The nighwatchman's son and daughter have completed high school. The son has his own bicycle shop in the New Capital, and the daughter is married to a man with a small restaurant near the bus station in the New Capital. Of the Old Town Washerman's six children, one is a baby, the next two youngest are in school, the next oldest boy works with his father, the oldest boy is a government clerk in the New Capital, and the oldest daughter is married to an engineer in Balakati. There has been considerable upward mobility in both families.

REFERENCES

Ames, Elinor W., and Kalindi Randeri. 1965. Some Differences in the Child Rearing Practices of Indian and Canadian Mothers. *Indian Psychological review* 2 (1):15-18.

Ames, Michael. 1969. Modernization and Social Structure: Family, Caste and Class in Jamshedpur. *Economic and Political Weekly* 4 (28-30):1217-24.

Bronfenbrenner, Urie. 1963. The Changing American Child - A Speculative Analysis, pp. 347-56 in *Personality and Social Systems*, edited by N. J. Smelser and W. J. Smelser. New York: Wiley.

Carstairs, Morris. 1967. *The Twice-Born: A Study of a Community of High Caste Hindus*. Bloomington: Indiana University Press.

Geertz, Clifford. 1963. *Peddlers and Princes: Social Change and Economic Modernization in Two Indonesian Towns*. Chicago: University of Chicago Press.

Inkeles, Alex. 1963. Social Change and Social Character: The Role of Parental Mediation, pp. 357-65 in *Personality and Social Systems*, edited by N. J. Smelser and W. J. Smelser. New York: Wiley.

Kennedy, Beth C. 1954. Rural-Urban Contrasts in Parent-Child Relations in India. *Indian Journal of Social Work* 15:162-74.

LeVine, Robert A., Nancy H. Klein, and Constance R. Owen. 1967. Father-Child Relationships and Changing Lifestyles in Ibadan, Nigeria, pp. 215-55 in *The City in Modern Africa*, edited by H. Miner. New York: Praeger.

Mencher, Joan. 1963. Growing Up in South Malabar. *Human Organization* 22 (Spring):54-65.

Minturn, Leigh, and John T. Hitchcock. 1966. *The Rajputs of Khalapur, India*. New York: Wiley.

Murphy, Lois. 1953. Roots of Tolerance and Tensions in Indian Child Development, pp. 46-58 in *In the Minds of Men*, edited by G. Murphy. New York: Basic.

Nimkoff, M. F. 1960. Is the Joint Family an Obstacle to Industrialization? *International Journal of Comparative Sociology* 1:109-18.

Poggie, John J., and Robert N. Lynch, eds. 1974. *Rethinking Modernization: Anthropological Perspectives*. Westport, Connecticut: Greenwood.

Prothro, Edwin T. 1961. *Child Rearing in Lebanon*. Cambridge: Harvard University Press.

Rudolph, Lloyd I., and Susanne H. Rudolph. 1967. *The Modernity of Tradition: Political Development in India*. Chicago: University of Chicago Press.
Sable, Alan. 1973. "Paths Through the Labyrinth: A Study of Educational Selection and Allocation in an Indian State Capital." Doctoral dissertation, Harvard University.
Seymour, Susan. 1976. Caste/Class and Child-rearing in a Changing Indian Town. *American Ethnologist* 3 (4):783-796.
Shah, A. M. 1974. *The Household Dimension of the Family in India*. Berkeley: University of California Press.
Singer, Milton. 1972. *When a Great Tradition Modernizes: An Anthropological Approach to Indian Civilization*. New York: Praeger.
Taylor, William S. 1943. Behavior Disorders and the Breakdown of the Orthodox Hindu Family System. *Indian Journal of Social Work* 4:163-70.
———. 1948. Basic Personality in Orthodox Hindu Culture Patterns. *Journal of Abnormal and Social Psychology* 43 (January):3-12.
Whiting, Beatrice B., and John W. M. Whiting. 1975. *Children of Six Cultures: A Psycho-Cultural Analysis*. Cambridge: Harvard University Press.
Whiting, John W. M., Irvin L. Child, and William W. Lambert. 1966. *Field Guide for a Study of Socialization*. New York: Wiley.

Alan Sable received his Ph.D. in sociology from Harvard University in 1973. During 1962-63 he taught at Lucknow University, India, as a Fulbright Tutor of English and from 1965-67 was a Junior Fellow of the American Institute of Indian Studies, during which time he conducted research on the schools in Bhubaneswar. Dr. Sable has taught sociology at Harvard University and the University of California at Santa Cruz. Currently he is a clinical sociologist in private practice in the San Francisco Bay Area. His publications include a book on Bhubaneswar's educational system, PATHS THROUGH THE LABYRINTH: EDUCATIONAL SELECTION AND ALLOCATION IN AN INDIAN STATE CAPITAL, S. Chand and Company, Ltd., New Delhi, 1977.

Chapter 7 is based upon Dr. Sable's 1965-67 research in Bhubaneswar and is an effort to describe the ways in which Bhubaneswar residents are responding to expanded educational opportunities and to explain what factors determine whether or not children stay in school.

7

Indian Education:
A View from the Bottom Up

Alan Sable

A great deal has been written about Indian education. Every respectable research library in India or the West possesses a plethora of works on the topic. One characteristic of these writings has been their "top down" approach. Whether couched in the splendidly arrogant rhetoric of a Macaulay or set forth in the dessicated statistical tables of a planning commission report, analyses of India's educational system typically have a pontifical tone that manages to convince at one level while at the same time leaving the reader with the suspicion that all is neither as simple nor as clear as it appears at another. What is lacking is explication of the concrete, the sort of analysis that proceeds not from some all-encompassing abstract viewpoint, but rather from immersion in a specific situation, a view from the "bottom up," as it were.

As a graduate student in sociology I spent more than eighteen months in Bhubaneswar doing research on its educational system. I wanted to understand selection for and allocation to both primary and secondary educational institutions in the city: Which students attended which schools, for how long, and why? To unravel these deceptively simple questions various research techniques were employed: Many hours were spent in informal conversation with students, dropouts, teachers, parents, and educational administrators; data were systematically gathered on enrollments, facilities, curricula, budgets, and attrition rates of each of the city's schools, and on the caste and parental occupations of students and dropouts; finally, a set of formally structured interviews were conducted with ninety male students and their fathers and ninety male dropouts and their fathers from three representative high schools.

The material so gathered became the basis for an examination of enrollment and attrition patterns in Bhubaneswar. It also provided the opportunity to analyze the Indian educational system from an unusually modest perspective, that gained from observing its operation in a single city. My findings concerning enrollment and attrition patterns in Bhubaneswar have been reported elsewhere (Sable 1977). Repeating them here is not the intention of this chapter. What I want to do instead is to address certain issues critical to Indian education that bear upon themes central to this volume. I will do this by employing data almost exclusively from Bhubaneswar.

This chapter includes three sections. The first, "Educational Planning from Below," is an investigation of educational planning in India not as it is done from above by planners in Delhi and elsewhere but as it is done "from below" by parents and children in Bhubaneswar who must decide whether or not, how, when, and where to enter the educational system, how many resources should be allocated to schooling, and for what purposes they or their children are to be educated. The second section, "Schooling for its Own Sake?", is a discussion of an issue often raised by people who deplore the state of Indian education, the fact that parents and students have allegedly come to value schooling not for its own sake but only as a means to a good job. The third section, "Educational Equality and Inequality in Bhubaneswar," is an examination of the extent to which equality of educational opportunity is found in Bhubaneswar. Providing equal educational opportunity is ostensibly a central goal of Indian educational planners and politicians. The degree to which this goal has been achieved and the extent to which it is shared by the people of Bhubaneswar are the focus of this section. In keeping with the central themes of this volume, all three sections are concerned with the relationship of the educational system to the culture and society that surround it and the political and economic structures that interact with it. These relationships are described and analyzed concretely here. More general theoretical analyses are left to the volume's concluding, integrating chapter.

EDUCATIONAL PLANNING FROM BELOW

Recognition of the need for rational educational planning is widespread among the people of Bhubaneswar. Virtually everyone in the city with children is aware that education can be a costly investment, although its tangible and intangible returns can be very high. I found that people of all social ranks were quite willing to discuss their educational plans with me. I also discovered that few of them were inhibited about revealing the social and economic calculations that underlay these plans. This, of course, greatly facilitated an understanding of how and why people make particular educational decisions.

Economic considerations are extremely important in the educational planning of Bhubaneswar's residents. First of all, they must consider the direct costs of schooling. All schools in Bhubaneswar charge tuition and fees, although at some schools, girls and children of the so-called "backward castes and classes" are exempted from these costs by state government regulations. Books, supplies, and decent clothing must also be provided by children's parents, and although regulations exist providing for free distribution of these things to children of the poor, supplies are grossly inadequate and often made available only when informal "contributions" are made to teachers. The direct costs of schooling are also inflated by the fact that many parents feel it necessary to supplement official schooling with private tutorials, for which fees must be paid.

About two-thirds of the families I interviewed in Bhubaneswar were spending between 20 and 30 percent of their monthly cash income on their children's schooling; almost one-quarter are spending *more* than one-third of their cash incomes in this way. Interestingly enough, almost all the fathers I spoke with could indicate the exact amounts spent for their children's schooling, frequently breaking the costs down into such components as school fees, books, supplies, clothing, and even "contributions." But the direct cost of schooling is not the only factor affecting educational planning in the city. Especially among the poor, it is the indirect, or "opportunity costs," of schooling that seem to be the major cause of attrition.

Most of Bhubaneswar's children attend school. Without having made a complete census of the city, it is impossible to determine the number of non-schoolgoers exactly. However, my estimate is that, at the time of my study, 5 percent of the New Capital children, 10 percent of the Old Town children, and 10 to 15 percent of the village children never enroll in school. However, while only a small fraction of Bhubaneswar's children remain completely outside the educational system, many attend for just a few years. Using school enrollment records, I determined that in the city as a whole about one-third of those beginning primary school do not finish. Primary school attrition rates vary by section of the city and socioeconomic group. The rate is 95.7 percent in tribal and untouchable enclaves, 53.4 percent in village schools, 34.7 percent in Old Town schools, and 20.2 percent in New Capital schools. The attrition rate among laborers' children is 88 percent, among craftsmen's children 78.8 percent, and among peasant's children 61.3 percent.

The cause of this attrition, as explained by the people themselves, is primarily economic. Some spoke of the direct costs of educating their children beyond the primary stage: "How can I afford high school fees and books, which are twice or three times those of primary school?" asked one man. But most emphasized the indirect or opportunity costs of keeping their children in school past the age at which they could be economically productive. One laborer explained:

> My son left school last year when he was ten. He was in Class 4 then. He was big enough then to begin to work with me in the capital as a haulier. Why should I pay for him to be in school when he could be earning money? We are a poor family and need his income to help us live.

Even if children's work does not bring a cash income, people frequently are aware that their labor can have value. A farmer told me:

> My boy is eleven and my girl nine. They have been to school for several years, but now I will withdraw them. They are big enough to help us with our work. The boy can tend animals, and the girl can help in the house. When they were little they went to school, and the teacher watched over them. Now that they are grown, they should work. One has to work to live.

Those who remove their children from school are not unaware that this virtually excludes them from the opportunity of obtaining any but manual work. "My son will be a sweeper just like me," said one man. "What else can he do if he has no schooling?" "None of our children have been to school beyond the second class. They will all be poor," said another. Such people simply perceive, and indeed have, no other options.

For the roughly two-thirds of Bhubaneswar children who complete the full five years of primary school and go on to secondary school, there are certain options: which school to attend, (in some cases) what course of study to pursue, and what plans to make for beyond high school. As in the case of those who only go to primary school, the educational plans of high school students are closely tied to economic considerations, and educational choices anticipate occupational aspirations and possibilities. Particularly among high school boys and their fathers there is a very great emphasis on the practical job opportunities that educational credentials bring.

Certain sectors of the job market in Bhubaneswar, as elsewhere in India, are tied very closely to the educational system. Virtually all positions in state and central government offices require educational credentials and have employment policies based upon a systematic coordination of level and type of employment and level and type of educational credential. Public sector industries and the educational system itself operate in a similar manner. Professions such as law and medicine are legally restricted to those with the requisite credentials. At the same time, educational credentials are largely irrelevant to employment in several important occupational sectors in Bhubaneswar: agriculture, small and medium scale trading, the priesthood, and almost any form of manual labor. Indeed, possession of anything higher than a Primary School Certificate virtually excludes a person socially and psychologically from these sorts of occupations, except in a managerial position.

One consequence of the close association between educational credentials and specific employment opportunities is that children and their parents can plan their schooling in a very rational manner. As a result, those who do not or cannot aspire for their sons to have white-collar positions do not tend to send them beyond primary school, whereas parents who have such aspirations for their children can see clearly what must be done. Virtually all the high school boys and fathers interviewed knew exactly which positions and what salaries could be obtained with each of the various types and levels of educational credentials available through the Bhubaneswar educational system. Not *one* of the 180 high school students, dropouts, or fathers I interviewed gave educational and occupational aspirations that did not correspond with each other.

While those pursuing high school and more advanced educational credentials are thus informed about the job possibilities theoretically open to them, they are also well aware that a serious unemployment problem affects the more educated portion of the Indian population. As a consequence, and also undoubtedly as a result of the vagaries of their own academic performance, many high school students and their fathers display a good deal of flexibility in their educational and occupational plans. Frequently, this flexibility is the result of pragmatism. For example, about half way through my study, newspaper articles began appearing that predicted a large surplus of engineers in India within the coming five years. Immediately, there was a marked decrease in the number of respondents at Bhubaneswar's elite Demonstration School who indicated their intention of attending engineering school; medical college became the most popular choice. Such flexibility demonstrates a rational pragmatism unfortunately not always matched by educational planners above.

Flexibility and pragmatism are also reflected in the realism people display in assessing which educational or occupational goals may reasonably be achieved. Frequently fathers and sons explicitly related their future plans to how well sons might do in their certificate and degree examinations. "If my son gets good marks, I will send him to medical or engineering college. If he does poorly, then he will just go for a B.A.," said one father. It is widely felt that certificate and degree examination results are difficult to predict. Held only after the end of each stage of education, very good students sometimes do quite poorly, while poor students do quite well. However, the results of these examinations are closely related to educational and occupational opportunities, and once the results are known, students and parents can predict with a high degree of accuracy what possibilities are open to them.

Approximately 70 percent of students pass the High School Certificate Examination. Those who fail are allowed to take the examination two more times, and I estimate that by the third try between 85 and 90 percent of the students are successful. For those who are not, a drastic downgrading of educational and occupational aspirations occurs. Those whose families own property typically revert to farming or shopkeeping. Those whose families are not so fortunate seek the low level jobs available to holders of the Middle School Certificate. Among students who pass the examination, those with high marks almost invariably decide to pursue highly desirable professional occupations such as engineering and medicine and apply for admission to appropriate academic programs; the rest, who do not have the marks to obtain admission to the highly competitive pre-professional and professional programs, pursue standard "academic" college courses of study instead. What is impressive is the degree to which good examination results seem to channel students into what are currently the most desirable professions. Almost 70 percent of those I interviewed indicated that they would enter these professional programs if they received high examination marks *regardless of whether or not that was their original aim*.

Another extremely important factor affecting educational and occupational aspirations is the student's own socioeconomic status. As we have seen, the very poor, without exception, realizing their financial limitations, simply do not aspire to occupations requiring educational credentials. Among those who do attempt to improve their socioeconomic position through schooling, there is a very strong pattern to aspire just "one step" higher. Thus, 85 percent of high school students whose fathers had no schooling or only primary schooling aspired only to obtain the High School Certificate; 73 percent of those whose fathers possessed High School Certificates aspired only to obtain a Bachelor's degree; and 94 percent of those whose fathers had college degrees wanted professional or advanced degrees. Occupational aspirations, closely related to educational ones, showed a similar "one-step-higher" pattern.

Another crucial feature of educational and occupational planning in Bhubaneswar is the way in which it is coordinated within families. Almost no high school boys reported that they planned their educational and occupational futures themselves. The family, and especially the father, seems to play an extremely critical role. If the father is dead or absent frequently, or if he is uneducated himself, an elder brother or uncle is often involved. There also is variation in the amount of input the child himself has. In about one-quarter of the families I interviewed, the fathers arrived at such decisions on their own and ordered their sons to pursue certain educational and occupational tracks. In the majority of families, however, although fathers still had a predominant influence, students were consulted.[2] As one man explained: "It is something like our system of arranged marriages. The father knows his son and the job market and the schools. He tries to arrange what is best." Ironically, perhaps, my study revealed that Old Town and village boys tended to have more freedom regarding their educational and occupational choices than New Capital boys because fewer Old Town and village fathers were themselves educated and familiar with the school system and job market. In fact, such fathers frequently indicated that they gained their knowledge of these things from their sons.

One consequence of the involvement of fathers and other older men in educational and occupational planning is that plans may be coordinated for the entire family. Thus, for example, a family with limited financial resources can invest them in whomever seems to have the best educational and occupational prospects. A farmer explained: "My eldest son is not good at studies. He will become a farmer. But my second son, who is good, I will try to push through high school and college and into government service." Another strategy is to have older children support younger siblings, escalating the level of investment and aspiration with each child. One student at an elite private school described the particularly elegant example of this that his family was able to achieve:

> I am the youngest of four. My eldest brother received his High School Certificate and became a clerk. He helped my second brother to finish college and become a higher level government servant. They both helped my next brother become an engineer, and he is now paying my fees. My father is dead now. He was a tenant farmer, but he taught his sons to care for each other.

Coordination of educational and occupational plans on a familial basis also provides a certain hedge against the vagaries of the employment market for the educated. As one high level civil servant pointed out:

> Of course I will not place all my sons
> in the same field. The way things are,
> that is very dangerous. One will be an
> engineer, another a doctor, and another
> a government official. At least one of
> them in that way will always be a success.
> So I will then be secure in my old age.

Although it is essential to stress that occupational aspirations play a fundamental role in people's educational planning in Bhubaneswar, they are not the only factor. This is particularly true for girls. Even among the middle and upper groups who send their daughters to high school, the expectation is that very few will permanently pursue an occupation: Ninety-eight percent of the fathers I interviewed said that they expected that their daughters would not be permanently employed, but marry "instead." However, since educated young men increasingly demand educated wives, schooling and educational credentials have become almost as necessary for girls as for boys among certain middle and upper level socioeconomic groups in the city. Table 7.1 indicates the wide disparities that exist in this respect; some groups send most of their daughters on to high school while others send almost none.

TABLE 7.1
Girls' Attrition Rates by Fathers' Occupations

Fathers' Occupation	Estimated % of Girls Who Leave School before Class 6 (the First Year of High School)
High Level Government	8.4
Middle Level Government	16.3
Low Level Government	72.4
Large Entrepreneur	7.9
Middle Entrepreneur	32.0
Small Entrepreneur	89.3
Big Peasant	40.1
Small Peasant	82.8
Laborer	94.6
Skilled Worker	91.3
Priest	37.2
Professional	15.3

Parents who educate their daughters do so partly in order to assure that they will be able to arrange marriages to educated young men with secure and relatively high-paying jobs. Thus, educational planning for daughters is as pragmatic and instrumental as it is for sons. For both boys and girls schooling is coming to be required for social as well as economic reasons. The notion that it is socially necessary to send children to school has even begun to appear among the very poor in Bhubaneswar. One woman living in the city's worst slum told me:

> Of course I send my children to the school. People would think I neglected their growth if I did not. They will only stay in school a few years. Our family has no money. But they will be in school like the children of other parents who care for their children properly.

Among virtually all but the very poor, school attendance has become socially mandatory, although the level of schooling required varies with socioeconomic status. Among village and Old Town peasants, for example, it is primary schooling that is expected, whereas among low and middle level government servants in the New Capital, children typically attend at least until the end of high school, and college attendance is extremely widespread at least among boys. Even the rich, whose children have no practical need of educational credentials, find schooling socially *de rigeur*. "My sons will inherit my business," said one extremely successful, though totally unschooled, entrepreneur.

> They don't need degrees to become clerks like the others. But I don't want people to think they are *junglee* (crude and rustic), so I am educating them at the best schools in Bhubaneswar. People with my wealth must educate their children. How can we be rich and illiterate? People would laugh at us.

Clearly, educational planning from below entails many factors: economic, occupational, and social aspirations; the pressure of finances and neighbors; and the range and scope of educational opportunities and the relationship they bear to the job and marriage markets. If one steps back to generalize about the process in Bhubaneswar, several features stand out. As a whole, the city's people are clear and forthright about the things that affect their educational plans and choices. Typically, people understand both the costs and benefits of schooling with remarkable accuracy and are well informed about the options (if any) open to them. There is a noteworthy flexibility evident in their willingness to adjust educational and occupational plans according to fluctuations in the job market and the vicissitudes of educational careers. Underlying everything seems to be a powerful pragmatism with regard to schooling.

SCHOOLING FOR ITS OWN SAKE?

Both indigenous and foreign observers who have noted the highly pragmatic attitudes of Indians toward schooling have tended to react with disapproval. Some commentators see this pragmatism as the root of educational problems in contemporary India. Such attitudes, they argue, somehow preclude "real" learning or stand in the way of "valuing learning for its own sake." Others, seeking to explain the high degree of pragmatism, argue that it stems from the introduction of an educational system into India that is essentially foreign and has little relationship to indigenous culture or social structure. My research in Bhubaneswar indicates that both of these prevalent views of Indian education are erroneous.

Virtually everyone I spoke with in Bhubaneswar saw schooling in pragmatic terms. This was especially true of those who were seriously attempting to obtain educational credentials. Among the high school students, dropouts, and their fathers who were systematically interviewed, recognition of the important connection between schooling and employment opportunities was virtually universal. For example, only three of ninety students and eight of ninety dropouts agreed with the statement: "The results of the High School Certificate Examination do not mean very much to me. I want a job that does not require good examination results." Only one of ninety students' fathers and four of ninety dropouts' fathers agreed with the statement: "The results of the High School Certificate Examination do not mean very much to my son. He wants a job that does not require good examination results."

When asked to assess the importance of various factors contributing to "success in life," almost everyone placed great emphasis on the amount of schooling and examination results. Table 7.2 indicates the responses of students and dropouts; fathers' responses were almost identical to their sons'.

TABLE 7.2
Respondents' Assessment of the Importance of Various Factors in Accounting for Success in Life

Factor	Percentage and Number of Respondents Rating Factor as Essential			
	Students		Dropouts	
	#	%	#	%
Amount of Education	86	95.6	85	94.4
Examination Results	87	96.7	85	94.4
Ambition	22	24.4	20	22.2
Intelligence	27	30.0	23	25.6
Hard Work	31	34.4	34	37.8
Caste	18	20.0	16	17.8
Karma	14	15.6	16	17.8
Good Horoscope	24	26.7	20	22.2
God or Fate	1	1.1	1	1.1
Relatives in Important Places	19	21.1	22	24.4

Although the perception of education's practical utility is virtually universal among high school students, dropouts, and their fathers, appreciation of its intrinsic value apparently is not. When asked about the reasons for going to school, large differences emerged between students and their fathers on the one hand, and dropouts and their fathers on the other, with students and their fathers answering "to learn" about twice as often as dropouts and their fathers. Similar results were obtained when people asked to volunteer their notion of the prime value of schooling. Perhaps most telling of all were the data that emerged when respondents were forced to choose between instrumental and noninstrumental statements regarding education. Table 7.3 lists some of these statements and the choices made by high school students and dropouts. The attitudinal differences between these two groups are striking, with students showing a marked preference for noninstrumental attitudes and dropouts showing a marked preference for instrumental attitudes.

TABLE 7.3
Choices Between Instrumental and Noninstrumental Attitudes Toward Schooling

	Students #	Students %	Dropouts #	Dropouts %
Choice One:				
My father is sending me to school so that I can learn to live with others.	4	4.4	1	1.1
My father is sending me to school so that I will be able to get a good job.	10	17.8	58	64.4
My father is sending me to school to learn new things.	70	77.8	31	34.4
Choice Two:				
The reason that education is so important is because it opens a person's mind to many things.	65	72.2	10	11.1
This is ture, but the chief reason that education is so important is because having some qualification gives a person a better chance in life.	24	27.8	80	88.9
Choice Three:				
Schools should teach only those things necessary to prepare students for the exams for their occupation.	18	20.0	77	85.6
No. Schools should teach other things as well, even though they are not needed in occupations or for exams.	72	80.0	13	14.4

My research thus indicates that, contrary to the assumptions of many who have commented on Indian education, instrumental attitudes do not necessarily preclude valuing schooling for its own sake. Furthermore, the strong attitudinal differences between students and their fathers and dropouts and their fathers suggest that valuing schooling for its own sake is a critical factor in staying in or dropping out of school. The implication clearly is that valuing education intrinsically is essential to moving through the Indian educational system.

The data I collected also shed some light on assertions regarding the supposed isolation of the educational system from the indigenous culture and social system. Men and boys who placed a high value on learning *per se* were not distributed randomly among the city's high school student and dropout population. Not surprisingly, given the importance such attitudes apparently have for remaining in the educational system, boys who valued learning tended to be the sons of educated fathers, that is, of men who themselves had successfully passed through the system. But some boys with the requisite attitudes had fathers who were totally uneducated or had attended school for only a few years. A very great proportion of this group belonged to two particular castes, Brahmans and Karans. Furthermore, one occupation, the priesthood (including both "household" and temple priests) had the highest proportion of men of any group who valued learning *per se*: Over 90 percent of such fathers scored highly on this dimension of the questionnaire, although none of them had had more than four years of formal schooling.

These data suggest that the indigenous culture and social structure are not at all irrelevant to India's "Western-style" educational system. In particular, at least certain caste and occupational groups seem to possess to a disproportionate degree the kind of values that facilitate successful functioning in the educational system. This has been inferred by some Indian social historians on the basis of the relative overenrollment of such groups as Brahmans and Writer's castes in 19th century schools.[3] My data substantiate this inference and suggest that because of their cultural traditions certain castes and occupational groups still enjoy an advantage over others in competing for educational rewards.

It is important to point out that attitudes supportive of learning *per se* are present among all social groups in Bhubaneswar. Even illiterate untouchables whose children had no real chance to attend school for more than a few years frequently expressed a recognition of learning as an intrinsically valuable thing. One such man, for example, said to me: "I am so sad that I have no money to send my children to school. What a wonderful thing to be able to learn, to understand."

It is also important to make clear that the cultural advantage apparently enjoyed by groups such as the Brahmans and Karans does not derive solely from the attitude they hold toward learning. The styles and methods of intellectuality employed in the schools resonate with those of these groups far more than with those of other groups. The memorization and chanting characteristic of local pedagogy, for example, closely parallels that of the Brahmanical religious and educational tradition. And the centrality of reading and writing directly mirrors the traditional occupational skills of the Karans. Even more concretely, approximately 80 percent of the city's teachers are themselves Brahmans or Karans, with all this implies about the subtle—and not so subtle—effects this has upon the culture of the classroom. If schools were oriented toward imparting practical agricultural skills, for example, presumably the intellectual styles of other groups would predominate in the schools, and their children would enjoy the sorts of advantages now enjoyed by children of Brahmans and Karans. This line of reasoning was suggested to me by a low caste peasant who said:

> Of course we do not do well at school. They teach Brahman things, things from books and things to memorize. We know how to plow and plant and prepare crops and reap. We are intelligent at these things, as intelligent as the Brahmans, or even more so. If schools taught these things, then our children would do well.

My research demonstrates that people in Bhubaneswar do not go to school solely for the economic and social advantage it brings, and if they do so, they tend not to be able to sustain attendance. Like any social institution, successful participation in Bhubaneswar's schools requires a degree of intrinsic engagement. It is also apparent from my research that the city's educational system articulates most

closely with certain elements of the indigenous
culture, in particular, the "high culture" and "academic" traditions of groups such as the Brahmans and
Karans. At the same time, the style and content of
schooling is quite remote from other social and cultural traditions, in particular, the teaching and
learning of practical agriculture, commercial and
craft skills. Such cultural biases, of course, are
found in most educational systems but often go unnoticed. However, no understanding of Bhubaneswar's
educational system is possible unless they are kept
firmly in mind.

EDUCATIONAL EQUALITY AND INEQUALITY IN BHUBANESWAR

The educational attitudes and planning strategies of the people of Bhubaneswar do not exist in a
vacuum. Officially, the educational system to which
these attitudes and strategies are directed is supposed to provide equality of educational opportunity.
India's Constitution sets as a prime national goal
the establishment of "a democratic system of education offering equal educational opportunity to all
irrespective of caste, creed, sex or economic position." As in all societies, this goal is far from
being achieved. This section describes the patterns
of educational inequality that exist in Bhubaneswar
and discusses their main causes and dynamics.

Bhubaneswar's thirty-five primary and secondary
schools differ greatly in size, staffing, facilities,
curricula, and clientele. It is this that lies at
the heart of the educational inequality that exists
in the city. At one extreme are four small, single-teacher lower primary schools[4] enrolling only about
eighty boys and girls from enclaves of the socially
outcast. At the other extreme are three large, well
staffed and equipped "English medium"[5] schools that
serve about 10 percent of the city's children, primarily those from upper socioeconomic groups. In
between are the city's twenty-eight "Oriya medium"
primary, middle, and high schools which enroll about
85 percent of Bhubaneswar's school children on a
neighborhood basis. Hence, the system can be most
simply conceived of as a mass one, with appendages
at the bottom and the top for the socially deprived
and for the elite. About 10 percent of the city's
children, who never enroll in any school, are completely outside the system. To understand the system, it is necessary to look separately at each of
its three main components: the enclave schools,

the English medium schools, and the neighborhood schools.

Three of the four enclave schools are one-room mud huts wihout plumbing or electricity; the fourth is simply an open covered platform in the midst of a crowded municipal Sweeper's settlement. Common to all the enclave schools is their location in large enclaves of the socially outcast: the Sweeper's colony, two small tribal villages, and a squatter's slum of crowded *bustees* (shacks). The enclave schools are all small. The largest has just thirty-seven pupils officially enrolled, though only about half that number attend regularly. They are all single-teacher institutions offering only the first three years of the primary school curriculum. Instruction is poor: I discovered that none of the students at any of these schools even knew the complete Oriya alphabet. Because their parents cannot afford it, almost no students go on to nearby upper primary school. In one enclave only two children had done so in the previous five years.

The enclave schools are not necessary geographically. All are quite near to much better equipped and staffed upper primary schools. The reason for their existence is purely social. Both the enclave residents and their neighbors agree that separate schools are desirable. The enclave residents feel that their children would be unwanted at the nearby upper primary schools. "Our own school is best. Why should our children go to the Brahmans' school where they will be laughed at?" I was asked by an untouchable enclave resident. This preference for separate enclave schools is shared by their neighbors: A man who lived near to the squatter's area said he was happy that his children didn't have to go to school with "the children of theirs and other bad people who live in the bustees."

Many tribal and untouchable children in Bhubaneswar attend regular Oriya medium schools and a few even attend the elite English medium institutions. In fact, there are approximately five times as many untouchable and tribal children in the neighborhood as in the enclave schools. High caste parents generally indicated that they heartily approved of the presence of such children in their schools. Acceptance and even support of integrating tribal, untouchable, and higher caste children thus coexists with approval for separate schools when there exist large, physically distinct enclaves with their own identities. Consequently, it would be very simplistic to analyze the situation as one of either rejection or acceptance of the children of marginal groups in schools. Both situations exist.

At the opposite end of the city's educational spectrum are the English medium schools. Two of these are missionary institutions, though heavily subsidized by the Orissa government. The third English medium school is supported and operated by the Central Government's National Council for Educational Research and Training as a model institution. It is attached to the Regional College of Education which serves the entire eastern region of India, an area with a population of approximately 160 million people. The Demonstration School, as it is known, has a staff and physical plant that would compare favorably with all but the very best American or European secondary institutions. The Convent and Stewart Schools are more modestly endowed, although their facilities are superior to any of the Oriya medium schools.

All three English medium schools employ curricula far more thorough and advanced than that provided in the Oriya medium schools. In recognition of this, their graduates are allowed to go on to college directly, without the one year preuniversity course of studies required of students from the Oriya medium high schools. The teaching staffs of all three English medium schools come from throughout India, and the missionary schools have several European teachers as well. One-third of the teachers have post graduate degrees, and one in eight has a foreign degree.

The clientele of the three English medium schools is drawn mostly from the privileged: Enrollment statistics indicated that 89.6 percent of the fathers of Convent School students, 81.4 percent of the fathers of Stewart School students, and 59.3 percent of the fathers of Demonstration School students were either high level government officials, large entrepreneurs, or professionals. Clearly, these are elite institutions. Non-Oriya residents of the city (mostly central government civil servants) also tend to send their children to the English medium schools. As a result, there are many non-Oriya castes represented at these schools, and it is difficult to compare the caste composition of these schools with that of the Oriya medium schools where, of course, virtually all of the students are Oriyas.

In keeping with their socioeconomic background, the male students of the English medium schools invariably intend to continue their schooling beyond the Higher Secondary Certificate. More prefer the prestigious and attractive professional schools that prepare them for careers as engineers or doctors over the general undergraduate colleges whose graduates are all too often unemployed. My survey indicated that about one-fourth hoped to attend the Indian Institute of Technology or other high quality elite institution, and about a tenth hoped one day to do advanced work abroad.

If they draw their students primarily from the ranks of the local representatives of national and regional elites, the city's three English medium schools also prepare them for their future roles. The very national composition of the student bodies and teaching staffs facilitates this orientation, as does the use of English as the medium of instruction. Textbooks and curricula stress national, rather than local heroes and identity. The academic tracking system is also oriented toward national rather than local institutions.

The origin and development of the three English medium schools also reflect their relationship to the city's elite groups. When the New Capital was planned in the early 1950s, planners and civil servants felt that it was necessary to provide English medium schooling "for the children of high level government officers." Accordingly, the Orissa Education Department approached the educational authorities of the Baptist and Roman Catholic Churches, who ran elite English medium schools in Cuttack, and asked them to open branches of the Cuttack Stewart and Convent schools in the New Capital. When these authorities pointed out that they did not have the funds to open new schools, the Education Department volunteered to subsidize the construction and operation of the schools. Between 1952 and 1964 the state government disbursed subsidies to these two private schools equal to approximately one-third of what was expended on all the Oriya medium schools combined, though the latter schools enrolled approximately ten times as many pupils.

The history of the Demonstration School also shows the effectiveness of elite pressure upon the educational system. The Demonstration School is a model institution operated by the central government. In order to provide an alternative to the usual academically-oriented Indian high school, the Demonstration School was designed as a "Multipurpose" institution, that is, one that offers vocational as well as academic courses of study. To accommodate vocational courses of study, the school was equipped with machine shops, agricultural equipment, and even a domestic science unit. However, at the time I was in Bhubaneswar, these were largely unused because less than 5 percent of Demonstration School students were enrolled in vocational courses. Furthermore, a fierce struggle was going on at the school between the headmaster, who sought equal enrollments in both academic and vocational courses of study, and local educational authorities, who thought that the facilities should be used, in the words of one of them, "to provide the best academic training possible to the children of officials posted here." Just as I left Bhubaneswar, the headmaster resigned; within two years the Demonstration School officially abandoned its commitment to offering vocational as well as academic training and became an exclusively academic institution.

Admission to English medium schools depends on financial resources and academic ability. The Stewart and Convent Schools charge fairly steep fees: approximately 500 rupees per year for secondary school in a city where the average family cash income is perhaps double that per annum. Fees at the Demonstration School are about a third of this, but prospective students have to pass a difficult English test before being admitted. This, in effect, eliminates all those whose parents have not been able to afford to send them to the English medium Convent or Stewart Schools for their first several years' schooling. In these ways, English medium schooling becomes the preserve of those of upper-middle and upper income and class status.

The truly mass educational system in Bhubaneswar is its network of twenty-nine Oriya medium primary, middle, and high schools. These schools enroll strictly on a geographical basis and, hence, their clientele represents all but the top and bottom of the class and caste structure of their respective neighborhoods. Table 7.4 shows the variation in father's occupation among the village, Old Town, and New Capital neighborhood schools. Because this table aggregates the schools in the three sections of the city, it underrepresents the diversity of individual schools and the social segmentation that exists even among the neighborhood Oriya medium schools. Table 7.5 lists the caste background of students of the Oriya medium schools in different sections of the city. Again, because of aggregation, diversity and segmentation are underrepresented.

One of the most interesting effects of socioeconomic segmentation is that the schools in the

TABLE 7.4
Occupation and School Enrollment:
Neighborhood Schools

	Percentage of Children in		
Fathers' Occupation	Village Schools	Old Town Schools	Capital Schools
High Level Government	-0-	0.6	99.4
Middle Level Government	0.5	5.9	93.6
Low Level Government	7.0	15.0	77.9
Middle Entrepeneur	19.4	35.5	45.2
Small Entrepeneur	13.7	13.7	72.6
Big Peasant	42.9	32.1	25.0
Small Peasant	52.3	26.2	21.5
Laborer	23.2	29.0	47.8
Skilled Worker	13.4	25.8	60.8
Priest	5.0	95.0	-0-
Professional	-0-	5.0	95.0

TABLE 7.5
Caste Composition of the Neighborhood Schools

	Village Schools	Old Town Schools	Capital Schools
Brahmans	4.3	34.0	24.3
Karans	13.5	8.4	28.4
Middle Caste	52.8	32.1	25.1
Low Caste	16.0	22.1	15.8
Tribals/Harijans	10.4	1.4	2.0
Others/None	3.4	1.5	4.4

various parts of the city have markedly different atmospheres, reflective of their social and cultural contexts. In the village and Old Town schools, for example, almost all the teachers wear traditional dress, *dhotis* or *lungis*. By contrast, in the New Capital neighborhood schools, teachers wear the white shirts and slacks of their government clerical counterparts. In the Old Town and village schools there is also a certain social intimacy: Teachers and headmasters know most student's castes and their father's occupations. In the New Capital schools, by contrast, only when caste names were obvious or children's fathers held especially prominent positions, were teachers aware of their students' backgrounds. Several times I witnessed village and Old Town students touch their teacher's or headmaster's feet in the dramatic Hindu gesture of respect. I never saw this happen in a New Capital school and was told—indeed, assured—by several headmasters that they would not "permit" such a gesture.

Another source of variation among the neighborhood schools is the differing resource of their sponsoring agencies. The Old Town and village schools are operated by the Notified Area Council, Bhubaneswar's municipal government (see Chapter 2). Most New Capital schools are run by the state government financial assistance. As a consequence, the schools differ considerably in physical facilities and staff. The Old Town and village schools generally do not have electricity and plumbing, for example, whereas the capital government schools do. The teaching staffs at the capital government schools are more highly paid and on the average possess higher academic qualifications. There is also considerably more instructional equipment. On the other hand, because of the New Capital's population growth, the capital government schools are much more overcrowded than the village and Old Town schools. In several New Capital schools classes are doubled up in rooms. This is a considerable handicap given the widespread use of mass chanting as a pedagogical technique.

In trying to assess possible differences among the neighborhood schools in educational quality, I compiled extensive and detailed data on physical facilities, instructional equipment, staff qualifications, overcrowding, etc. I was puzzled because no clear pattern emerged. An extremely blunt but helpful comment from a professor at Utkal University in Bhubaneswar clarified the situation. In response to the sheets of data I showed him, he said: "Mr. Sable, you obviously do not understand our educational system at all. What difference do all these figures make? There is only one thing that matters about an Indian school, either to school children or to their parents. That is the pass rate (the proportion of students who pass the Primary, Middle, and High School Certificate Examinations). If you want to judge differences among our schools, look for differences among our schools, look for differences in their pass rates." As illustrated in Table 7.6, I found that there were no great differences. By this all-important measure, Bhubaneswar's network of neighborhood Oriya medium schools seemed to offer children roughly equal educational opportunity and the educational system appeared remarkably egalitarian. This statement must immediately be qualified by noting that enrollment and attrition rates differ markedly among different socioeconomic groups and different parts of the city, especially at the primary school level (Tables 7.7 and 7.8).

TABLE 7.6
Examination Pass Rates in Neighborhood Schools

	Primary School Certificate Exam.	Middle School Certificate Exam.	High School Certificate Exam.
Village Schools	92.2%	84.4%	66.7%
Old Town Schools	95.1%	82.8%	70.8%
Capital Schools	95.4%	81.1%	70.3%

TABLE 7.7
Primary School Attrition Rates by Section of the City and Type of School

School	Attrition Rates (Class 1 to Class 5)
Enclave School	95.7%
Village Schools	53.4%
Old Town Schools	34.7%
Capital Schools	20.2%

TABLE 7.8
Primary School Attrition Rates
  by Fathers' Occupations

	Attrition Rates (Class 1 to Class 6) % from all Schools
High Level Government	8.3
Middle Level Government	12.4
Low Level Government	51.7
Large Entrepreneur	7.7
Middle Entrepreneur	25.0
Small Entrepreneur	75.5
Big Peasant	35.5
Small Peasant	61.3
Laborer	88.0
Skilled Worker	78.8
Priest	38.7
Professional	15.2

The data suggest two important and interrelated observations: (1) *For those who have not dropped out of the system,* Bhubaneswar's network of Oriya medium neighborhood schools offers remarkably equal educational opportunities. (2) On the other hand, primary school attrition is both severe and closely associated with belonging to certain socioeconomic groups. Strongly differential levels of educational attainment hence occur in Bhubaneswar, but—leaving aside for the moment the provision of markedly superior English medium educational opportunities to the city's elite groups and markedly inferior Oriya medium ones to tribal groups and untouchables—the source of this situation does *not* lie principally in the differential provision of educational opportunities to various sectors of the city and hence to various sectors of the populace.

This has several important implications. It appears that simply providing more and more schools, although that is needed because of overcrowding, will not appreciably increase educational equality. In Bhubaneswar at least, the problem is no longer the provision of schools, but rather the economic, social, and psychological barriers that prevent a considerable proportion of the city's children from making use of them. My research suggests that were the system to become more vocationally oriented, it would attract many of those who now simply see no reason to educate their children. Furthermore, given the direct and opportunity costs of schooling, universal enrollment for more than a token period seems impossible to achieve in the city as long as the school fees and cost of books, materials, uniforms, etc., must be borne by the families of the poor. Provisions for removing these costs, which exist already in official statute, would have to be strictly implemented and the children of the poor perhaps even paid to attend school for schooling to be a bearable investment for them or their parents.

If we now step back and very briefly recapitulate what we have seen in this "view from below," a complex picture emerges. We have seen that the educational system of this small city mirrors its rich social and economic diversity. Particularly striking is the fact that the system makes special provision both for the privileged and for the deprived in a way that effectively perpetuates their respective social positions. At the same time, in an almost stereotypically Indian paradox, this "elitist" system is also in many respects strikingly egalitarian, providing roughly equivalent educational opportunities to the vast majority of its clients.

We have also seen that throughout the city and in virtually all social groups there is a highly realistic recognition of the practical importance of schooling for securing and enhancing social and economic status and that on the whole families appear to make impressively rational use of the educational opportunities available to them. Little evidence exists of cultural resistance to this Western-style institution, and some of the most "traditional" groups were found to be best equipped for success within it. Old Town and New Capital residents were found to share the same approach to education: pragmatism, flexibility, and rational planning; socio-economic and in some cases cultural background, rather than residence, was most important in determining educational opportunity, aspiration, and achievement.

What strikes this observer most about Bhubaneswar's educational system and its clients are their mutual flexibility and adaptability. On the one hand, the system has accommodated itself impressively well to the city's complex stratification system. Similarly, the people of the city have for their part adapted well to this elaborate, "modern" institution. Virtually all perceive the practical value of schooling. Most use the system rationally, even with savvy, and certainly with flexibility.

It is difficult to say to what degree the city's educational system is a harbinger of change. Certainly in the Old Town for the first time a generation is arising that is largely literate, with all the cultural, economic, and social consequences that may bring. Furthermore, for many families in the Old Town (and some in the New Capital) this will be the first generation whose sons will possess the educational credentials to enter the world of "modern" salaried employment and social status. And yet, precisely because the city's educational system has adapted so well to its social structure, much of the change it brings will be subtle and gradual, more on the order of evolution than revolution.

NOTES

1. As explained in Chapters 1 and 2, Bhubaneswar includes several formerly rural villages within the city limits.
2. My study showed that boys' mothers, most of whom are themselves uneducated, have no direct role in educational planning, although they sometimes intervene. In one family, for example, a mother successfully objected to plans to send her son away to boarding school.
3. The Karans are Orissa's writer's caste, the caste whose members traditionally served as scribes. Just as all Brahmans do not make their living from the priesthood, many Karans derive their income from other occupations. But like priestly service for Brahmans, "writing" is culturally deemed the work appropriate for Karans.
4. Lower primary schools include classes one to three of the five-year primary school program. Upper primary schools offer classes one to five. Middle schools contain classes six and seven; high schools, classes six to eleven.
5. Schools that employ English as the medium of instruction are called English medium schools; those that employ Oriya, Oriya medium schools.

REFERENCES

Sable, Alan. 1977. *Paths through the Labyrinth: Educational Selection and Allocation in an Indian State Capital*. New Delhi, India: S. Chand and Company, Ltd.

Part 4
Economic Adaptations

James M. Freeman received a Ph.D. in anthropology from Harvard University in 1968. He is currently a professor of anthropology at San Jose State University, San Jose, California. His research interests in South Asia are religion, urbanization, life histories, untouchables, and humanistic aspects of change and adaptation. He has conducted two field research projects in India: (1) a sixteen month study of an urbanizing Hindu temple village in 1962-1963; and (2) a twenty-two month follow-up study of the same village in 1970-1972. He has published several articles on India as well as two books: SCARCITY AND OPPORTUNITY IN AN INDIAN VILLAGE, Cummings, Menlo Park 1977; and UNTOUCHABLE: AN INDIAN LIFE HISTORY, Stanford University Press 1979. His post-doctoral research and writing on India have been supported by fellowships from the American Institute of Indian Studies (1970-1972), the Social Science Research Council (1976-1977), and the Center for Advanced Study in the Behavioral Sciences (1976-1977).

Chapter 8 is based upon materials collected by Dr. Freeman during his two fieldwork periods in India. It is particularly valuable in that it examines socioeconomic change over a ten-year period in one village that has been affected by the construction of the New Capital.

8

The Widening Economic Gap: An Urban Indian Example

James M. Freeman

In recent years income disparities have widened, not only between rich and poor nations, but also within poor nations, where the affluent few accumulate most of the wealth. This situation applies particularly to the Orissan villagers on whom I report in this chapter. Modernization and urbanization, far from alleviating the plight of the poor, have increased the income gap between them and the affluent. No solution to their plight is foreseeable.

Kapileswar is a temple village and suburb of Bhubaneswar (see Chapter 5). Despite over two decades of growth and urbanization since Bhubaneswar was designated the state capital of Orissa, only 20 percent of the villagers in Kapileswar live without fear of starvation. This chapter examines, first, the effects that the growth of the New Capital at Bhubaneswar has had on the economic condition of Kapileswar; second, why these effects occurred; and finally, the significance of these effects. I gathered the data during a sixteen-month field study of Kapileswar in 1962-1963 and a twenty-two month follow-up study in 1970-1972.[1] I collected data by conducting a detailed census of every household of the village, interviewing villagers, observing economic activities, and recording life histories of villagers.

THE SETTING

The Physical Environment

Bhubaneswar lies in a fertile rice growing tract of eastern India. Because of population growth during the past century, inherited landholdings have been subdivided and fragmented into parcels so small that even most landholders barely have enough to support them. Over half the families of Kapileswar are landless. Natural disasters aggravate their plight: striking on the average of six out of ever ten years, cyclones, droughts, floods, and epidemics destroy life, crops, and property *(Census of India* 1961:11-12, 28).

Natural disasters hit the poor hardest. About 20 percent of the villagers live on the brink of starvation. They lack both food reserves and cash to pay for even the cheapest medicines. If ill and unable to work, they do not eat. About 60 percent subsist at a slightly higher, but still marginal, level. Only the highest 20 percent live comfortably, without fear of starvation. Despite the growth of the new city, the starving poor have at present few employment opportunities and little or no chance of improving their economic condition. Although the poor are of all castes, the lowest castes have the highest percentages of persons in desperate economic straits.

With the construction of the new city, many villagers seized new economic opportunities. Between 1950 and 1965, Bhubaneswar experienced rapid growth: some villagers helped build new houses, roads, and public buildings; others became civil servants or businessmen. Many outsiders migrated to the new city, taking up residence in nearby villages such as Kapileswar. After 1965, however, the growth of the city leveled off, and so did employment opportunities for the people of Kapileswar. The economic fluctuations of the new city directly affected occupational selection and school attendance. In this chapter I examine why, despite the apparent opportunities that the new city offered, the plight of the poor was not better in 1971 than it has been in the previous decade.

The Urbanizing Village of Kapileswar

Kapileswar is a multicaste village which had a population in 1971 of 2,869 persons (594 households).[2] Table 8.1 shows the caste distribution of households in Kapileswar. The village lies adjacent to the old section of Bhubaneswar, a pilgrimage center famous for its ancient temples (Panigrahi 1961). The Kapileswar temple is a satellite of the main temple of Bhubaneswar, called Lingaraj. Both the Lingaraj and Kapileswar temples, like others in India, not only provide a livelihood for persons of many castes who take care of the deities and properties of the temples, but also have many social, political, and educational functions (Aiyer 1946; Bhardwaj 1973; Misra, 1961; Ramesan 1962; Stein 1960; and Vidyarthi 1961).

TABLE 8.1
The Caste Distribution of Households in Kapileswar, 1972

Caste Name	Households #	Households %	Individuals #	Individuals %
Native Residents				
High				
Khuntia (Brahman)	13	2.2	76	2.7
Misra (Brahman	11	1.9	56	2.0
Other Brahman	3	.5	12	.4
Mallia	225	37.8	1,063	37.3
Middle				
Khandait (Militia)	11	1.9	66	2.3
Guria (Confectioner)	10	1.7	80	2.8
Sunar Bania (Goldsmith)	11	1.9	52	1.8
Potoli Bania (Betel Seller)	3	.5	34	1.2
Teli (Oilpresser)	17	2.9	99	3.5
Chasa (Cultivator)	18	3.0	101	3.5
Gauda (Herdsman)	9	1.5	46	1.6
Kamar (Blacksmith)	1	.2	5	.2
Badhei (Carpenter)	2	.3	8	.3
Low				
Kumbhar (Potter)	25	4.2	95	3.3
Keuta (Inland Fisherman)	21	3.5	111	3.7
Barik (Barber)	3	.5	14	.5
Untouchable				
Dhoba (Washerman)	4	.7	15	.5
Bauri	100	16.8	456	15.9
Hadi (Sweeper)	11	1.9	80	2.8
Totals: Native	(498)	(83.9)	(2,469)	(86.3)

TABLE 8.1 (cont'd)

Caste Name	Households #	%	Individuals #	%
Outsiders				
High				
Brahman (many surnames)	28	4.7	95	3.3
Karan (Scribe)	8	1.3	36	1.3
Middle				
Guria (Confectioner)	5	.8	24	.8
Sunar Bania (Goldsmith)	3	.5	15	.5
Teli (Oilpresser)	4	.7	22	.8
Other business castes	6	1.0	26	.9
Gauda (Herdsman)	1	.2	3	.1
Chasa (Cultivator)	5	.8	15	.5
Khandait (Militia)	5	.8	15	.5
Badhei (Carpenter)	1	.2	5	.2
Low				
Kumbhar (Potter)	2	.3	17	.6
Keuta (Inland Fisherman)	4	.7	13	.5
Nolia (Sea Fisherman)	22	3.7	109	3.8
Untouchable				
Hadi (Sweeper)	2	.3	5	.2
Totals: Strangers	(96)	(16.0)	(400)	(14.0)
Totals: Village	594	99.9*	2,869	100.3*

*Percents do not add to 100 because of rounding error.

Until the middle of the twentieth century, the Kapileswar temple dominated the economic, ritual, and political life of the village: nearly three-quarters of the villagers received some economic benefit from the temple. Several castes held tax-free paddy lands and tax-free house plots for the performance of obligatory, specialized, interdependent, hereditary services in the temple.[3]

A hereditary trustee and his relatives, members

of a privileged temple servant caste called Mallia, controlled the Kapileswar temple, its endowed properties, and its paddy fields. Found only in Kapileswar, the Mallias are the largest caste of the village, with 1,063 persons (37 percent of the village population). Their hereditary occupation is service to the deity of the temple.

The untouchable Bauri caste contrasts sharply with the Mallias. The Bauris are the second largest caste of the village, with 456 persons (16 percent of the village population). Stigmatized from birth as spiritually defiling pollutors of "clean" high caste people, the Bauris, as well as other untouchables, historically lived in segregated wards of Kapileswar. High castes denied them the use of public wells, as well as entry to schools, shops, and high caste temples and forced them to perform the most despised and foul jobs of their society. Landless and impoverished, the Bauris worked primarily as agricultural day laborers for the landed and wealthy high castes of the village.

Contemporary Indian laws, as well as the Constitution of India, prohibit discrimination against untouchables. Although Indian federal and state governments have spent millions of rupees and made countless efforts to improve the economic and social position of the untouchables, a wide gap remains between legislation and successful social reform. In Bhubaneswar, as in other Indian cities, untouchables experience no obvious public discrimination. In Kapileswar, three miles away, the old ways persist: untouchables enter neither shops nor village temples, although by law permitted to do so, because they fear economic reprisal (see, e.g., Freeman 1976:611-17). The contrasting economic responses of Mallias and Bauris to urbanization illustrate the widening gap between the poor and the affluent.

The Mallias: Occupational Improvement

The Mallias, the largest caste of the village, have moved into more diverse kinds of occupations than any of the other groups, in part because of different levels of wealth and education among them. The wealthiest are the best educated and have the highest percentage of civil servant clerks; middle income or less well educated Mallias are temple servants (the caste occupation), and when that is insufficient for survival, they become unskilled laborers, performing jobs incompatible with their caste status.

Between 1953 and 1971, the numbers of Mallias holding civil service jobs rose from three to sixty-three (25 percent of the Mallia male work force). Educational achievement increased rapidly as Mallias prepared their sons for government service, which they considered prestigious employment. Correspondingly, fewer Mallias worked as temple servants; the temple could not support the numbers of Mallias qualified to do temple service (see Freeman 1971: 1-12; 1975:124-33).

In the mid-1960s, as the growth of the New Capital slowed down, government jobs in Bhubaneswar became scarce and difficult to secure. This explains Mallia employment patterns: the government hired thirty-three Mallias during the five peak growth years of 1960 to 1965, but only fourteen during the next five years. Unemployed Mallias with high school and college educations opened small food stores and tea shops. Although less highly regarded than civil service, the tea shop business appealed to many Mallias because it was consistent with their identities as high caste temple priests who distribute sacred food to pilgrims. Before 1950, Mallias owned eight shops; by 1971, they had opened another twenty-nine shops, including seven that failed because of insufficient capital.

The growth and decline of city job opportunities also affected Mallia agricultural practices. In 1971, 54 percent of the Mallia households owned paddy lands, but only 31 percent worked their own land or even supervised it. Their indifference to agriculture reflected not resistance to new influences, but rather selective adaptation to them: hiring laborers or sharecroppers to work their lands, the Mallias themselves became civil servants or businessmen because both occupations carried greater prestige than did cultivation. As government jobs declined, so did Mallia attendance in high school and college. A few youths returned to farming their own lands; others said they would soon follow.

In summary, the Mallias select occupations that conform to caste ideals associated with ritual purity and prestige. The exceptions, such as the seven men out of a work force of 252 men who are unskilled construction workers, come from families that are so poor that their only choice is to work at demeaning jobs or starve. Table 8.2, a summary of caste selectivity, shows the contrasting responses of six castes of the village to employment opportunities in the New Capital.

Caste Occupations in an Urban Setting

Like the Mallias, almost every caste of the village has used its caste occupation or training as a springboard for seizing new opportunities in the New Capital. Most earners either have continued in their caste occupations or have adapted or commercialized caste occupational skills to new situations: Potters sell pots, Herdsmen tend cattle and sell milk, Barbers cut hair, Inland and Sea Fishermen sell fish, business castes run businesses, Cultivators experiment with cash crops, Sweepers work as municipal garbage collectors, and Goldsmiths fashion ornaments.

The Bauris: Occupational Stagnation

Bauri workers hold several different jobs concurrently, but unlike the more affluent Mallias, most Bauris have failed to leave their occupations of seasonal agricultural laborer and unskilled construction worker. After twenty years in an urban setting, only two persons out of a work force of 269 Bauris have acquired new skills. In this impoverished caste, over half the earners are women.

The Bauris do not refuse to change jobs; rather, they cannot because they are poor. Mallia landowners live off the earnings of their paddy lands while learning new skills, seeking new jobs, or educating their children for new jobs. The Bauris lack such an economic cushion. Only eight of the one hundred Bauri households own land: three and one-half barren, unproductive acres.

Six Bauri households have no able-bodied workers; their earnings are from begging and collecting wood and leaves. The remaining ninety-four households all earn a living from agriculture: eight are landowning households whose workers are also sharecroppers; fourteen are landless sharecropper households whose members earn 50 percent of the harvest; the remaining seventy-two are landless households of agricultural laborers who earn 8 to 12 1/2 percent of the crop cut. From the point of view of the Bauris, the landless sharecroppers are well off because their share of the rice may last them up to ten months, while the agricultural worker's share rarely lasts longer than four to six months.

Since 1962, Bauri landholdings have declined from four and one-half acres to three and one-half, and the number of sharecroppers, from fifty-seven to

TABLE 8.2
Household Occupations of Six Castes
 Whose Earners Resided in Kapileswar in 1971

	No. of House-holds	No. of Land-owners	Aver. Size of Ld/Hold. (acres)	Unem-ployed	Reli-gion	Govt. Serv.
Native Residents						
Khuntia Brahman	13	12	7.39	0	(13)	3
Mallia	225	(117)	1.26	4	124	51
Oil-presser	17	12	5.4	0	0	1
Bauri	100	(8)	0.04	0	0	0
Outsiders						
Brahman	28			2	0	22
Sea Fishermen	22			0	0	0

twenty-seven persons, but the number of agricultural laborers has increased from 203 to 230. In landowning and sharecropping households, the percentage of earners who work as agricultural laborers rather than sharecroppers increased from 33 to 93 percent. This shift occurred because high caste landowners dismissed Bauri sharecroppers to avoid the effect of new land laws that enable actual cultivators of a plot of land to claim it as their own. Many landowners cultivate their own lands, hiring agricultural laborers (see also Bailey 1963:74-75; and Sharma 1973:87-92 on evasions of land laws). As civil service opportunities decline, more high-caste landowners can be expected to do their own cultivation, throwing more Bauris out of work.

Since 1962, the percentage of nonagricultural wage laborers among Bauris has declined from 89 to 81 percent of the Bauri work force because road and house construction jobs in the city have declined. Although a few more Bauri men worked in the stone quarries in 1971 than was the case in 1962, the opportunities for quarry work have decreased: in 1962, men quarried stones every day; by 1971, they

Shops	Mkt.	Prof. &Skil. Labor	Unskil. Cons. Labor	Agri. Own Land & Sr/Cr.	Agri. Labor	Sell Fish	Other	Collecting
2	0	0	0	6	0	0	3	0
26	13	0	16	43	5	0	48	0
2	10	0	1	7	0	0	6	0
0	(16)	2	(86)	(21)	(72)	0	28	(90)
1	0	0	1	0	0	0	3	0
1	1	0	0	0	0	(22)	0	0

found quarry work only one out of every two or three days.

Those who are not able-bodied male adults work at less strenuous jobs. Women gather leaves, grass, and bundles of wood. Young children, the elderly, and the lame fetch or collect coal cinders from the railroad beds and broken scraps of iron and glass which they sell for a fraction of a rupee. In 1971, 138 persons from seventy-eight households collected fuel and other items for a living. By contrast, the only Bauris with modern skills were two automobile mechanics who worked in the New Capital.

In summary, castes like the Mallias are best able to take advantage of the economic opportunities presented by the New Capital economy, often in ways that are compatible with both caste occupation and self-image. The Bauris, by contrast—limited by lack of wealth, contacts, and education—continue to do simple unskilled labor as their fathers have done for generations. Obviously, the Bauris have gained far less than the Mallias; the economic gap between them has rapidly widened. In some parts of India, including Orissa, untouchables have benefited economically or politically from legislation prohibiting discrimination against them (Bailey 1957: 211-27; Cohn 1955:53-77). In Bhubaneswar, however, ingrained exploitative aspects of caste and their economic consequences remain as strong as they were twenty years ago. Bauris continue to be channeled into unskilled, poorly paid jobs that deny them anything more than basic subsistence earnings.

Reasons for Occupational Successes and Failures

The success or failure of the occupational adaptations of castes depends not only on wealth but also on the type of city that develops, what it offers, and what it needs. Because it is primarily an administrative center, not an industrial complex, the New Capital needs civil servants, small businessmen to cater to them, and garbage collectors, but it does not need temple priests or steel workers. The Kapileswar castes that benefited from the new city were those whose skills fitted, or could be adapted to, the particular urban environment of Bhubaneswar. The Bauris suffered because they had no specialized caste occupation: poor people of nearly all castes do unskilled labor. When the New Capital was built, contractors hired unskilled laborers from many castes; the Bauris had no special claims to these jobs and now compete for scarce opportunities with workers from other castes.

The Sweepers, by contrast, once were as poor as the Bauris but have made substantial economic gains because they have a highly specialized occupational niche that is indispensable for the city as well as the village. The Sweepers are both assured of employment and protected from encroachment by the poor of other castes. Because of the polluting character of the work, only a Sweeper will work as a sweeper. Thus, the Sweepers benefited precisely by retaining their hereditary polluting occupation. However, in so doing, they perpetuated the stigma associated with their caste.

The response of the Sweepers, as well as the Mallias, shows that caste occupational adaptations are related to the symbols of caste. The economically exploitative aspects of caste, which help to maintain caste hierarchy, are reinforced by symbols of pollution and purity by which caste boundaries are carefully demarcated and certain jobs and activities isolated as symbolic of different caste identities.

As caste perpetuates differences, so caste

itself is perpetuated by the ways in which the opportunities of the New Capital are presented to the villagers, are perceived by them, and are acted on by them. Adaptations to urban life are often cited as breaking down caste distinctions. The caste-reinforcing aspect of urbanization has been less frequently mentioned. The New Capital is changing the village of Kapileswar and its castes, but in turn the villagers are making the city an extension of their caste-based village community.

THE DISTRIBUTION OF WEALTH IN KAPILESWAR

Land, Wealth, and Income

I used three indicators to measure the distribution of wealth in Kapileswar: the amount of cultivable land owned, the amount of wealth owned other than land (other wealth), and annual household income, based on the average number of adults in a household. An explanation of this last indicator is given in Table 8.5. For each of the three indicators, I used a nine point scale. Using a fourth cumulative scale, I then combined the measures of land, other wealth, and income. These data are given in Tables 8.3 through 8.6.

To classify landowners into low, middle, well-to-do, and wealthy categories, I used villager estimates of the amount of land needed to support a family of five (see Table 8.3). The villagers assume that if a household has rice, an adult male consumes between .5 and .6 kilograms of husked rice per day, 180 to 215 kilograms per year (396 to 473 pounds). Adult female consumption is .4 kilogram per day, 140 kilograms per year (308 pounds). Since unhusked paddy is slightly more than double the weight of husked rice, the annual consumption per adult is twice that of husked rice.[4]

A family of five with one adult male, one adult female, and three children consumes between 1,300 and 1,600 kilograms (2,860 to 3,520 pounds) of unhusked rice annually. Kapileswar's paddy yields per acre range from 270 kilograms (594 pounds) on poor land to 720 kilograms (1,584 pounds) on good land. Average local yields of about 500 kilograms per acre (1,100 pounds) are higher than the 1970-1971 all-Orissan average of 390 kilograms (858 pounds) per acre.[5]

To be supported solely by produce from average paddy lands, a single adult needs to own and to

TABLE 8.3
Acres of Cultivable Land Owned per Household

Land Scale Classification Acres Household	1 No Land 0	2 Low .1-.24	3 Low .25-.49	4 Low .5-.99	5 Middle 1-2.9	6 Middle 3-4.9	7 Well-to-do 5-9.9	8 Well-to-do 10-19.9	9 Wealthy Over 20	Totals
Native Residents	266	3	21	31	113	36	21	1	6	498
Outsiders	77	2	1	0	7	2	5	1	1	96
Entire Village	343	5	22	31	120	38	26	2	7	594
	No Land	Low (Under 1 Acre)			Middle (1-4.9 Acres)		Well-to-do (5-19.9 Acres)		Wealthy (Over 20)	
Totals	343	58			158		28		7	594

TABLE 8.4
Wealth Owned Other Than Land per Household*

Wealth Scale Classification	1 Very Low	2 Very Low	3 Low	4 Low	5 Middle	6 Middle	7 Well-to-do	8 Well-to-do	9 Wealthy	Totals
Rupee Value	0-99	100-499	500-999	1000-4999	5000-9999	10,000-19,999	20,000-49,999	50,000-99,999	100,000+	
Households										
Native Residents	5	162	109	133	37	28	16	4	4	498
Outsiders	12	49	13	14	3	1	2	1	1	96
Entire Village	17	211	121	148	40	29	18	5	5	594
Rupees	Very Low (0-499)		Low (500-4999)		Middle (5000-19,999)		Well-to-do (20,000-99,999)		Wealthy (100,000+)	
Totals	288		269		69		23		5	594

*The figures above are based on estimates of the value of such items as houses which are evaluated in terms of the number of rooms, whether built of stone or mud, and whether built with stone, metal, tile, or thatch roofs; income property other than paddy lands; luxury items such as bicycles, wristwatches, radios, electricity, running water; implements such as plows and carts; and kind and number of livestock. Jewelry was not included because it was not possible to estimate the amount or value per household.

TABLE 8.5
Annual Income per Household Based on Average Number of Adults per Household*

Income Scale Classification	1 Starvation	2 Starvation	3 Low	4 Middle	5 Middle	6 Well-to-do	7 Well-to-do	8 Wealthy	9 Wealthy	Totals
Rupee Value	Under 125	125–249	250–499	500–749	750–999	1000–1749	1750–2499	2500–4999	5000+	
Households										
Native Residents	6	22	178	143	51	78	14	6	0	498
Outsiders	1	3	28	23	12	17	7	4	1	96
Entire Village	7	25	206	166	63	95	21	10	1	594
Rupees	Starvation (0–249)		Low (250–499)	Middle (500–999)		Well-to-do (1000–2499)		Wealthy (2500+)		
Totals	32		206	229		116		11		594

*This table shows the annual income per household based on the average number of adults per household. An adult is defined as anyone who is 15 years of age or older; children are considered as follows: ages 10–14=.75 adult; ages 2–9=.5 adult; children under 2=.25 adult. Thus a household of two adults and three children whose ages are five, nine, and twelve is considered to contain 3.75 adults. A determination of annual household income on this basis makes possible an estimate of how many households earn an income which is below the subsistence level for an average adult.

TABLE 8.6
Cumulative Wealth per Household Scale
  (Combines Land, Other Wealth, and Income Scales)

Cumulative Scale Classification Households	3-6 Privation	7-14 Low	15-20 Middle	21-24 Well-to-do	25-27 Wealthy	Totals
Native Residents	101	306	82	4	5	498
Outsiders	26	56	13	1	0	96
Entire Village	127	362	95	5	5	594
Percentage	21.5	60.7	16.1	.8	.8	99.9

personally cultivate nearly .7 acre; a family of five needs about three acres. The villagers' estimate is close to that of Misra and Sinha (Misra 1961:110-11; Sinha 1971:58) In the District of Puri, where Kapileswar is located, the average plot is about .3 acres.
  Table 8.7 shows that only 10.6 percent of Kapileswar's 594 households own enough paddy land to be supported solely by it. The need for outside sources of support accounts in part for both the occupational diversification and the multiple job holding of the people of Kapileswar.

TABLE 8.7
Households Owning Above and Below the Land
  Survival Figure of .7 Acre per Adult
  (Three Acres per Five-member Household)

	Native Residents		Strangers		Entire Village	
	No. of Households	%	No. of Households	%	No. of Households	%
Above	54	11	9	9.4	63	10.6
Below	444	89	87	90.6	531	89.4
Total	498	100	96	100	594	100

Throughout Orissa, less than 20 percent of the landholders own more than 60 percent of the total land in the state (see Sinha 1971:58). Similarly, in Kapileswar, land inequalities are pronounced: Table 8.8 shows that nearly 30 percent of the land is owned by one percent of the households, and nearly 60 percent of the households are landless.

TABLE 8.8
Total Acres Owned by Landowners of Different Size Holdings

Acres	No. of Households	%	No. of Acres Owned	%
Landless	343	57.5	0	0
Under 1 Acre	58	9.8	24.53	3.1
1.0-4.9 Acres	158	26.6	335.43	43.1
5.0-9.9 Acres	26	4.4	166.50	21.2
10.0-19.9 Acres	2	.3	28.0	3.6
20 Acres and up	7	1.2	223.0	28.9
Totals	594	100	777.46	99.9
Average Size Landholding:	1.30 Acres			

As Table 8.4 shows, the range in wealth other than land is also great: from households of homeless beggars and widows who own nothing to households whose wealth exceeds Rs. 100,000 (more than U.S. $13,000) and who own many luxury items.

Table 8.5 shows the annual income per household. In Bhubaneswar in 1971 an adult could barely survive, eating one meal a day or every other day, on about Rs. 250 a year, or about Rs. 20 a month. Although this is an exceedingly low estimate, with no allowance for clothes, household items, medicine, money to rent a room or repair one's dwelling, or other basic expenses, some thirty-two households in Kapileswar (about 5 percent) have earnings below this bare subsistence amount. These people are starving. Another third of the households—the low-income households—subsist marginally. When they work, the people of these households earn enough to eat; but if they miss a day of work because of illness, they do not eat. The people of the remaining households—middle income, well-to-do, and wealthy—live free from the threat of hunger.

Table 8.6, a twenty-seven point cumulative scale that includes nine points from each of the three scales of wealth (Tables 8.3 through 8.5), provides an overall assessment of the wealth of each household in Kapileswar. One-fifth of the households fall in what I term a privation category characterized by three features: bare survival or below survival income, little or no additional wealth, and little or no land. The households in this category have no protection from loss of income resulting from unforeseen (though frequent) disasters. The households (over 60 percent) in the low category live under conditions only slightly better, while the remaining households in the upper three categories live comfortably.

Overall wealth of households varies greatly with caste. Table 8.9 summarizes the contrasts among six castes of Kapileswar that are representative of wealthy, middle, and poor castes generally. I have already demonstrated that the great disparities in land owned, wealth owned, and income earned have influenced the direction of occupational change in Kapileswar.

Debts and Land Transfers

In June 1971, I collected data on 159 households that were then or had been in debt between 1968 and 1971.[6] Of these households 104 were in debt in 1971. The villagers expected other households to incur new debts just before the November harvest, when food becomes scarce.

The impoverished Bauris had the highest number of households in debt (forty-six), but their outstanding loans were small, averaging only fifty-nine rupees per household. Other Bauri households were refused loans because they were thought to be bad credit risks. Bauri landowners and sharecroppers with assured employment and income were able to get loans twice as large, on the average, as those obtained by agricultural wage laborers. Professional moneylenders and employers, mostly Mallias, furnished over 80 percent of Bauri loans, charging 25 percent or more annually, payable in paddy or cash. For short-term loans and loans with mortgages,

TABLE 8.9
Comparison of the Wealth of Six Castes of Kapileswar

	No. of House-holds	Land Owned			Wealth Other Than Land			Avg. Annual Income			Cumulative Score	
		Total Acres per Caste	Avg. Acres per House-hold	Rank in Vil-lage	Total Rupees	Avg. Rupees per House-hold	Rank in Vil-lage	Total Rupees	Rupees per House-hold	Rank in Vil-lage	Avg.	Rank in Vil-lage
Native Castes												
Khuntia Brahman	13	103	7.92	1	415,000	31,923	1	18,800	1,446	1	18.30	1
Mallia	225	308.2	1.37	9	876,440	3,859	7	160,546	714	12	10.09	11
Oilpresser	17	91.3	5.37	2	357,250	21,015	2	18,600	1,094	4	14.29	3
Bauri	100	3.5	.04	22	53,900	539	23	50,724	507	23	7.15	24
Outsiders												
Brahman	28	81.3	2.9	4	53,900	1,925	13	32,440	1,159	3	10.57	10
Sea Fishermen	22	.2	.01	23	6,600	300	25	11,638	529	21	6.73	26

A Bauri grandmother harvests her landlord's paddy.

KAPILESWAR VILLAGERS

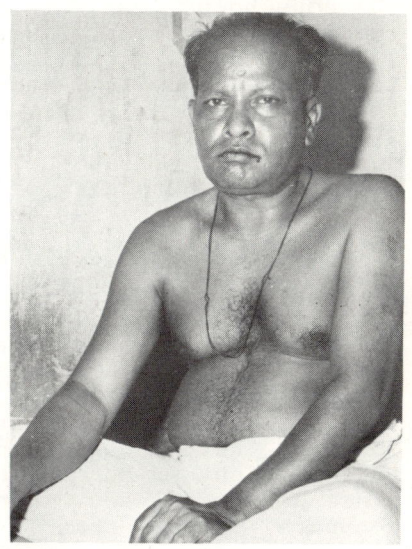

A wealthy landowner.

A Mallia-caste betel seller in his Old Town shop.

interest rates, were 37 percent. Significantly, over 60 percent of the ninety Bauri loans were exclusively for food.

Similarly, the Mallias, the second largest group of debtors, took out forty-six loans, nearly half of them for food; only four were for business, and only one for cultivation. Twenty agricultural castes took loans, two-thirds for agriculture, less than one fifth for food. The remaining nineteen households that took loans cited food scarcity more frequently than any other reason (42 percent).

Between 1950 and 1971, eighty-three households in Kapileswar bought more land than they sold, while 101 households lost more land than they gained. The remaining 410 households showed no gain or loss in landholdings. The villagers bought 84.7 acres of cultivable paddy land and sold 98.15 acres, for a net loss of 13.45 acres. The villagers also sold slightly more house plots and dry lands than they bought, for a net loss of .91 acre. Land sales thus show that the building of the New Capital has not led to great increases in the wealth of the village as a whole.

About 20 percent of Kapileswar's households, categorized as well-to-do or of the economic ascent, have retained their lands, but their gains are canceled out by the many more households on the economic decline who are selling their lands not only to other villagers but also to outsiders. Selling paddy lands does not necessarily indicate economic difficulty. With an expanding city and inflated land prices, eighteen households have sold lands to finance new businesses. But this sort of activity accounts for less than 10 percent of Kapileswar's 187 land sales. The most frequently cited reason for land sale was to pay for rituals: sixty-one sales (33 percent) financed marriage and funeral ceremonies; forty-one sales were for food; twenty-four were to repay loans; ten were for medicine; and twelve financed litigation. The overwhelming majority of land sales failed to bring in capital for investment. They simply staved off economic disaster or enabled families to perform their social obligations on ritual occasions.

PORTRAITS OF STARVATION AND AFFLUENCE

The numerical data of this paper give some idea of the magnitude of poverty and the range of wealth in Kapileswar. But this account would not be complete without presenting glimpses of what poverty as well as affluence is like for the individuals who experience it. The following reports are from interviews and full-length autobiographies that I collected from Kapileswar villagers, and from events that I witnessed.

A Bauri's View of Starvation

Muli sits on the veranda of his windowless mud and thatch hut. He is a forty-two year old Bauri, slender, ravaged by a lung disease, and too ill to work. He is supported by his wife, who left at dawn to transplant paddy in the fields of an Oilpresser. Rain falls softly from black monsoon clouds; the dirt road outside Muli's house is an impassable swamp of mud. Although midday, Muli has eaten nothing since the previous night, for he has no food in his house. Despite his hardships, Muli says that he has seen worse times, and he describes one of them to me:

> Before the harvest came in November, rice became very scarce; prices rose, and no one would lend us rice. We could not find any work, so we had no money to buy food. In order to survive, we dug up roots and stole yams from the fields of wealthy landowners. Even then, we were hungry. We ate one meal a day, or none. Sometimes we ate one meal every other day.
>
> Right at harvest time, my infant son developed boils. They soon spread to my body, all over, except my face. It was severe and painful. I could not walk because of the pain, so I could not harvest paddy at the one time we could expect to have steady work. My father, mother, and brother went to cut paddy. Mother resented that my wife and I were earning nothing, and she refused to give us any food. But my sister stole food from the kitchen and fed us. We sat at home in agony, covered with boils. Whenever my mother found us eating, she scolded us and told us to leave: "Two people will sit in the house and eat," she said, "and there is their son, who requires two to three coins of sugar each day! So we feed three people every day from our earnings. Why

aren't you looking after your own stomaches? We cannot feed you anymore!"

Each night my wife cried under my feet. And we both prayed to God to cure us.

One morning I hobbled to the hospital, hoping to get some help from a doctor whom I knew. But he had been transferred; another doctor was there whom I did not know. I was a man of small caste, an untouchable, so I despaired. How could I talk to an important man like that? I turned away and returned home.

I was such a lucky man that my boils, instead of going away, got bigger day by day, and so did those of my wife. Meanwhile my mother scolded us more and more.

My wife could no longer stand the scolding. One morning she borrowed some berries from a neighbor and sold them in the village. Even though she was in terrible pain, she worked; I couldn't do that. So I stayed home and took care of our infant son. I borrowed some sugar on credit from a high caste shopkeeper. I mixed the sugar with water and fed it to my son two to three times that day. When my wife returned, she nursed him. With the money she earned I went to the market and bought rice, sulphur, and cocoanut oil. It was very painful for me to walk. My wife boiled the sulphur and oil together, spread the hot past on our boils, and soon they burst, and pus drained out. Throughout the day, up to that time late at night, we had not eaten anything. Now we ate. That night, for the first time in weeks, we were able to sleep without horrible pain and with our bellies full.

But the boils returned. We survived like this for one month, with my wife working while I took care of our child, feeding him sugar water until his mother returned late at night and nursed him. Sometimes during that month we were able to eat even twice a day. My mother saw this and was jealous. She picked quarrels with my wife, screaming: "Who took my fuel, my rice, my vegetables? You did!"

Finally, my wife could stand this no longer, and answered harshly: "Who is taking your property? Whose pubic hair cares for your property?" This was a grave insult to give to one's respected superior, so my mother hit her, and they fought, screaming curses at each other: "You daughter of a whore! You cholera-eaten corpse! Leprosy will eat away your fingers!"

Crises of an Affluent Oilpresser

The crises of the poor center on starvation; those of the wealthy focus on costly litigations and labor disputes. Jogi, forty-five years old, fat and balding, complains that the Bauri laborers who cultivate his twenty-five acres of paddy land are greedy: "They want to be paid one bundle of paddy for every ten they cut instead of their proper wage—one for twelve." He pauses to daub lime paste on a shiny green betel leaf which rests on a polished red stone slab, sprinkles the leaf with slivers of areca nut, spices, and tobacco, deftly folds the leaf into a cone, and pops it into his mouth. Each day he chews over 100 of these betel concoctions, spending twice as much for his habit as the households of his workers spend each day for food.

Jogi sits near me on a blue and white cushioned mat in a room on the second floor of his ten-room stone house. Above him an electric overhead fan turns slowly; at his side a large table radio blares film songs. While Jogi's household is one of ninety-two in the village that has electricity, and one of the twenty-five that has running water, few if any of the others have a profusion of luxury items such as Jogi's household: five wrist watches, three bicycles, two overhead fans, a large radio, a bottled gas stove, a toaster, a refrigerator, a shower, and a latrine with a flush toilet under construction.

On the first floor of Jogi's house, a narrow corridor leads from the front reception room past storerooms stacked with bags of rice to the kitchen area where Jogi's wife is preparing the midday meal: rice, lentils, two vegetable curries, and fish curry.

This is typical fare for Jogi's household, in which expensive items, such as meat and fish, are served nearly every day.

I ask Jogi why he hires inefficient wage laborers instead of more highly skilled sharecroppers, who produce higher yields and better profits. He shakes his head petulantly and says:

> I used to hire sharecroppers. But two years after the great fire in Kapileswar (1959), my Bauri sharecroppers told me that they would no longer give me my owner's traditional one-half share, but only one-fourth. They got their idea from a new law which said that they only had to give their masters one-fourth, and that they couldn't be thrown off the land if they had worked it for several years. Nevertheless, I evicted them, and in revenge they took the entire crop for themselves. My lands were three miles from the village, so I could not watch and stop them. The next year, they forcibly occupied my lands, cultivated them, and again took my entire crop for themselves. I took them to court to get back my land. It took three years for the case to be decided, and during that period the Bauris retained control over the crops, which they harvested. But in 1962, the court ruled in my favor. The Bauri people could not read or write; they had no written proof that they had been the traditional sharecroppers of my lands. So the court ordered them evicted, and I hired some wage laborers who are now giving me trouble. If they don't accept the payment I give them, I'll hire other workers to replace them next year.

Jogi's other sources of income helped him weather the loss of income from his crops. He is a moneylender who runs a cloth shop in the market of the New Capital. In 1946, Jogi's father started an inheritance dispute over property worth one quarter of a million rupees. By 1972, the case had dragged on for some twenty-six years, costing Jogi upwards of Rs. 20,000. The case is now in the higher courts. When I asked him whether the case was worth the time and money involved, Jogi shrugged: "We have won in the higher courts, but of course the other side is appealing. Perhaps my grandchildren will benefit from the result."

CONCLUSION

Wealth, Opportunities, and Constraints

By village standards, the wealthy and well-to-do households of Kapileswar, which are the primary recipients of benefits from the New Capital, maintain high standards of living and are avid consumers of new products and luxury items. Their wealth gives them much greater flexibility than the poor in choosing new opportunities. The New Capital has provided the wealthy with the opportunity to try new occupations, products, and life styles, and the wealthy have benefited immensely.

By contrast, the development of the New Capital has not been good to the poor of Kapileswar. Despite twenty years in an urban boom town environment, 60 percent of the households of Kapileswar remain poor, virtually landless, uncertain of an income, and unable to benefit significantly from the opportunities that the New Capital affords. Most of the loans the villagers take out are simply for food or medicine, not for starting businesses or furthering their children's education. The villagers have sold more paddy lands than they have bought; only the three business castes and one Brahman caste own more land in 1972 than they did in 1950. The paddy lands of Kapileswar, even those that in principle are inalienable temple trust lands, are gradually passing into the hands of outsiders. Although incomes have increased, few families have made the transition from poor to middle-income or well-to-do status.

The economic constraints that prevent the poor from taking advantage of the New Capital include: first, an unequal distribution of land, which results in a small number of households owning most of the land; second, an unequal distribution of wealth other than land, which results in only a few households of the village having money for investments in business or education; third, a preponderance of low-income households dependent on occupations with uncertain and fluctuating employment opportunities; fourth, high interest rates on loans that undermine a household's ability to accumulate wealth; fifth, natural disasters that occur at least every other year, hitting the poor harder than the wealthy. The poor have no food reserves. Calamities and crop destruction lead to soaring food prices, to hunger, to widespread emigration from Kapileswar, to selling land and ornaments, and to increased indebtedness. The poor spend much of their daily wages repaying loans at 37 percent interest that they were forced to take out in order to eat.

Faced with such crises, many households became locked into a descending spiral from which they cannot escape and which pulls them below the survival level. Usually this occurs when a combination of disasters, such as drought and illness, hit at the same time. Once ill and unable to work, earn, and eat, weakened by hunger, malnutrition, and disease, the poor of Kapileswar consider themselves fortunate if they survive at all.

Implications

For two and a half decades national and state governments of India have been committed to improving the economic and social condition of their people, and in many places they have achieved notable successes (Randhawa 1974). The failures described in my study do not imply that urbanization and attempts at economic improvement elsewhere in Orissa or in India generally necessarily result in, or are foredoomed to, failure, but rather that failure can result from extreme conditions of poverty and scarce resources, as well as from specific adaptations of caste groups.

The Bauris of Kapileswar say that they are worse off economically than their relatives in villages several miles from the New Capital. I believe their claim is plausible for four reasons. First, in urban villages like Kapileswar, cash wages are replacing payments in paddy, but the buying power of cash is less than that of paddy, both because of monetary inflation and because farm cash wages usually are paid after the harvest when the price of paddy is lowest. Just before the harvest, when paddy is scarce, cash earners who need paddy must buy it at high prices. Second, as lands around the New Capital increased in value, speculators bought them up. Village grazing lands became the sites of housing developments. Bauri cattleherding youths lost their jobs. The inflated price of paddy lands prevented the few Bauris with money from buying them. Third, by turning to construction work in the New Capital, the Bauris of Kapileswar became dependent on the unpredictable, fluctuating capital construction trade.

Bauris in rural villages remained in lower paying but more secure agricultural occupations. Finally, people of other castes competed with Bauris for scarce urban construction jobs. Lacking a caste-protected occupation, the Bauris have no certain source of income. Ironically, adaptation to Bhubaneswar's urban setting may well have resulted in less economic improvement for them than their rural counterparts were experiencing.

Few anthropologists or rural sociologists reporting on economic development and urbanization in India have arrived at conclusions as bleak as mine. Might my conclusions reflect, therefore, my personal convictions rather than dispassionate analysis? Mamdani's critical evaluation of the Khanna Project, a population control study in western India, is a devastating object lesson that shows how an investigator's implicit values and assumptions may predetermine and invalidate his conclusions (Mamdani 1972). Such a criticism hardly applies to my study because my conclusions, instead of confirming the expectations I had prior to the study, contradicted them and made them untenable.

Clearly, the data I gathered, and the way I arranged them, reflected the problems I examined. The results, however, were *not* at all what I had anticipated. Rather, they disproved my every assumption. When, in 1962, I began the first of my two field studies of Kapileswar, I never anticipated writing about starvation among the urban poor. I planned to study the effect of the growth of the New Capital on the religious life-styles of Hindu temple priests in Kapileswar. My interest was in religion, not economics. Postulating a traditional-versus-modern dichotomy, I assumed that the values and life-styles of these privileged castes were incompatible with the new life-styles offered by the new city, that the priests would resist the influence of the city, and that their religion would disintegrate under the impact of urbanization. I believed, by contrast, that the less privileged lower castes and untouchable castes, with less commitment to old life-styles, would seize the economic opportunities and benefits offered by the city, and, in so doing, would significantly alter their life-styles.

All of my assumptions were wrong. The priests did not resist; instead, they adapted rapidly and well to the new urban complex at their doors, doing so without losing their religious life-styles. Most of the lower castes and untouchable castes failed to benefit from the new city, and the economic gap between them and the traditionally privileged high castes widened rather than narrowed.

Furthermore, I found that economic and political events profoundly affected the Kapileswar temple, the major topic of my religious research. I was compelled by these findings to abandon not only my original assumptions, but also the perspective from which I had hoped to study the urbanization of Kapileswar. Placing greater emphasis on economic factors and processes of adaptation, I returned in 1970 for a two-year restudy of Kapileswar, the results of which are summarized here and in my 1977 publication.

High caste and low caste villagers who have read or been told about the information and conclusions of my study say they consider it an accurate assessment of their economic situation. Still, recalling Mamdani, did the villagers simply tell me what they thought I wanted to hear, or should hear? If my conclusions had been based solely on surveys and interviews, I could have been misled by informant responses. But my conclusions were also based on observations, not only on farming and other daily activities, but also of the effects of disasters.

For example, these observations led me to realize that I had at first underestimated the importance of both disasters and seasonal fluctuations in the availability of food in assessing the economic situation of the villagers, particularly those only barely surviving. At first glance, many poor households did not appear to be in desperate economic straits. In following their fortunes over two to three years, a vastly different picture emerged, for it was not one crisis, but a combination of crises brought to a climax by natural disasters, that brought these households to ruin and accounted for their failure to benefit from the opportunities of the New Capital.

In summary, the conclusions reached in this study were not those I had anticipated. I wish that the poor of Kapileswar were not as badly off as at present I think they are, and I would personally be quite happy if new studies employing different perspectives and more data could prove my conclusions needed to be modified.

NOTES
1. The research upon which this chapter is based was supported by a Senior Faculty Fellowship of the American Institute of Indian Studies, 1970-1972. Preparation of this paper was aided by a fellowship from the Center for Advanced Study in the Behavioral Sciences, 1976-1977, with funds from the Andrew H. Mellon Foundation. I am grateful to both the Institute and the Center for their generous support. I am also indebted to my research assistant, Harihar Mallia, who is a native resident of the community that I studied.

Portions of this chapter are from my book, *Scarcity and Opportunity in an Indian Village*, and are used by permission of Cummings Publishing Company. The book contains additional data supporting the conclusions of the present paper.

2. In this chapter I use the term "household" to mean, following Shah's definition, a residential and domestic unit composed of one or more persons living under the same roof and eating food cooked in a single kitchen (Shah 1974:8). Almost all of the 594 households of the village consist of exclusive kinship units. The three exceptions are wealthy households in which a personal servant also resides. For the purposes of this study, the servants are listed separately from the households in which they work.

3. See Cahpter 5 for a more extensive discussion of the Kapileswar Temple and its decline.

4. The Bureau of Statistics and Economics, Government of Orissa, considers cleaned rice to be 65 percent of the green rates of paddy (Government of Orissa 1972:4). Villagers who can afford them eat other foods with nutritional value, including wheat, potatoes, brinjals, plantain, taro, fish, goat meat, lentils, green vegetables, tomatoes, mango, guava, and jackfruit (see also Care-Orissa 1972).

5. The average yield in Orissa in 1970-1971 was 960 kilograms per hectare (2.47 acres), or about 390 kilograms per acre. This is a decline from the 1963-1964 yield of 1,000 kilograms per hectare and is less than the all-India average (Care-Orissa 1972: 46-47; Sinha 1971:56-58).

6. Some individuals were reluctant to discuss their debts because they were embarrassed by them, while moneylenders did not wish to discuss the loans they gave. Accordingly, the number of debtors and lenders is probably much higher than my figures indicate.

REFERENCES

Aiyer, V. G. Ramakrishna. 1946. *The Economy of a South Indian Temple*. Annamalainagar, India: Annamalai University Press.

Bailey, Frederick G. 1957. *Caste and the Economic Frontier*. Manchester: Manchester University Press.

————. 1963. *Politics and Social Change: Orissa in 1959*. Berkeley: University of California Press.

Bhardwaj, Surinder Mohan. 1973. *Hindu Places of Pilgrimage in India*. Berkeley: University of California Press.

Care-Orissa. 1972. *Planning for Better Nutrition in Orissa*. Care-Orissa.

Census of India, 1961.

————. 1966. *Orissa. District Census Handbook, Puri*. Cuttack, India: Orissa Government Press.

Cohn, Bernard. 1955. The Changing Status of a Depressed Caste, pp. 53-77 in *Village India*, edited by McKim Marriott. Chicago: University of Chicago Press.

Freeman, James. 1971. Occupational Changes among Hindu Temple Servants. *Indian Anthropologist* 1 (November):1-13.

————. 1975. Religious Change in a Hindu Pilgrimage Center. *Review of Religious Research* 16 (Winter):124-33.

————. 1976. The Untouchable Tragedy. *The Geographical Magazine* (London) 45 (July): 611-17.

————. 1977. *Scarcity and Opportunity in an Indian Village*. Menlo Park, California: Cummings Publishing Company.

Government of Orissa. 1972. *Report on the Sample Survey for Estimation of Loss in Yield Rates of Khariff Crops Due to the Flood and Cyclone of 1971 in Orissa*. Bhubaneswar, India: Bureau of Statistics and Economics.

Mamdani, Mahmoud. 1971. *The Myth of Population Control*. New York: Monthly Review Press.

Mishra, Sadasiva. 1961. *Economic Survey of Orissa*, Vol. 1. Cuttack, India: Government of Orissa, Finance Department.

Panigrahi, Krishna Chandra. 1961. *Archaeological Remains at Bhubaneswar*. Bombay, India: Orient Longmans.

Ramesan, N. 1962. *Temples and Legends of Andhra Pradesh*. Bombay, India: Bharatiya Vidya Bhavan.

Randhawa, Mohinder Singh. 1974. *The Green Revolution*. New York: John Wiley and Sons.

Shah, A. M. 1974. *The Household Dimension of the Family in India*. Berkeley: University of California Press.

Sharma, Hari P. 1973. The Green Revolution in India: Prelude to a Red One? pp 77-102 in *Imperialism and Revolution in South Asia*, edited by Kathleen Gough and Hari P. Sharma. New York: Monthly Review Press.

Sinha, B. N. 1971. *Geography of Orissa*. New Delhi, India: National Book Trust.

Stein, Burton. 1960. The Economic Function of a Medieval South Indian Temple. *Journal of Asian Studies* 19 (2):163-76.

Vidyarthi, Lalita P. 1961. *The Sacred Complex of Hindu Gaya*. Bombay, India: Asia Publishing House.

Dr. Harish Chandra Das holds two M.A. degrees, one in anthropology and one in Hindustani classical music. From 1962 to 1971 he served as a collaborator in the Harvard-Bhubaneswar study, undertaking surveys of several villages affected by the growth of the New Capital. His Ph.D. thesis, "Sub-Urbanization of Two Orissan Villages," was submitted to Utkal University in 1971 under the final guidance of Professor Laxman Mahapatra who had replaced Professor A. Aiyappan as chairman of the Department of Anthropology. Dr. Das's first official employment was as Curator of Anthropology in the Orissa State Museum in Bhubaneswar. He is currently Superintendant of the State Museum.

Chapter 9 focuses upon economic changes incurred by one of the five villages that is contiguous to the New Capital. Dr. Das first surveyed the village of Nuapalli in 1964 and has continued to do research there since that time.

9 | The Economy of an Urbanizing Village

Harish C. Das

This chapter deals with the changing economy of Nuapalli, a multicaste village on the periphery of the New Capital.[1] This traditional village has been exposed to both modernizing and urbanizing influences since the shift of the state capital to Bhubaneswar in 1948. Situated three miles to the northwest of the Bhubaneswar Railway Station (see Figure 1.2) and covering a vast tract of land (including probably the biggest forest in Puri District), it is an area into which the capital is expanding. In recent years, the fringes of the residential area of the village have come to be spotted with the large buildings of The Regional College of Education, The Central Poultry Farm, The Regional Research Laboratory, Utkal University, and a portion of Units VII and VIII of the New Capital. The residential area of the village has not been included in the New Capital thus far. However, a national highway, which passes through the village, stands at the northern and northwestern border of the residential area.

My concern in this chapter is to identify some of the effects of the expansion of the New Capital upon the occupations of the villagers of Nuapalli.[2] The traditional occupations of the villagers can be broken down into those that apparently have been affected by the growth of the New Capital; those which seem to have lost importance; those which seem to be permanently inflated, by which I mean those that have been highly attractive for at least one or two generations; and those which appear to be temporarily inflated, by which I mean those that were in great demand as the new city developed but whose long-term viability is highly questionable. The categories of new occupations are familiar ones and need no introductory explanation.

217

UNAFFECTED TRADITIONAL OCCUPATIONS

Certain occupations of the village, such as paddy cultivation and moneylending, remain apparently unchanged even after the advent of the New Capital.

Paddy Cultivation

Paddy cultivation, the mainstay of the villagers, has not been inflated as an occupation although there is a high demand for rice. The traditional methods of cultivation are still employed, and about 70 percent of the households are directly or indirectly engaged in this type of work. Villagers of all castes are agriculturists. Some castes cultivate land in addition to their traditional callings.

As elsewhere in rural Orissa, there are three types of paddy cultivators in Nuapalli: owner-cultivator, sharecroppers *(bhaga chasi)*, and those who cultivate on a contract basis *(sanja chasi)*. Owner-cultivators may be divided into two groups, landowners who engage agricultural wage laborers for cultivating their fields but do not work in the fields themselves and landowners who work in their own fields. Owners who are rich, who have other occupations, or who for some reason cannot personally cultivate their land, the aged, sick, and widowed, and those who have lost or have been forced to sell their oxen give their land to others for cultivation on a sharecropping or contract basis. Cultivation by contract is usually practiced for the second crop, that subsequent to the main harvest, and for other subsidiary crops. Whatever may be the yield from the field, the owner of the land gets his contracted quantity of the produce from the cultivators. In some cases, the owner may prefer to contract for cash.

For the cultivation of paddy fields, manpower, draft animals such as bullocks, tools, and seeds are all necessary. For want of one or more of these, owners give the land to other neighbors on a sharecropping basis. The terms have been standardized over time: The owners pay all the taxes and take half the produce; the sharecroppers supply draft animals, farming equipment, and labor in return for the remaining half of the produce. Sharecropping is arranged on an ad hoc basis. It is not a system of permanent landlord/tenant relations; no long-term contract is made between the sharecropper and the landowner. The arrangement is such that the sharecropper cultivates for one season only. If both parties agree, the arrangement may continue for years. However, fluctuations in manpower or resources in one household or the other, dissatisfaction with each other's conduct, or some change in social situation are liable to alter the arrangement.

Nuapalli lacks irrigation facilities, whereas the low-lying land of the neighboring villages is irrigated by the Daya West Branch Canal yielding double rice crops. The attempt of the Bhubaneswar Block Development Office to introduce Japanese methods of cultivation in Nuapalli failed due partly to the apathy of the villagers but mainly to the lack of irrigation facilities. In 1966 the Orissa University of Agriculture and Technology set up a demonstration experiment of improved methods of cultivation in the Bhubaneswar Block which included Nuapalli. In the first year, two Karans and one Khandait of the village cultivated their fields in accordance with the advice of the agricultural experts, but their attempts were unproductive. The advisors had not responded to their request for fertilizers. However, in recent years the villagers have experimented more intensively with high yielding varieties of rice. The villagers of Nuapalli resisted the Block Development Office and the University when these organizations tried to insist that they adopt improved methods of cultivation. But when they themselves experimented and achieved good results, they resolved that they would continue the new procedures in the future.

Moneylending

Moneylending remains, as always, an attractive traditional occupation. Moneylenders continue to play an important role in village economics. Poor villagers run to them in time of need, particularly to facilitate the purchase of bullocks and food and to help finance marriages and the like. In cases where a large sum is borrowed, property is mortgaged.

The system of moneylending is interesting. When a debtor approaches a moneylender, he states the amount he needs and what he has to offer as collateral. The moneylender replies callously that he is short of money because borrowers have not repaid him. Although he is as eager as the debtor to make the transaction, he bargains in a traditional manner. Ultimately, he makes a loan in accord with the borrower's need and the value of the collateral. Usually gold and silver ornaments or brass utensils are kept by the moneylender against the loan. It is customary to offer the borrower only one-half or one-third the value of the collateral at an interest rate of 36 percent per annum. If the borrower fails to pay the interest, the creditor can sell the items taken as collateral when the accrued interest reaches the value of the original loan.

Nuapalli has three unlicensed moneylenders. One is a Khandait, one a Karan, and the other a Saora (of tribal origin). The Khandait moneylender links this occupation with shopkeeping. If the borrower gets a loan from him, he is expected to purchase food and other necessities from the moneylender's shop. Thus, the moneylender/shopkeeper gets a double benefit.

The Karan moneylender is a landowning cultivator. He will make a loan in cash or paddy against the same kind of collateral as the Khandait at the same rate of interest. The headman of the Saora ward acts as a moneylender only for the people of his community. He appears to be liberal in dealing with his borrowers; he makes small loans on good faith and only in the case of big amounts demands collateral. I have no reliable way of estimating the volume of transactions by moneylenders because they are discrete in discussing such matters with others.

DISAPPEARING TRADITIONAL OCCUPATIONS

Two traditional occupations that are quickly disappearing are bamboo growing and livestock keeping and raising.

Bamboo Growing

Nuapalli was once rich in bamboo groves. The tracts around the village residential areas and the nearby forest were full of bamboo groves. However, with the gradual extension of the New Capital, many of these areas were cleared. This resulted in the elimination of many bamboo groves. The Saoras, for example, had grown bamboo on a large scale on government land lying to the north of their ward, but these groves were cut down when the Regional College of Education was built in 1964. Similarly, a large number of groves planted by Gaudas (milkmen) were felled when the Central Poultry Farm was built.

Nuapalli villagers who had always supplied themselves with bamboo now have to purchase it from the interior villages for their household use. Furthermore, the Saoras and Bauris of the village, who had made a living selling jungle bamboo to outsiders during the first few years of the New Capital's construction, are no longer allowed to enter the jungle. During a recent visit to Nuapalli in 1975 I did not find a single person pursuing this occupation.

Livestock Keeping and Raising

Livestock is as important an economic asset of the villagers as land. There is a common saying in the village that livestock is a bestower of lives to the villagers. Bullocks and buffalo are used in ploughing and carting; cows provide milk which is partly consumed in the village, but the major portion of which is sold to people in the New Capital; and cowdung is used as fertilizer and fuel. Most of the cultivators who owned wetland possess a pair of bullocks, and some have more than one pair. Even cultivators with small plots of land and sharecroppers need draft animals on occasion, although in fact many people have idle bullocks.

Table 9.1 reveals that cows, goats, and chickens are more common than other domesticated animals. Cows and buffalo are mostly raised by the Gaudas (Milkmen) since the selling of milk is their traditional occupation (see section on Temporarily Inflated Traditional Occupations). The number of chickens a household owns is highly variable over time. Chickens are raised mostly for sale to butchers outside the village.

I learned from the villagers that the Gaudas previously had had more buffalo and that the number of buffalo was steadily decreasing. Buffalo milk has a higher fat content than cow milk and thus may easily be watered down. Since buffalo are really more profitable than cows, it is surprising that only a few households keep them. The only possible explanation is the lack of sufficient fodder to feed the animals. Villagers used to collect fodder from the nearby forest but are now prohibited from doing so.

Sheep and goats are generally kept by farmers and are raised mainly for their meat. The meat consumed in the village is derived from these animals or is purchased from the New Capital market.

TABLE 9.1
Distribution of Livestock in Nuapalli in 1964

Kind of Livestock	Number of Livestock	No. of Livestock-Owning Households	% of Households Owning Livestock
Bullocks	239	106	53.5
Buffalo	53	4	2.02
Cows	275	109	55.05
Calves	285	112	56.5
Chickens	398	67	33.8
Goats	416	83	41.9
Sheep	0	0	0

Bullocks and cows are the most important livestock in the village and are usually purchased from the Harirajpur Market near Khurda Road Railway Station. An experienced and usually elderly villager accompanies the purchaser to the market for the selection and final purchase of an animal. The method of haggling and bargaining is interesting. The seller names a price for the cow or bullock which is usually more than one and one-half times the fair price. The elderly person who acts as middleman consults both parties and tries to make them accept a price somewhere between the two figures. If the price fixed by the middleman is not accepted by the seller, the buyer may go to some other shop. At this point, however, the middleman names a price somewhat higher than the earlier offer. A mutually satisfactory price is in this way finally arrived at. Before money is exchanged, the buyer and the elderly person examine the teeth, tail, head, horns, and general physical condition of the animal once again.

Due to decreased grazing land, a lack of pedigreed bulls, and improper nourishment, however, the general condition of the village cattle is not good. Nor does the common practice of crossbreeding cows with scrub bulls provide improved calves. Furthermore, the nearby jungle which used to provide fodder for cattle is fast receding and is not open for public use, and the grazing land set aside for the village is devoid of grass.

PERMANENTLY INFLATED TRADITIONAL OCCUPATIONS

There is a whole category of traditional occupations that have become increasingly attractive in recent years and will probably remain so. These I refer to as "Permanently Inflated Traditional Occupations," and they include wage labor and shopkeeping.

Wage Labor

The traditional economy of the village and the growing economy of the New Capital have created an increased demand for labor. Prior to the advent of the New Capital, labor was mainly employed in the agricultural sector. The construction of raods and buildings and public health work offer new opportunities to the laboring class of the locality.

Table 9.2 lists the percentages of agricultural and urban wage labor recruited from the village. The table reveals that 43 percent of the working-age persons in Nuapalli are engaged in wage labor. The lower percentage of female wage laborers, particularly in agriculture, is due to the fact that higher caste people in the village consider it humiliating for their women to work as laborers. Whatever female labor is available is drawn from the lower caste Bauri and Saora tribes. The people of the village who work as wage laborers prefer agricultural work to that offered in the more urban environment of the new Capital because it is the work to which they are accustomed. They also prefer to be paid in kind as agricultural wage laborers usually are.

TABLE 9.2
A Sample Working-Age Population of Nuapalli Engaged in Agricultural & Urban Wage Labor in 1964

	Male		Female		Total	
	No.	%	No.	%	No.	%
Urban Wage Labor	16	5.4	16	5.9	32	11.3
Agricultural Wage Labor	79	27.0	11	4.7	90	31.7
Total	95	32.4	27	10.6	122	43.0

In addition to work in the agricultural sector, many lower caste people who could have been expected to constitute the bulk of the labor supply in the New Capital are engaged in more remunerative occupations such as wood cutting or stone cutting (see the next section on "Temporarily Inflated Traditional Occupations").

Shopkeeping and Peddling

Shopkeeping is not a new enterprise in the village, but with the establishment of the New Capital, it has been inflated. Now the volume and variety of retail goods are much greater than previously. They are supplied by shopkeepers in the village, itinerant traders and merchants, and shopkeepers in the New Capital.

There are three types of shops in Nuapalli: grocery shops, tea shops, and confectioneries. Grocery shops sell spices, rice, sugar, pulses, flour, wheat, ciagarettes, tobacco, cheap medicines, kerosene, mustard and coconut oil, and ordinary stationery items such as slates, pencils, white paper, chalk, and ink. Tea shops sell prepared tea and a variety of sweets and cakes. The items found in a confectioner's shop are fried rice, fried paddy, puffed rice, flat rice, and sweets.

Shopkeepers store in their shops those items that are most frequently required by the villagers. Since the volume of transactions is very small, they neither maintain a special room for their wares, nor arrange things in a systematic manner as is being done in the big shops of the New Capital. One room of a house facing the road is used as a shop. The shopkeeper generally sits at a small desk, the drawer of which is used as a cash box. Articles are kept around him in ordinary tin containers and handmade wodden baskets. In imitation of the racks and showcases of big shops in the New Capital, some shopkeepers keep articles on wooden planks set in the walls with pegs. Recently, wooden cabinets have been introduced into the village.

Almost all shopkeepers purchase commodities wholesale from the merchants of the New Capital on credit. Each weekend, they pay the wholesalers what is due and purchase materials for the coming week.

Nuapalli has seven shops, two of which are owned by outsiders living in the village and five by life-long residents of the village. Customers are drawn from the village only. The approximate

annual incomes from shopkeeping are furnished in
Table 9.3 The data presented in that table are derived from statements of the shopkeepers themselves.
I suspect that income from this source is greater
than the table suggests. However, since I had no
reliable way of estimating that income, I had to depend on the shopkeepers' own statements.

TABLE 9.3
Approximate Annual Incomes from Shopkeeping
in Nuapalli in 1964

Castes Owning the Shops	Year of Opening	Approximate Annual Incomes	Type of Shop
Gudia	Old Shop	Rs. 600	Confectionery
Gudia	Old Shop	Rs. 1,800	Confectionery
Khandait	Old Shop	Rs. 1,250	Grocery
Oilman (outsider)	1953	Rs. 1,400	Grocery
Gudia (outsider)	1955	Rs. 1,200	Grocery
Gauda	1960	Rs. 780	Grocery
Khandait	1964	Rs. 500	Tea Shop

   In addition to these shopkeepers, several Gudia
villagers (Confectioners) peddle their wares in the
village twice daily, in the morning and in the afternoon. They sell baskets full of cheap sweets, fried
rice, fried paddy, and cakes. None of them ever
venture to sell their products in the New Capital
because they know well that their products, being of
inferior quality, will not sell there.
   A small retail trade is carried on by numerous
peddlers from outside the village. They bring cheap
stationery items, biscuits, dried fish, and other
cheap odds and ends to the village, exchanging them
for rice or cash. Some specialized peddlers, such
as sellers of earthenware pots and umbrellas, and
traders in cloth, also visit the village from time
to time. Vegetables and fish are bought at the New
Capital market. The villagers seek out the merchants of Bhubaneswar mainly for large orders and
for major purchases during marriage, death, or other
religious ceremonies.
   The prices of things in the village are higher

than in town because the village shopkeepers have a lower merchandise turnover than New Capital merchants. The acceptance of payment in kind, however, increases the shopkeepers' profit margin because they can accept grain, for example, at a rate of exchange below the price at which they can sell it.

During my 1975 visit to Nuapalli I found many more shops with a wider variety of goods. Shops are now sometimes decorated with electric lights and beautiful showcases. The shopkeepers' incomes appear to be greater now than they were during my detailed survey in 1964. In short, trade is flourishing in this community.

TEMPORARILY INFLATED TRADITIONAL OCCUPATIONS

There are four inflated traditional occupations that presumably will lose their importance in the village economy in the near future due either to a depletion of resources or the presence of a substitute. These are wood cutting, milk selling, carting, and brinjal (eggplant) cultivation. More restrictions on the use of forest products and the clearance of the jungle for the expansion of the New Capital will cause a diminution of the wood supply; as suppliers of milk, local residents will not be able to compete with New Capital suppliers; motorized vehicles are replacing carts; and unauthorized brinjal cultivation in the deforested area will not be permitted to continue for very long.

Wood Cutting

Business in wood has gained considerable importance since the establishment of the New Capital. Before the town sprang up, firewood was available in abundance near the residences of the wood cutters, and, as a consequence, the supply exceeded the demand and income from this source was very small. The New Capital has increased the demand for wood and provided a close market. In fact, the collection of firewood has become an important source of income, and more energy is put into it than ever before.

The collection and sale of firewood is the traditional occupation of the Saoras of Nuapalli. Before the establishment of the New Capital, they used to collect wood from the present town area and sell it in distant villages where there is no jungle. Now the New Capital provides a closer and larger market for it.

The Saoras usually collect untrimmed branches which they bind into small bundles. Each such bundle contains eight pieces of wood. Ten bundles make a headload for a man, and eight bundles a headload for a woman. The price of a headload containing eight bundles was Rs. 1 in 1960, Rs. 2 in 1965 and Rs. 5 in 1975. In other words, the price of firewood has increased fivefold in the last fifteen years.

To meet the increasing demand for firewood, the Bauris adopted this occupation during the beginning years of the construction of the New Capital. Unlike the Saoras, they deal in trimmed and split wood. They collect the untrimmed firewood from the forest, process it, bind it into bundles containing eighty pieces (one *pana*), and sell it in the town. The price per pana of stickwood six inches long was forty paise and that of split wood one and one-half feet long was Rs. 2.50 in 1965. In 1950 the price was about half that amount. By 1975, although the price had more than doubled what it had been in 1965, the volume of transactions had greatly decreased because of the restrictions put on the use of forest products.

I estimated the earnings of wood cutters, based on their own statements, as follows. If one person works twenty-five days each month, his income is Rs. 600 per annum. For two months of the year, however, most wood cutters are engaged in agricultural pursuits. Thus, a person's net earnings would be Rs. 500 per annum. In fact, the earnings of wood cutters are fairly good. The approximate annual income of the Saora and Bauri wood cutters is presented in Table 9.4

TABLE 9.4
Approximate Annual Incomes from Wood Cutting in Nuapalli in 1965

Caste/Tribe	No. of Households	Male	Female	Total Persons	% of Total Working Age Bauris & Saoras	Estimated Annual Earnings
Bauri	36	41	40	(81)	73.6	Rs. 44,500
Saora	41	55	66	(121)	85.2	Rs. 67,000

As indicated in the table, the Saoras and Bauris of Nuapalli have been able to earn a fair amount from this source and achieve at least a minimally acceptable standard of living. In addition to this, a few Saoras and Bauris earn a great deal from supplying logs to people from outside the village.

Since the establishment of the New Capital, the Government of Orissa has placed stringent restrictions on wood cutting in the forests in the vicinity of the New Capital. These restrictions on the use of forest wood led some people to resort to illegal means of gathering wood. The response, for instance, of the wood cutters of Nuapalli to restrictions placed upon their traditional occupation has been to ignore and defy them. Because there are no trees outside the restricted forests, they have continued to enter these forests despite the restrictions. When caught, they have bribed the forest staff and have so far avoided being prosecuted by the government. Thus, their response has been to continue cutting wood in their traditional manner and to resort to bribery whenever necessary. Although they have to pay fines and bribe the forest guards, they continue to collect wood as the income is alluring.

An extreme response to these conditions was the formation of an illegal business organization by five Saoras and four Bauris of the village. In June 1964, they reached an understanding with the forest staff who allowed them to cut two cartloads of log wood every day in closed forest areas and to carry these to the village at night. In addition, the guards promised to warn them if a forest officer was on duty in the vicinity. In return, they promised to pay the guards Rs. 100 per month.

This illegal organization was an unusually enterprising response to the external pressure that had restricted the traditional occupations of the wood cutters. Since it was a profitable business, the members decided to continue despite the restrictions. In fact, their potential monthly earnings were extremely good. The market price for one cartload of wood was Rs. 35 to 40 in 1965. They could make at least Rs. 1,400 if they worked only twenty-five days each month. Deducting from this sum about Rs. 60 for bullock fodder and to pay laborers occasionally to split wood and Rs. 100 for bribes to the forest staff, they could earn Rs. 1,240 each month. Divided equally among nine men, this sum would give each man Rs. 138 per month, which for these people was a very good income.

These nine members were caught cutting wood in

June of 1965 by a forest officer and were fined, but after two weeks had elapsed they began working in the restricted area again. They were soon caught again. This time their attempt at private enterprise was squelched for good. Their attempts, however, indicate that the wood cutters of Nuapalli, feeling they have been mistreated, are perfectly ready to defy the government even if it means bribing forest guards and cutting wood illegally.

The wood cutters of Nuapalli have experienced a sudden boom in the firewood business, but at the same time the forest area around them is decreasing. In other words, the source of their boosted income will be short-lived, and the end of available jungle will mean the loss of a traditional source of income, the loss of a saving occupation for impoverished families, and for women the loss of their economic contribution to the household.

Milk Selling

Milk selling has become a profitable business for the milkmen of Nuapalli owing to the increased demand for milk in the New Capital. Before the town sprang up, milk by-products such as curd and ghee had a ready market in the nearby villages and the temple town of Bhubaneswar, but milk itself was not in great demand.

My 1964 survey of Nuapalli indicated that there were thirty-five milk sellers; thirty of these were Gaudas (Milkmen), three Saoras, and two Karans. Eighty-five percent of the milkmen sold milk to a fixed clientele in the New Capital. Some supplied milk to middlemen who frequented the village daily on bicycles, while some of the customers were drawn from the village itself. In the New Capital milk was delivered to government officials at their residences with payment made usually during the first week of the month. The daily supply of milk was estimated to be 140 litres, and the quantity was doubled by diluting it with water or powdered milk. Pure milk in Nuapalli is rare; in almost all cases, it is adulterated.

The operation of a milk business involves the whole family of a milkman. Young boys and girls take the cows out to graze, women feed and milk them twice a day, and adult males sell the milk. Straw, boiled paddy husk, and water constitute the main fodder for the cattle. I did not come across a single milkman who used a high yielding blended fodder.

Hence, the quantity of milk produced is not very great.

A follow-up inquiry in 1966 already indicated a decrease in the number of milk sellers from thirty-five to twenty-two. The main reason for the decrease in this inflated traditional occupation was the inability of indigenous milkmen to compete with government milk-selling centers in the New Capital which supply pure milk in bulk. Customers in the city prefer the unadulterated milk from the Government Milk Center. Furthermore, considering the number of cows, the quantity of milk produced in the village is very poor. Unsystematic methods of raising cattle, decreased grazing land, and a lack of good breeding bulls may account for the poor condition of the cows, which in turn results in low levels of milk production.

Carting

Carting was undertaken as an occupation by many of the Bhubaneswar area at the time of the construction of the Bhubaneswar Air Field during World War II. Carts were in demand to transport stone and other materials required for the construction of roads and buildings. The need for carts was intensified when construction of the New Capital began. At that time trucks could not be used because roads did not exist, and villagers quickly responded to this new demand. With the development of the new city, however, fast-moving vehicles have come into use for transportation.

During the period from 1940 to 1955, construction work in the Bhubaneswar area made carting a desirable occupation that was within the range of villagers' traditional skills. Villagers were largely able to meet the developmental needs of that period. With the growth of roads and the preference for swifter and heavier transport afforded by trucks, villagers now find that a formerly useful and profitable occupation is becoming outdated. There was a temporarily inflated demand for old skills which are now being rejected.

Brinjal Cultivation

The cultivation of brinjal (eggplant) is not a new thing to the people of the Bhubaneswar area, but brinjal has only been cultivated in large quantities in the deforested areas of Nuapalli and Bharatpur since the establishment of the New Capital. The villagers like to cultivate brinjal because it requires little money and little labor. They plant seedlings in July during the rainy season and harvest the brinjal from about October until January. During this period, they pick the vegetables about three times a week and sell them to middlemen in the field, in the village, or at the New Capital market. The cultivators sell on a wholesale basis and in 1964 received from Rs. 5 to Rs. 15 per basket. The brinjal baskets are about four feet in diameter and one foot deep, but the packing and the size of the brinjals vary. The middlemen take surplus brinjals to Cuttack and Khurda for sale.

In 1964, thirteen Gaudas, seventeen Karans, and six Saoras cultivated brinjal in the Bharatpur forest which covers an area of about eighteen acres. In addition, some cultivators of Nuapalli planted it in large quantitites in their kitchen gardens. On the basis of cultivators' statements, the approximate annual income from this source was calculated to be Rs. 9,000. In 1965, the number of cultivators had increased compared to previous years, but the yield was poor due to meager rainfall. Since 1966, however, the forest has been closed to unauthorized cultivators. Despite stringent restrictions, some villagers are still cultivating brinjal in the deforested area.

This source of income for the villagers of Nuapalli will be short-lived for the forest lands upon which they depend are decreasing and their use growing more restricted. In fact, the end of these boom days is already in sight. The end of these sources of income will force villagers into the modern economy of the New Capital. Their ability to adjust successfully to such a change will depend upon their present efforts to take advantage of new occupations available in the city.

NEW OCCUPATIONS

The New Capital has made available several new occupations to the inhabitants of Nuapalli and neighboring villages. The new occupations adopted by the villagers include various government and private jobs, contracting, and the renting of their poorly equipped houses to outsiders.

Government and Private Jobs

In 1964, sixty-seven persons from Nuapalli were in government service. One of them was a clerk in Cuttack, and others were peons and watchmen mostly at the Text Book Press in Bhubaneswar. Annual earnings from jobs of this kind were estimated to be Rs. 7,000. During my 1975 visit to Nuapalli, I found more young men, particularly from Karan and Khandait castes, employed in the New Capital. Some young men have recently graduated from Utkal University and are in search of jobs.

Renting Houses

With the advent of the New Capital, outsiders came to the nearby communities seeking low-rent quarters in which to live. Nuapalli housed a few such persons during the time of my survey in 1964. In 1975, I found many outsiders living in the thatched houses of the village at rents ranging from Rs. 20 to Rs. 30 a month.

Because there is a shortage of housing in the city, newcomers attempt to live in the surrounding villages. The villagers are aware of the situation but are unable to provide well-furnished houses due to a lack of funds and knowledge of urban amenities. However, in recent years, five Khandait households have constructed furnished houses for that purpose.

Contracting

Contracting, particularly for the construction of roads, culverts, etc., has become a new avenue of income for a few villagers. Two Karans of the village were in this occupation at the time of my 1964 survey, having adopted this occupation in 1948 when the New Capital was first being built. At that time outside contractors came into the village to recruit coolies to clear jungles and construct roads for the New Capital; in the course of time they entrusted the work to these two individuals, who were paid regular salaries. Once they were experienced in the work, however, the two Karans started contracting independently. In 1957, they became licensed contractors and constructed culverts and small roads in the New Capital. One of them briefly ceased contracting in 1960 when he incurred a loss but resumed the work in 1963. The other contractor continued in his work, proving to be a first-class contractor. He has constructed a two-story building of his own in the New Capital and runs his business very successfully.

CONCLUSION

Under the impact of the New Capital the traditional economy of Nuapalli has undergone change; the occupations of different castes have multiplied and diversified. A basically static village economy has come into contact with an impersonal, competitive economy and has been disturbed, if not revolutionized, as a result. Some traditional occupations have remained unchanged, some have lost importance, and some have been temporarily or permanently inflated. All the while, new occupations have crept in, making the village economy a truly mixed one.

NOTES

1. The village was intensively surveyed in 1963-64 under the guidance of Dr. Cora Du Bois, Professor of Anthropology at Harvard University. The research was financed by the National Science Foundation of the United States. Since that time, occasional visits to the community and to other village groups now part of the New Capital have helped to supplement my knowledge of on-going changes. In addition, I have studied the communities of Siripur, Baragad, and Laxmisagar which lie within the boundaries of the New Capital in order to provide a comparative perspective on the issues discussed.

2. Editor's note: Dr. Das has studied carefully four of Nuapalli's six wards *(sahi)*. His 1963-64 population count for these is as follows:

Saora ward *(sahi)*	250
Gauda ward	243
Bauri ward	190
Gad Ward (mixed)	520
	1,203 people

Richard and Doris Taub first did research in Bhubaneswar, Orissa in 1962-1964. That research served as the basis for Richard Taub's Ph.D. dissertation in sociology at Harvard University and as the basis for the first major publication from the Harvard-Bhubaneswar project, BUREAUCRATS UNDER STRESS, University of California Press, 1969. Together, the Taubs have authored AMERICAN SOCIETY IN TOCQUEVILLE'S TIME AND TODAY, Rand McNally, 1974, and more recently, ENTREPRENEURSHIP IN A SOCIALIST SOCIETY: SMALL-SCALE INDUSTRIES IN INDIA, University of California Press (forthcoming). The latter publication is based upon interviews undertaken in 1971 and 1975 with small-scale industrialists in three states of India. The Taubs returned to Orissa for that purpose, working this time in Cuttack rather than Bhubaneswar. Currently, Richard Taub is an associate professor of sociology at the University of Chicago. Doris Taub manages litigation support for complex litigation.

Chapter 10 derives from the Taubs' comparative investigation of small-scale industries in India. It focuses upon a set of industrial entrepreneurs in Cuttack, Orissa's industrial and commercial center, and their ties with the state government in Bhubaneswar. Thus, it extends the discussion of economic change and development beyond the immediate environs of Bhubaneswar to a city twenty miles away.

10

Cuttack Entrepreneurs

Doris L. Taub and Richard P. Taub

Orissa ranks low among India's states not only in numbers of small industries, but on most other measures of prosperity. Ninety-four percent of its population is classified as rural, more than in any other state. With 20 percent of its population literate, it ranks eleventh among seventeen states. It is twelfth in income per capita (*India Pocket Book of Economic Information* 1970:38).

Another measure of Orissa's conservatism is that although the Orissan temples are important tourist attractions, they remain virtually the only major Indian temples that do not let foreigners—even those certified by Indian authorities to be orthodox Hindus—inside even their outer walls. That this rule has persisted, despite national legislation to the contrary and, on occasion, very great pressure from political leaders, is an indicator of the strength of these traditional feelings and the power of those who hold them.

Cuttack is the state's largest city, with a population of 200,000; but just as the entire state has a rural quality, so Cuttack city itself feels to the visitor more like a congeries of small towns squeezed in together than it does like a small city. The main streets are broad, though unpaved, and lined with shops; but behind them lie thousands of tortuous paths, snaking their way into hundreds of village-like enclaves as removed from city life as if they were in the countryside. The principal means of transportation are bicycles, bicycle-rickshaws, and feet. There are no tall buildings, department stores, or anything else one associates with urban life—except crowds.

Taken as a whole Orissa is a poor state, ranking toward the bottom of the states on many dimensions. Its general situation is replicated in the

235

small-scale industrial sector.

THE INDUSTRIES

"If you can learn why Orissa is so inhospitable to industry, you will have performed a great service," a young lawyer told us. "Industries here always wither and then die, even those that have had brief periods of prosperity."

A mood of depression compounded by lassitude hangs over much of Orissa's industry. It is here that one begins to understand the self-reinforcing character of a depressed economy and the fragility of enterprise in such a setting. Orissa has neither the capital resources to sustain privately-owned industry nor the purchasing power to provide adequate nongovernment consumption. Most of the successful industries are run by industrialists who earned their money elsewhere and were looking for a new investment, or by those who already had access to large markets such as Calcutta or Madras. So delicate is the economic balance on which many industries rest, that small changes, for example in government policy, can generate radical changes in fortune.

The depressed state of Orissa's industries is quickly apparent to an observer. Its major industrial estate is half vacant, the empty sheds monuments to numerous failed enterprises. At the time of our visit, a once-prosperous medium-scale industry manufacturing automobile batteries had just collapsed, a result of being dropped from the State Trading Corporation's list of authorized suppliers. Without the export business channeled to it by STC, the company could not stay alive. Many of the other companies on the industrial estate are only marginally operating. For example, a supposed manufacturer of bicycles derives most of his income from renting cycle-rickshaws, assembled at his plant, to laborers on a daily basis. Still other manufacturers derive their income primarily from black-marketing their controlled-price raw material allocations.

To choose fifty-six industries for our Orissa sample in 1971, we had to draw eighty-two names from the *Directory of Industries* compiled in 1967. Of the eighty-two, thirteen had definitely failed, another seven were unknown to people in the neighborhood listed, two had to be replaced because they were cooperatively owned, and two had to be replaced because they were large-scale industries. Of the

forty-five industrialists we were finally able to
locate and interview, three had gone out of business,
five more were in the process of failing, and another twenty were barely holding their own. To illustrate, let us take a closer look at the industries
themselves.

THE PROSPEROUS RESPONDENTS

In all, ten respondents of the forty-five could
be called prosperous. Eight of these had accrued
their capital in areas other than the industry for
which we interviewed them. Seven of them had followed the classic third-world pattern (and the pattern of developing Germany in the nineteenth century), earning their wealth in commerce and turning to
industry as another source of opportunity.

Of the ten, five came to Orissa from outside
the state, and still rely on their outside contracts
for marketing. Three others belong to minority
groups—two are Muslims and one's mother tongue is
Telugu, the language of the adjacent state to the
south—leaving only two who are unambiguously part
of mainstream Orissa culture. If Orissa were the
only state we had studied, we would be tempted to
attribute some defect to "native" populations in India, emphasizing both the virtues of pariah (in the
Western sense) capitalism, and suggesting either
that migrants had more vitality because they uprooted themselves to seek better opportunities, or that
the uprooting process itself might free one from the
weight of traditional ties, making innovation easier.
All of this may in some measure be true, but the
patterns are certainly different in our other two
states.

The most well-to-do person in our sample, and
certainly one of the wealthiest in the entire state,
is a Marwari, that is, a member of a business community whose origins are the inhospitable desert
lands of Rajasthan. Marwaris have migrated all over
India, succeeding in trade, moneylending, and to a
somewhat lesser extent, manufacturing. This man's
factories, located in a village with a railway line
and near rich deposits of fire clay, produced glasses, bottles, fire bricks, and ceramic bathroom fixtures. The glass products are sold primarily in
South India; the others have an all-India market.
The manufacturer also holds the Orissa franchise
for the manufacture of Coca-Cola. He makes the Coke
bottles in his glass factory. In addition, he owns

rental property. This respondent acknowledges a
gross annual income (turnover) for all of his factories combined of more than Rs. 20 million ($3 mil-
lion), and an overall investment in machinery and
raw materials of approximately the same amount. His
three large factories, which employ about four thousand workers, occupy fifty acres, dominating the
village.

   He appeared in our sample because he also owns,
in joint partnership with the Government of Orissa,
a fourth factory established to manufacture ceramic
tiles. This factory, a small-scale unit with an investment of Rs. 750,000 in machinery and raw materials, was created as a demonstration project to encourage others to set up similar enterprises and to
provide local employment. It is a failure. Its imported machinery is allegedly defective, producing
ripples and bubbles in many of the tiles. The defective tiles could be sold in an expanding construction market, our respondent reported, but are
bypassed in the current market because better tiles
are easily available. The machinery now lies idle.
The factory building is used to store the Coke bottles.

   After Marwaris, the largest group of traders
and merchants in our sample comes from the state of
Gujarat. They are an austere group—strict vegetar-
ians, teetotalers, not given to display—whose religious beliefs have much in common with those of
the Gujerati Jains, whom Weber (1958b:199-201ff.)
singled out as a group whose ideology had consequences for capital accumulation much like those of Cal-
vinist Protestantism. This group, too, has migrated
all over India. One of the two Gujaratis in our
sample was among the ten most prosperous. His small
factory, however, was but a sideline, supplying simple bicycle parts to his family shop. He also
owned a large and successful general store, as well
as property.

   Two men from Bengal are also in this prosperous
group. One, a soap manufacturer, sold his product
primarily in the large Calcutta market. The other
operates a successful sawmill. The mill, because of
which he fell into our sample, is one of several
owned by his family, also successful timber contractors, licensed to harvest timber from the forests.
The soap manufacturer was a grocery and soap whole-
saler in Calcutta before he entered manufacturing.
The sawmill operator also began his industry after
establishing his career in trade, the timber trade.

   The fifth respondent in this category is another

outsider, one of three Punjabis in our Orissa sample. He and his brothers, refugess displaced after Partition, came to Orissa with little but energy and mechanical skill. The respondent came at the invitation of a raja who had hired him to set up a sugar mill but who was soon after deposed. He realized he would have to do something on his own. First, he sent for his brothers to join him. Each of the brothers had received a small sum of money from the Central Government for refugee relief after Partition. When these sums were pooled, the brothers had a small stake available. They built an ice factory in a village ninety miles from Cuttack, near a major source of fish. Fishermen using their ice could then transport their catch to much more distant markets, and the brothers flourished. Then the fish changed their habitat, probably in response to the changing water conditions that resulted from persistent cyclones in the area. The brothers lost their market for ice, so they converted the ice factory into a cold storage unit. Since local farmers did not at that time plant anything that required cold storage, they canvassed the countryside, distributing seed and persuading the farmers to plant potatoes that might then be stored in the cold storage. When a nearby oceanfront area was developed into a port, the brothers opened a restaurant in the port town. They also had run a gas station near the ice factory, but (in a fashion familiar to Americans) it was bypassed by a national highway built to carry iron ore to the new port. This family reports its annual gross income from all its enterprises as Rs. 250,000.

Two of the minority-group successes are Muslims, of which there were seven among our Orissa respondents. Although Muslims can be found in most occupations in India, they clearly dominate a few areas: leather products, rubber products, and tobacco products. That Muslims should be active in the leather trade is not surprising. Leatherwork is an unclean occupation for Hindus, and the only other large groups of leatherworkers across India are the untouchables. The manufacture of rubber products seems to have evolved naturally from the kinds of skills and techniques required in leatherwork. Then too, similar products—sandals, for example, as well as industrial supplies such as flexible couplings—can be made from both of these materials.

The affinity of Muslims for the manufacture of tobacco products is not so obvious, but is undeniable. Three such industries appear in our sample, two of them in Orissa: a manufacturer of a tobacco-based product that is mixed with molasses, lime powder, and numerous secret ingredients for use as a toothpaste, called *gurakhu*; a producer of inexpensive leaf-wrapped cigarettes; and a manufacturer of a product chewed after meals for its refreshing taste, made of chopped betel nuts mixed with spices and/or tobacco, called *seeval* or *supari*. The owners of all three are Muslims.

The gurakhu manufacturer reports annual sales, almost all of them in Calcutta, of Rs. 3.5 million ($650,000). His family has been manufacturing gurakhu for more than a hundred years, and theirs is a well-known brand. The second prosperous Muslim repairs and retreads tires. He also has income from extensive property holdings. The last of the well-to-do minority-group manufacturers is a family who make gold jewelry and sell it in their retail shop. Their mother tongue is Telugu. The family comes from an area within what is now Orissa, but are culturally part of the people from the state immediately to the south, Andhra Pradesh. Of the group, their enterprise is the one that might least be considered manufacturing. The family is not involved directly in the production of the jewelry, which is handmade by goldsmiths. They subcontract their orders to village craftsmen, devoting most of their energies to running the store, the largest of its kind in Cuttack.

The remaining two of the ten prosperous manufacturers are both native to Orissa and speak Oriya as their mother tongue. The first is a baker, manufacturing cookies (bisquits) and white bread (double-roti) for the local market. His fleet of rickshaws and his truck rush freshly baked goods to local shops daily. The baker is the only manufacturer in our entire Orissa sample who has succeeded by providing consumer goods solely for local consumption. He reports an annual gross income of Rs. 1.4 million on an investment of Rs. 500,000 (income just under $200,000 on a $70,000 investment). He entered the bakery business after participating in a family-owned wholesale grocery business, and he continues to have an interest in that enterprise.

Both of the Oriya respondents know that they are exceptional, and the second is bitter about it. "You cannot do business in Orissa," he said. "The government is run by foreigners (people from outside the state) and they do not have the best interests of the people at heart. The only people who thrive here are outsiders: Punjabis, Marwaris, and Bengalis.

The rest of us suffer, and government officials do not care."

This respondent has the exclusive Orissa agency for several popular products of which the state government is a major purchaser. He reports his gross annual income as Rs. 10.8 million ($1.2 million). Although he has remained in business for a long time, his real successes have come when the men he supported held important political office. During those periods, government agencies were ordered to purchase his products, even if these were not entirely appropriate to their needs. When his cronies are defeated, his fortunes decline. For some time, he had run two other small-scale industries, one of which sold almost its entire output to the government, and the other of which sold a substantial part to the government. In addition, the respondent had obtained government certification as an approved supplier for the second industry. Approved suppliers must be used by nongovernment enterprises purchasing products with government loans. Since the list of such suppliers may be very short, depending on the particular product, and potential buyers numerous, such certification is highly coveted. At the time of the interview, however, he had just closed these two industries. The government began to manufacture the first product itself, and the respondent's second industry had been removed from the list of approved suppliers when a new group came to political power.

INDUSTRIES AND POLITICS

Although political chicanery plays an important part in the prosperity of many private individuals in India and, probably, in most democratic capitalist nations as well, its impact in Orissa is particularly visible and dramatic because the sources of successful industrial growth there are so meager. Others of our respondents have tied their fortunes to political leaders in Orissa with less success than the respondent we described. In general, they have had brief periods of prosperity, but because they established their industries when their friends came to power, they never learned either how to manufacture their product efficiently or how to compete for business in the marketplace. Consequently, when their sponsors left office, their industries floundered.

The government of Orissa is the largest buyer

of goods and services in the state, and its spending habits ripple widely through the economy. This is true in many economies, including that of the United States. But because, in Orissa, everyone depends on government orders, with little opportunity to make real money otherwise, the impact of the government's decisions—giving the contract to this one and not those other three seems more marked. When the state was constructing Paradip Port and its connecting superhighway, anyone who owned a moving vehicle thrived. Some people who did not even own a moving vehicle bid on the contracts to transport ore anyway. On the strength of being awarded such a contract, they were able to purchase one or more trucks on credit, repaying the loan with a share of the money they made on the job.

All of the prosperous respondents except the Muslims have political connections that are essential to the conduct of their business. Some of them engage in outright fraud. Others make generous political contributions in order to gain access to scarce raw materials. Everyone needs the cooperation of the government in one way or another. For example, the soap manufacturer needs mutton tallow and other oils, and the baker needs flour, sugar, and cellophane. These commodities are periodically unavailable at any price. The glass manufacturer set up his tile factory in partnership with the government, and he needs them to grant licenses for the import of his machinery. The Punjabi does not need regular assistance from the government, but he contributes regularly to all political candidates so that whichever one wins, the government will not interfere in his operation. There is no way to manufacture in Orissa without involvement, formal and/or informal, with the government.

THE OTHER INDUSTRIES

It is difficult to conceive of most of the remaining enterprises in our sample from Orissa as industries at all. Most of them are run by craftsmen who produce goods to order, or provide a service with hand tools. They do not have the capital to produce inventories or even, in many cases, to purchase raw materials for the items they have contracted to produce. Many were listed as industries to augment government lists and thereby enhance the appearance of official performance.

A number of our industries, for example, might

more properly be called services. Here, a customer brings his good to the businessman, who does something to it and returns it. In this category are three tailors, one dry cleaner, one man who repairs electric motors, one who repairs musical instruments, three printers, and eight millowners. Let us look more closely at this last category.

Seven of the mills are located in villages. For approximately Rs. 3,000, one can buy the basic milling machine and connect it to a power line. Local agriculturalists bring their grain, mostly rice, to the miller, and wait while it is hulled, watching closely to be certain that none is stolen. These businesses are seasonal and dependent on agricultural yields. Two of them were languishing. One businessman had had his electricity disconnected because he had never earned enough money to pay the bill. Unfortunately, he did not know he was eligible for a concessional rate as a seasonal user. He had borrowed money from a moneylender to buy the machine and was sinking more deeply into debt, trying to earn the money to pay back the loan by doing day labor.

A second was victim to progress. A former official of the Department of Industries had taken a loan from his sometime employer and opened a mill down the road from the victim. The new mill used more modern machinery, and could process a variety of agricultural products, such as coconut and split peas, in addition to rice. This modern mill was thriving, with a long queue at the door, and machinery whirring. We began our interview there, thinking it was the mill in our sample. Only later did we learn that the dilapidated building, owner languishing on a bench in front, was the mill we sought.

All but one of the millers in our sample provided traditional services in a traditional context, although they did it more efficiently than do users of the old hand-pounding method for rice. None of these millers had enough capital to buy grain, process it, and sell it in the market themselves, and none of the seven had more than one employee.

The rural setting was brought home to one of us in the course of interviewing one of the millers. It was a long walk to the interview, and since a foreign social scientist, interpreter in tow, is a novelty, we were soon followed by a substantial proportion of the residents (an experience we both became accustomed to after awhile). We therefore had to conduct the interview in front of a large crowd. The crowd was so large, in fact, that a snake charmer came by, playing his flute as the sun set, shadows lengthened, and his cobra undulated. Soon a group of women returned from the forest, where they had been collecting wood all day, heads piled high with twigs that they would sell in the village. They leaned their bundles up against walls and trees, sat down to rest, and watched the snake, the crowd, and us. We, in turn, watched the snake, the shadows, and the people watching us, and had a hard time remembering to conduct the interview. One should not, however, equate the bucolic nature of the setting with some conception of timeless, changeless India. The lone dirt road to this village led straight to the gates, a mile away, of the glass factory we discussed earlier.

The eighth miller had located his mill in Cuttack. His milling operation was integral to his wholesale business. He was the only one who had enough capital to purchase grain, process it, and then sell it on the market. He was doing quite well financially, although a cut below the ten prosperous respondents we have described. His approach to his enterprise was modern: He estimated costs, had located his mill according to a preconceived plan, and chose his processes within the framework of the market. A Marwari, he was the only miller in our sample not working in his native village. His overview of the grain business and his detailed grasp of the national situation contrasted markedly with the orientation of the village millers.

A step up in the industrial scale were our six furniture manufacturers, whose factories were huddled together in one section of Cuttack. Five of them were carpenters who bid for small government contracts to make furniture for offices and the fancy guest houses the government maintains for traveling officials. Upon winning such a contract, which in most cases required a bribe of ten to fifteen percent of the total award, they would have to borrow money at twenty-five percent interest per month to buy raw materials. They increased their income with an occasional contract to provide furniture for a newly married couple. In those cases, they demanded an advance payment, which they would then use to buy their materials. All were following in the footsteps of their fathers, and they found it difficult to imagine what else they might do or might have done. Working and living together, some of them related to each other, they all knew about government contracts to be let, bargains in raw materials, and the like.

Only one of the carpenters could be considered an innovator, and that probably because he was pushed into the carpentry business by misfortune. He was the son of a former landlord *(zamindar)* who lost some of his property through land reform and some to political activity prior to Independence. The respondent had failed his examination for the B.A. Making a stab at the trucking business, he was fleeced by employees who claimed parts were defective that actually were sound. The employees sold the original parts, replacing them with inferior ones for which they received kickbacks. The business failed, and the respondent, in desperation, decided to set up a furniture factory because it seemed to him a business with a large profit margin per unit of sale and one that was simple enough that employees would be unable to cheat him. At the peak of the season (government contracts, in India as in America, are often let just before the end of the fiscal year, to use up money already allocated before the authorization lapses), he had seventeen employees, most of whom brought their own tools. Although his shop was located among the carpenters, neither he nor any of his employees was their castemate, and he seemed to stand somewhat apart from their close-knit group.

Because so much of his work is delegated, this respondent, unlike the other carpenters, is able to spend most of his time soliciting business while the manufacturing process continues. His business is the only one of the group that is at all differentiated in function. He began the business with an investment of Rs. 500 ($70) and has since bought land and constructed a building for Rs. 35,000 ($7,000). His business is growing modestly but steadily.

TRADITION AND MODERNITY IN INDUSTRY

When one looks at industries such as these at the microlevel, many of the sharp distinctions between modern industries and traditional crafts begin to blur at the edges, and this blurring helps us begin to understand the levels of complexity associated with the word "modern," even in the relatively unambiguous context of a factory, as, say, compared to that of a belief system.

A dramatic example of this issue is raised by the owner of a *chitralaya* in our sample. A *chitralaya* (literally, "abode of pictures") is a shop that manufactures costumes and scenery and rents them out for local theatrical events, traveling theaters, and dance troupes. This respondent first learned about *chitralayas* when he worked in one in his own village. Following the procedure so common in this poor area, costumers and set designers would take advances so that they could buy the materials for producing the stylized sets and costumes required for these events.

Later, our respondent moved to Cuttack, where he opened a *chitralaya* of his own, catering to a wider range of customers. He now owns the most successful such enterprise in the city, providing costumes and sets, inter alla, to those (few) Orissa artists who have become international figures and carry their own equipment with them abroad. He has systematically set out to build up his stock in costumes and sets so that they can be rented on demand, without the delays associated with fabrication to order. He has also developed systems whereby he can move the equipment from one troupe to another quickly so that he does not lose money while equipment stands idle. At the time of the interview, he had applied to the Department of Industries for a loan so that he could increase his stock of supplies and improve his methods of moving the materials from one group to another.

The traditional roots of this business are obvious. The theater for which the respondent is providing equipment is devoted to re-creating ancient Hindu religious tales in highly stylized form. Furthermore, the owner of the company is one of only two Brahmans in our Orissa sample. (The other is a printer.) While operating a *chitralaya* cannot at all be considered this man's "traditional occupation," nonetheless, it is a more logical choice than many alternative ones might be. Brahmans, in Hindu belief, are associated with and in principle responsible for both the conduct of religious ritual and that of education. The connection to the *chitralaya* seems apparent. Likewise, printing is, in all our states, an occupation heavily populated by Brahmans. This too is not a "traditional" occupation, but it is a logical and acceptable one, probably because of its association with literacy and the written word.

The problem we want to draw attention to is that the idea of modernity in the industrial context is usually tied closely to the use of machinery and the conversion of inanimate raw materials into power. Yet we have seen in our sample, for example, that almost all the millers, who certainly use power-driven machinery, are only modern in any sense *because* they use machinery. Embedded in their villages, following family or caste occupations, providing traditional services in return for traditional forms of remuneration, and serving a narrowly defined, bounded clientele, they are really rather close to most definitions we might formulate for the word "traditional."

By contrast, the owner of the *chitralaya*, who does not use power-driven machinery, has nonetheless developed a differentiated organization, rationalized and responsive to market conditions, and he attempts to use modern business management techniques (although he would not call them that) to increase both his business and his profits. Similarly, our one prosperous carpenter does not use machinery, but he has begun to develop the rudiments of a differentiated organization and, consequently, has taken a first step down a road that could conceivably transform furniture-making in Orissa without ever requiring the addition of machinery.

In our sample, we also have men who use power-driven machinery to produce traditional goods, such as certain farm tools and customarily-shaped cooking utensils. In Tamilnadu, one such manufacturer collects his raw materials, old, worn-out utensils, through traditional networks of small shops that take them in exchange for new pots. This manufacturer melts the old utensils down, casts them into ingots, and rolls them in his rolling machines. Then he cuts and stamps them in a series of power-driven presses. Since the pots are not his own raw materials, he is paid only for the operations he performs on them. After making them into new utensils, he redistributes them through the same network. Like the millers in Orissa, his relationship to his raw materials, and to his clients, is as traditional as they would have been if the work had been done by hand.

Conversely, one of our respondents, a graduate of Cambridge, manufacturers electronic components. The assembly of these components, however, is done entirely by hand by semiskilled workers. Even the soldering iron used to fuse the parts is heated in a fire, rather than by electricity. Much of Japan's industrial growth in the electronics field was fueled by just arrangements (Shinohara 1968).

The point is that industrial technology is only one of a series of variables that may in combination be important for understanding what modernity of industrial organization means. The "modernity" or "traditionality" of the product may count, but in other contexts the organization of the work may be what makes it modern; and modern organization may also provide the entrepreneur with a distinct competitive advantage as well. Weber (1958a:67ff) understood this well. Many of his intellectual successors, however, have not.

UNCERTAINTY

Fatalism is often associated with conceptions of traditional Hinduism, and we found this orientation toward the future among many of our poorer respondents in all states. A number of them commented on the uncertainty of the future, and we were struck by the psychology of scarcity, with its prospect of bad days ahead, that is most marked among our Orissa respondents. Even our most economically successful respondent in Orissa, the glass manufacturer, reported:

> Father always told me, one must build in such a way that he is always protected in his weakest position. That is, he can manage well in his worst possible time. Suppose I am doing ten lakhs (1,000,000) worth of business. I should not live at the ten lakhs level. For some misfortune may befall us in our business, and then I will be wretched. So I must live at the one lakh level, which I know is the minimum possible income I can have. . . . My business may have different fortunes, but I will not lose everything. . . .

This respondent is considering constructing several widely dispersed plants because he anticipates labor trouble in the future, and this is one way to halt its spread.

Uncertainty coupled with a sense of potential scarcity is, however, firmly based in reality. Life abounds with potential disasters, caused by both man and nature. We have already mentioned some ways in which the rhythms—sometimes vagaries—of government activity affect industrial life in Orissa. Other government activities, however, also have such consequences. The tire retreader in our Orissa sample, for example, has not bothered to uncrate the new high-speed retreading machine he purchased from Czechoslovakia, because the government has decided to start its own tire-retreading factory. Once the government's factory is operating, all government retreading jobs will obligatorily be performed there. Government demonstration programs that include starting up leather-goods factories have put many leather-workers out of business.

Government factories may or may not be well run. In any case, they always have the power to require that other government units purchase only from them. One unit in Orissa had to close because the government began to make and distribute the simple medicines that had been this manufacturer's product.

Likewise, the fear of nationalization, or at least of increasingly confiscatory taxation, also runs through respondents' reports of anxiety about the future. Many respondents have decided not to let their industries grow too large because to do so is to become visible and, consequently, a target for takeover, increased government scrutiny, or at least, inordinate demands for political contributions.

Present social instability and the threat of more in the future also makes our respondents anxious. Communal riots in the mid-1960s, for example, had serious economic consequences for the Muslims in Orissa. One tailor told us that he had expanded to the point at which he was ready to install a showroom and a try-on room and begin making ready-to-wear clothing. He lost most of his machines and other equipment during the riots, and he feels too discouraged to try for that level of achievement soon again.

Similarly, the gurakhu manufacturer has high walls and heavy steel doors around his factory. Guards stand at the entrance. He is now consciously restricting production. He reports that present demand for his product alone could enable him, if he wished, to hire half again as many employees as he now has, even if he did not have the finances in hand—which he does. However, he now has working for him only those people who did not try to sabotage his equipment during the last few riots. He does not know of any other test that will guarantee him safety if the riots start again. For the past three years, he has had to develop his own allocation system for customers since demand so far exceeds production. (In some measure, however, the company has always restricted production. The product has a short shelf life, and by keeping it in limited supply, they are able to guarantee its freshness.) Like the glass manufacturer, this respondent, too, is toying with the idea of opening factories in other states. Communal riots tend to be localized, and with factories in other areas, he would be able to continue manufacturing elsewhere even if the Orissa plant were shut down.

Nature, too, exacts a high toll from people in Orissa. We have mentioned flooding in the area, but this is not as serious a concern for businesses as are the regular cyclones that visit the coastal region. In the course of our interviewing in the Kendrapara area, a number of respondents mentioned that they were only then beginning to recover from the devastating effects of the cyclone of 1968. The day after we left that part of the state, another cyclone struck, killing thousands of people and uprooting many thousands more. Our assistant tried to visit the area shortly after the disaster and learned that people we had intended to interview were dead. Whole villages had vanished, and travel through the region was virtually impossible.

The cyclones had long-term effects as well. For example, the condition of the ocean and river bottoms changed, causing the fish to leave for another location. The livelihoods of many local fishermen, as well as of those (including one of our respondents) whose businesses were related to the annual catch, were destroyed.

Under such circumstances, one is impressed not by the fatalism of the inhabitants, but by the willingness of so many to try again. The ice manufacturer who converted his plant to a cold storage is one example. Another is a Muslim manufacturer of cast concrete products, whose factory was destroyed by the 1968 cyclone. In our interview, he told us how proud he was that in just three years he had built his business back to the level it had attained prior to the cyclone. We do not know what effect the 1971 cyclone had on him.

On the other hand, we should also note that many others of our respondents do convey only a limited sense of life possibilities. In some ways, they remind us of the small American shopkeepers described by Mayer and Goldstein (1961) and Vidich and Bensman (1960). One of the metalworkers in our sample hopes that if he makes more and more goods, in greater variety, customers may start to come. (Vidich and Bensman's shopkeepers add more and more to their product lines instead.) He even fills the street in front of his store with merchandise to attract the attention of customers; his location is not very good, but the best he can afford, and few people even pass by his shop.

The miller who watched all his customers go to the new, multipurpose mill down the lane is in much

the same position as the small American grocer who
loses his customers to the supermarkets (see also
Malamud 1957). We emphasize the American comparison
here because it is our view that the behavior of
many of our respondents, despite their alleged traditionalism and the supposedly massive cultural differences between them and contemporary Americans,
can, in fact, be understood, as their American counterparts can, simply by reference to objective cir-
cumstance, without resort to elaborate culturally-
based explanations. The ranges of behavior in both
countries are very great, a fact often missed by
those who utilize idealized formulations of "modern"
and "traditional" when making comparisons.

CONCLUSIONS

One must be wary of ascribing a constellation
of attributes and behaviors to people just because
they may appear traditional on one obvious dimension.
Lerner (1964), Inkeles (1974), and others see traditional people as having a limited perception both
of their own world and of the world outside. But as
with the village we described earlier that looked so
timeless and changeless when we saw it but whose
residents worked in the glass factory, things may
not always be only what they seem; and one may be
too eager to push people into categories that fit
one's theoretical (and sometimes stereotypical) conceptions, the more especially when the people themselves, eager to please, may cater to those precon-
ceptions. Let us illustrate.
In its efforts to augment the number of industries included in the directory, the Orissa Department of Industries had included a horn carver on the
list. He is an artisan who buys cattle horns, which
he polishes and carves into shapes both useful (pocket combs, pillboxes) and decorative (animals and other figurines). Sitting with his family in his little
shop, carving and polishing, he looks every bit the
ancient craftsman. His family works seven days a
week to produce goods that do not sell in great volume. In his interview, he manifests a sense of limited opportunity. Nonetheless, he has entered his
best work in a national contest, and he has won several prizes. He knows about the government handi-
craft stores scattered throughout India and in large
cities over the rest of the world. His goods are
displayed for sale there. He has also managed to
borrow Rs. 1,000 from the state Handicrafts Board.

He knows about export licenses. If he had the resources, he would print a catalogue and price list for customers who cannot come to his shop. His daughter is married to an engineer, and he plans for some of his sons to get government jobs.

This respondent began the interview by emphasizing that he was just a humble craftsman following his traditional occupation. Since both he and his shop fit that description in appearance, someone looking for "traditionalism" might easily be misled into romanticizing the life of the craftsmen in India, or reading more into the appearance than in fact was there.

Orissa's small industry activity corresponds closely to its general economic position. As in many other countries of the third world, the majority of its most successful businessmen are merchants and traders who have expanded their enterprise into industry. Without the resources to support capital investment or the wealth of potential customers to purchase consumer goods, those industries that succeed must have access to capital and markets outside the state. Because of the general level of poverty and the uncertain environment in which they work, many of the businessmen in Orissa appear to be constrained by tradition even when, in fact, they are more likely constrained by the limited opportunity structure.

We are led, furthermore, to recognize that conceptions of traditionalism and modernity must be multidimensional. Industries that use traditional means of production and/or manufacture traditional products may, nonetheless, have modern organizational structures. Others using modern machinery may make traditional goods and/or sell their products through traditional networks. Moreover, modern products may be produced by traditional means. In conclusion, then, we would not want to be obliged to locate any of these industries on a single traditional-modern continuum.

REFERENCES

Government of India. 1970. *India Pocket Book of Economic Information*. New Delhi, India; Ministry of Finance.
Government of Orissa. 1967. *Directory of Industries*, Cuttack, India.
Inkeles, Alex. 1974. *Becoming Modern*. Cambridge, Mass.: Harvard University Press.

Lerner, Daniel. 1964. *The Passing of Traditional Society*. Glencoe, Ill.: Free Press.
Malamud, Bernard. 1957. *The Assistant*. New York: Farrar, Straus, and Cudahy.
Mayer, Kurt B. and Sidney Goldstein. 1961. *The First Two Years: Problems of Small Firm Growth and Survival*. Washington, D. C.: Small Business Administration.
Shinohara, Miyohei. 1968. Japan, pp. 1-113 in *The Role of Small Industry in the Process of Economic Growth*, edited by Bert F. Hoselitz. The Hague: Mouton.
Vidich, Arthur J. and Joseph Bensman. 1960. *Small Town in Mass Society*. Garden City, N. Y.: Doubleday Anchor Books.
Weber, Max. 1958a. *The Protestant Ethic and the Spirit of Capitalism*. New York: Scribner.
    1958b. *The Religion of India*. Glencoe, Ill.: The Free Press.

Part 5
Tradition in Transition

11 | Some Conclusions: Sources of Change and Continuity

Susan Seymour

The decision to establish a new city of administration in Bhubaneswar has produced a variety of changes, some of which are rapid and irreversible, while others are more gradual and some yet barely discernable. The preceding ten chapters have tried to identify and examine some of these areas of change for the period from 1961 to the present (1979). This chapter will first review and synthesize some of those findings and will then address some broader questions about urbanization and sociocultural change in India as a whole.

The construction of the New Capital in Bhubaneswar has had certain immediate and irreversible effects upon the city and its environs. Most obviously, there is the physical presence of a new planned city that is an administrative, educational, and cultural center and that has been the impetus for rapid population growth. As Grenell points out in Chapter 1, Bhubaneswar's population has grown at an extraordinarily rapid rate—far greater than government administrators had predicted—from an estimated 10,000 in 1946 to over 100,000 by the 1971 census. Accordingly, inhabitants of the old temple town and the surrounding villages have come into direct contact with a new set of institutions and with thousands of strangers whose presence cannot be ignored.

Changes and adaptations in the economic sphere, and in particular in the occupational sphere, are some of the most apparent. During the first period of rapid growth, from 1948 to 1965, construction of the New Capital offered inhabitants of the Old Town and surrounding villages new occupational opportunities. There was, for example, an enormous demand for unskilled labor. Members of a variety of scheduled castes and tribal groups who were primarily agricultural laborers and sharecroppers responded to this demand and were thereby brought into a wage economy, bringing relief (at least temporarily) from an environment that regularly brings cycles of abundance and disaster. In addition, because the New Capital was planned primarily for government administrators, it came to consist largely of middle and upper caste, Westernized Hindus who had to rely on the surrounding population for a variety of traditional goods and services. Members of scheduled castes that specialized in menial services, such as Sweepers and Washermen, were therefore greatly in demand.

Other inhabitants of the Old Town and surrounding villages responded to the presence of the New Capital by moving into such new lines of business as shopkeeping, contracting, and rental of houses to an influx of civil servants. Some responded also by educating certain of their children for civil service positions that were perceived as bringing greater economic security as well as prestige.

These occupational shifts, however, have been subject to fluctuation. First, although there were several economic booms during peak periods of construction in the New Capital, after 1965 new construction declined and numerous laborers found themselves unemployed. Not all could return to their traditional work because meanwhile, landowners, in their efforts to comply with new land laws, were dismissing sharecroppers and tenant cultivators. In addition, other landowners who had been attracted to the New Capital, but who were also suffering from the shortage of jobs there, were moving back to the land. Land had also grown less plentiful because extensive areas had either been sold to or confiscated by the government in the planning and construction of the New Capital. Furthermore, as the demand for labor declined, local laborers found themselves in competition with laborers who had been imported from outside Orissa to expedite construction during the boom periods of growth. In the absence of housing, the latter group, which had been recruited but not planned for, established squatter colonies in zones interstitial to the Old Town and New Capital and competed with the local population for scarce jobs. The result was, as had been documented by Freeman in the case of Kapileswar village, that numerous people at the lower end of the socioeconomic hierarchy became economically worse off than before.

Economic spheres other than labor, also inflated by the construction of the New Capital, may well find such change temporary and may be expected to decline. Some businesses have been negatively affected from the beginning. As Das has pointed out for Nuapalli village, traditional businesses that depend on increasingly scarce resources, such as woodcutting and milkselling, cannot be sustained in the long run. Others, such as bamboo growing, have already experienced severe declines due to government regulations and confiscation of land. Civil service jobs in the New Capital have provided a new kind of employment and attracted much interest among the local population, yet they too are now in short supply. Nevertheless, as both Mahapatra and Freeman point out, these positions have had an impact upon traditional temple service occupations by attracting away members of the younger generation.

Construction of the New Capital has, therefore, produced a variety of economic changes in Bhubaneswar. In the occupational sphere, it has created both new jobs and an expanded market for old ones to which old residents have been highly responsive. At the lower end of the caste hierarchy, many people with specialized services have found an occupational niche for themselves in the new town; however, others without such specialties, who moved into the new cash economy under temporarily inflated conditions, now find themselves either unemployed or engaged in businesses that cannot be sustained. They cannot return to the land because land has become both scarce and valuable. At the middle and upper levels of the caste hierarchy, by comparison, many people have responded to new economic opportunities by moving into a *diversity* of occupations. As Freeman points out, higher status groups have been able to adapt to the new town more successfully because wealth provides the necessary flexibility to train for new occupations and to experiment with new businesses. Thus, movement into new occupations has tended to follow caste lines and to perpetuate traditional status differences, a topic to which we will return.

The kinds of economic developments that have taken place in Bhubaneswar and its immediate environs have had little impact upon the city of Cuttack twenty miles away. This is because the New Capital was deliberately planned to be an administrative center, not a commercial one, so as not to compete with Cuttack, which remains Orissa's primary commercial and small industry center. Nonetheless, Cuttack's economic growth is intimately tied to the New Capital. As the Taubs point out in Chapter 10, industries in Cuttack are largely dependent upon government contracts, which means that they tend to fluctuate with the vagaries of political connections and decision-making in the New Capital. For this and other reasons, an attitude of uncertainty and potential scarcity prevails in Cuttack and few small industries are prospering.

Residents of Bhubaneswar and its environs have been responding not only to new and fluctuating economic opportunities but also to educational ones. The New Capital was conceived as an educational and cultural center as well as an administrative one. In consequence, an array of educational institutions has sprung up. Although the majority of these are Oriya-medium primary and secondary schools that are not significantly different from those already existant in the Old Town and surrounding villages, the establishment of several English-medium primary and secondary schools and also several colleges and a university in the New Capital has increased the educational alternatives for people in Bhubaneswar. The pragmatic flexibility with which families have responded to these new alternatives is stressed by Sable in Chapter 7.

With all the schools now available in Bhubaneswar, most children can attend school and most do for at least several years. However, by the secondary level there are high rates of attrition that vary with residence and socioeconomic status. Scheduled caste and tribal enclaves have an exceedingly high attrition rate (96 percent), which declines for villagers (53 percent) and Old Town residents (35 percent). The lowest rate of attrition (20 percent) occurs in the New Capital. What these various attrition rates obviously suggest is that those persons making most effective use of the educational opportunities in Bhubaneswar are the already educated elite of the New Capital. Children from low status and illiterate parents are for the most part benefiting little. As Sable points out, these attrition rates do not indicate a lack of interest in formal education; indeed, most Bhubaneswar residents value schooling. Rather, patterns of attrition are associated with economic considerations and rational planning on the part of families.

Most Bhubaneswar families are *aware* of the relationship between formal education and employment opportunities. In particular, they know that if their children are to enter the attractive civil service system in the New Capital, they must be educated. Again, however, socioeconomic status is a critical factor that cross-cuts the old and new parts of Bhubaneswar. For lower status families the expenses associated with school are often prohibitive. In addition, many lower status children must stay home to tend to younger siblings and perform household chores while their parents are out working. By contrast, higher status families have more flexibility. They can send their children to school for that period of time which is consistent with considerations of sex, achievement, and career goals. Girls, for example, tend to be educated in so far as it is pertinent to arranging a good marriage. Boys are kept in school as long as they are achieving at satisfactory levels and are oriented to reasonable career goals. Fathers try to ensure their family's welfare by diversifying their educational investments: Sons are directed into a variety of fields, some that require high levels of formal schooling and others that do not. Higher status parents are sensitive to the fluctuating job market in Bhubaneswar and vary their children's education accordingly.

Sable identifies another relationship between caste status and schooling. Children from castes traditionally associated with learning for its own sake have lower attrition rates regardless of their parents' level of formal education or their current socioeconomic status. For example, Old Town Brahman and Karan fathers with no formal education value schooling and encourage their sons to do well. While there has been a shift in the context and use of learning, there appears to be some continuity in attitudes toward learning.

Some comparisons between the new schools that have come with construction of the New Capital and the old schools are pertinent. At the primary and secondary levels the majority of new schools are not significantly different from the old ones as measured by "pass rates"—i.e., their success in training students to pass various qualifying exams. The Old Town and village schools, however, are more intimate than the New Capital ones. Teachers know their students and their students' families, where they live, and what they do. The atmosphere of the more urban New Capital schools is, by comparison, impersonal and anonymous. In addition, the only three English-medium primary and secondary schools are in the New Capital and are attended almost exclusively by children of the administrative elite. They serve, therefore, to reinforce that status group. Altogether, Old Town and New Capital schools are producing an increasingly literate generation of young people who have the training to move into salaried positions.

Turning to children within the home, Seymour's study of family organization and childrearing practices in Bhubaneswar offers some insights into the educational and occupational choices people are making. Significant differences were found in the organization of households and in consequent child care between the Old Town and the New Capital, although low socioeconomic status cross-cuts these differences. In the Old Town people reside in kin and caste-based neighborhoods, where houses are densely clustered together and everybody knows one another. There are both a high proportion of joint households with several generations represented and large numbers of people pursuing their traditional caste occupations. In this intimate setting children grow up with a variety of potential caretakers and appropriate role models. As a consequence, parents seem little concerned to actively stimulate and teach their children; rather, children gradually acquire what they need to know simply by observing those around them. Family life is characterized by a laissez faire atmosphere in which children's activities are neither greatly restricted, nor particularly guided. In addition, Old Town children are allowed to remain dependent on others for general caretaking and attention for an extended period of time. They are being prepared for a highly interdependent, joint family life.

New Capital families, by contrast, are assigned houses in neighborhoods according to their civil service status, not on the basis of kinship or caste (with the exception of Sweepers). Most households are nuclear in structure as individual sets of parents and children have moved into town to take government posts there, leaving their extended kin behind. Houses are built on a Western suburban model, which means that they are separated by fenced yards. Consequently, children grow up in a more impersonal, heterogeneous setting where they are not surrounded by relatives and friends of the same caste. Under these circumstances of smaller, more isolated households, parents seem more concerned than those of the Old Town to actively instruct their children and encourage them to be more self-reliant. They cannot simply rely on their children's observing and gradually acquiring appropriate behavior to function successfully as adults.

These differences between Old Town and New Capital family organization and living conditions are reflected in different educational and occupational goals of both parents and children. In the Old Town, formal schooling, although valued by many, is not of as much consequence to most people as it is in the New Capital. For instance, if boys are to pursue traditional caste occupations, be it carpentry, barbering or priestly services, little formal, Western-style education is necessary. Even in those instances where boys are sent through secondary school and college in order to pursue civil service or engineering careers, the goal is to contribute to the joint family, not the pursuit of individual ambition.

In the New Capital, by comparison, formal, Western-style education is of greater consequence. Almost all middle and upper socioeconomic status parents send both sons and daughters through secondary school and frequently on to college. Not only do children attend school regularly, but they are tutored at home at night. Parents take an intense interest in their children's education, praising them for doing well in school and publicly chastising them when they do not. These parents have already made a break with their extended families by coming to the New Capital to pursue careers, and they hold corresponding ambitions for their children.

These Old Town—New Capital contrasts in childrearing and consequent behavior are cross-cut by low caste and socioeconomic status. Poor people at the bottom of the social hierarchy are subject to constraints that affect their childrearing practices, making them similar on both sides of town, regardless of family organization. Because they are poor, all able-bodied adults (men and women) work outside the home whenever they can find employment. Low status children are, therefore, frequently left in the care of other children or to fend for themselves. They become both more self-reliant and more responsible at earlier ages than their higher status counterparts in the Old Town and the New Capital, and due to their household responsibilities they are generally not in school.

The final focus, religion, is a particularly pertinent subject to examine since before the construction of the New Capital Bhubaneswar was principally noted for its temples and religious activities. Also, religion is an area where Western theories about the impact of urbanization and sociocultural change abound. The research by Mahapatra, Miller, Freeman and Preston is, therefore, significant in trying to determine what effects construction of the New Capital and its concomitant population increase are having. Mahapatra and Freeman both describe a decline in temple rituals and in the status of temple priests for old Bhubaneswar and Kapileswar village. They attribute this change to a number of factors, construction of the New Capital being one. As an instance, expansion of government jurisdiction into the Old Town has affected the temple-based hierarchy and system of power there. Although government intervention in temple management began in the nineteenth century under British rule, in recent years that process has been intensified.

Economic considerations account principally for the decline in temple rituals and services. Priestly families, whose temple lands were growing inadequate to support them and whose temple remunerations were decreasing in value by inflation, were offered new sources of income with the development of the New Capital. Many members of the younger generation were as a consequence, encouraged to acquire a formal, Western-style education and to seek secular employment. This, in turn, produced a shortage of practicing priests and hence a decline in temple rituals. Furthermore, the New Capital offered Old Town and village residents an alternative status system as many of the young, Western-educated elite came to prefer the prestige of the civil service hierarchy in the New Capital to the traditional, and now declining, prestige associated with temple services.

Despite a decline in temple services and temple rituals, there does not appear to be a general decline in religious beliefs and activities in the Bhubaneswar area. Miller's investigation, for example, of Old Town monasteries and holy men makes it clear that the traditional and venerated *guru-shisya* relationship persists. In addition, while some of the endowed monastic orders of the past have declined in wealth and functions since establishment of the New Capital, new ones have arisen. Miller documents the fact that high-ranking members of the New Capital government elite are involved in these monasteries as both patrons and disciples of specific gurus. Thus, interest in Hindu monasteries and holy men is not limited to the more traditional, nonwestern-educated population of Bhubaneswar. In consideration of this phenomenon, Miller argues that the *sampradaya*, with the *guru-shisya* relationship at its center, is one of the oldest and most adaptive structures of Hinduism and helps to account for that religion's persistence through time in Bhubaneswar as elsewhere in India.

Similarly, Freeman indicates that in Kapileswar village religion is not on a decline. While there may be a decline in the patronage of the temple and associated rites, religious activities of other kinds are flourishing. Villagers have been turning to new and more devotional forms of religious expression that do not entail elaborate and highly structured rituals associated with caste restrictions. Popular religious movements have not only attracted widespread village interest but are also attended and sponsored by Old Town and New Capital residents.

Preston's account of the rise of Chandi Temple in Cuttack also helps to affirm the vitality of religion in this part of Orissa. That temple, instead of languishing under the impact of urban growth and change, has flourished. Its growth in prestige and influence reflects the more commercial orientation of Cuttack by comparison with Bhubaneswar. Unlike the ancient temples of Bhubaneswar with their complex set of temple servants and caste duties, Chandi Temple has become associated with rich and devout merchants who help to sponsor city-wide, popular rituals that appeal to a wide diversity of urban residents. Thus, it has become a symbol of democratization of a religious institution once associated with a feudal social structure and again exemplifies the adaptiveness of Hinduism.

In this review we have tried to identify some of the principal areas of change and adaptation in Bhubaneswar that have been produced by the construction of the New Capital and the concomitant influx of new people into the area. What is perhaps most striking is the extent to which old institutions and ways of life persist in the face of extensive changes in the physical and social environment. For example, despite the introduction of new educational and economic opportunities, caste remains a viable institution. In fact, we have seen that in some respects the educational and economic effects of the New Capital have simply reinforced caste lines. Similarly, despite a preponderance of nuclear households in the New Capital, there is evidence that joint family ideals persist. Furthermore, although there have been some changes in the religious orientation of an ancient temple town and its environs, there is no evidence that Hinduism is in a decline or that religious institutions are being secularized in the face of rapid urbanization and socioeconomic change.

The fact that Western observers are *struck* by the adaptiveness and persistence of Indian institutions and attitudes in the context of rapid sociocultural change reflects the Western, ethnocentric viewpoint that urbanization and modernization imply changes that are linear and inevitable. It is commonly assumed, for example, that sociocultural change will occur in the direction of greater egalitarianism, secularism, individualism, materialism, and a more democratic political system. These represent Western values, and thus the term "modernization" has come to connote movement in the direction of Euro-American civilization. Different Western theorists stress different criteria to define modernization: e.g., Levy (1966) selects the increased use of inanimate sources of power (technology); Bendix (1967) focuses upon social changes similar to those of the eighteenth century industrial revolution; Lerner (1964:71) concentrates upon "the transition to participant society"; and Apter (1967) selects "self-conscious choice" and "rationality," as the major ingredients of becoming modern. By emphasizing certain directions in which nonwestern societies are assumed to move and qualities or values they are assumed to acquire, such theories focus attention upon structural differences and implied incompatibilities between the old and the new rather than upon processes of adaptation, and thus they produce an analytic gap between "tradition" and "modernity." Tradition and modernity then become static and opposed categories: i.e., to become "modern" requires discarding old institutions and ways of life.

Some recent views, emerging from observations and analyses of sociocultural change in complex societies, have pointed to the *continuities* between the old and the new, thus diminishing the presumed antithesis between more traditional and more modern ways of doing things (e.g., Geertz 1963; Mandelbaum 1970; Rudolph and Rudolph 1967; Singer 1972). In such societies as India, where there is a known long, rich, and complex past, it is difficult to ignore the dynamism and persistence of tradition despite centuries of political domination by outside rulers. Such recognition has led the Rudolphs to propose a dialectical view of change:

Conclusions

> If tradition and modernity are seen as continuous rather than separated by an abyss, if they are dialectically rather than dichotomously related, and if internal variations are attended to and taken seriously, then those sectors of traditional society that contain or express potentialities for change from dominant norms and structures become crucial for understanding the nature and processes of modernization (1967:10).

Yet even this view implies some antithesis between "tradition" and "modernity" and movement in a particular direction. Accordingly, we find ourselves in agreement with Singer's conclusion:

> Although no single comprehensive alternative theory has yet emerged to sweep the field, it seems to me likely that a new theory of modernization will articulate much more closely with a general theory of cultural change than does the classical theory of traditional and modern societies. It will not only go beyond the "traditional versus modern" dichotomy but will also transcend the bifurcation between cultural diffusion and cultural evolution and between "culture" and "society." Above all, it will be grounded on the comparative and historical studies of literate civilization as well as of primitive and peasant cultures (1972:384).

In the absence of such an alternative theory, we have in this volume, and in the Harvard-Bhubaneswar Project in general, tried to emphasize careful description of events and processes, avoiding as much as possible static categorization while trying to identify continuities with the past and adaptations of traditional structures to changing conditions.

Caste, to pursue a first example in some detail, has been a resilient institution in India (see Mandelbaum 1970: 427-520), and Bhubaneswar is no exception. The responses of Bhubaneswar residents to expand occupational and educational opportunities have been in large part according to caste lines. As others have noted, members of higher and more literate castes tend to shift to new professions requiring Western-style, formal education while members of lower castes tend to shift to new occupations requiring little such education (e.g., Gould 1970;

Singer, 1972). Caste provides an "adaptive structure" (Gould 1970: 72) in the context of a changing economy.

In the Old Town and surrounding villages people continue to reside in neighborhoods organized along caste lines. Although the New Capital, with its concentration of civil servants, has introduced a somewhat different social system into the area, there are clear continuities with the past. As city planner Koenigsberger predicted (Chapter 2), a new "administrative caste" hierarchy has developed with its own set of status symbols, such as size and location of house assigned and educational degrees attained. "Units" in the New Capital were designed to provide mixed housing for different levels of civil servants. However, houses were built in rows of similar house type, thereby ensuring that civil servants of similar status would reside near one another. In addition, a separate Sweeper Colony was established near the railroad tracks. And by not providing housing for other low status service castes, New Capital planners and government officials indirectly produced pockets of slum habitations in outlying areas of the new town.

There are, nevertheless, portents of change. While some upward mobility in the caste system has always been possible, for the first time members of low caste groups have access to the kind of schooling that can enable them to get higher status jobs in the government hierarchy where positions are based primarily upon achieved rather than ascribed criteria. Although many low caste families, for reasons already outlined, cannot take advantage of these new opportunities, some are doing so and will have the chance to alter significantly their socioeconomic status. In addition, members of enough different Old Town caste groups have become economically oriented to the New Capital, where transactions are more commercial than personal, that traditional jajmani relationships have seriously declined. The introduction of a cash economy has brought new opportunities to members of different caste groups and has reduced their traditional dependence upon one another. Further, the established dominance of Old Town priestly families is being undermined by a variety of factors, such as expansion of government jurisdiction into the Old Town and a competing system of power and prestige in the New Capital. In the long run, these kinds of changes may produce a significantly different, but nonetheless persisting system of stratification in

Bhubaneswar as elsewhere in India (e.g., Ames 1969; Chekki 1970; Srinivas 1966).

The joint family is another example of a resilient and adaptive Indian institution. Despite forecasts that the joint family was suited only to agrarian conditions and would decline in urban and industrial surroundings (e.g., Goode 1963), there is much evidence to suggest that such a decline is not inevitable (e.g., Ames 1969; Freed and Freed 1969; Shah 1974; Mandelbaum 1970). In fact, as with the case of caste, the joint family is a far more complex and varied phenomenon than Western scholars have often assumed. In the Bhubaneswar area, for example, some thirteen or fourteen different kinds of extended households have been identified. Not all of them meet the cultural and structural ideals of the joint family, but they are suggestive of the flexibility and adaptability of the Indian family system.

In the Old Town, joint households are not uncommon and joint family ideals prevail. Even families that are sending their sons through college and directing them into new forms of employment expect them to reside in the same households as adults and to contribute to the family's welfare. In the New Capital, as has been pointed out, the preponderance of households are technically nuclear, although they are more properly described as "supplemented nuclear" since in many of them there are a variety of extended kinsmen who come and go. In addition, many New Capital residents formerly lived in joint family households, continue to maintain ties with their joint family kinsmen, and will retire to their joint family estates. Thus, residence in the New Capital might best be viewed as simply one phase in the longer developmental cycle of Indian domestic groups (e.g., Gould 1968).

Nonetheless, there are again portents of change. In the smaller, nuclear families of the New Capital there is less segregation of the sexes and more of an emphasis upon a conjugal bond between husband and wife than in the Old Town and surrounding villages. With smaller, less formally structured households, more intense relationships between parents and children are developing. Girls, as well as boys, are being sent to school, and the age of marriage is being delayed accordingly. In addition, the emphasis that middle and higher status New Capital families place upon formal, Western-style schooling and subsequent professional careers is not easily compatible with joint family living arrangements.

Ambitious New Capital children will have to go where appropriate jobs are to be found, leaving their extended kinsmen behind. As in the case of caste, there are clear continuities with the past, but there are also suggestions of changing interpersonal relations and personal ambitions that may have far-reaching implications.

As a final example, in the case of religion there are in Bhubaneswar both clear continuities with the past and indications of important changes underway. Contrary to the views of such theorists as Weber (1958), Levy 1966; 1972), and Myrdal (1968), Hinduism has proved to be extraordinarily adaptive and compatible with urbanization and sociocultural change. For example, while there has been a decline in temple worship, no such decline in the activity of monasteries and associated gurus is evident. They continue to attract New Capital as well as Old Town residents. In Bhubaneswar, as in Madras City (Singer 1972), there has been a shift away from more formal, ritualistic forms of Hinduism and their associations with a rigid caste hierarchy toward more popular, devotional forms (*bhakti*) of Hinduism which bring together a variety of people regardless of rural or urban residence and regardless of caste status. Devotion is one of the three standard paths to salvation in Hinduism, and *bhakti* movements are very old, having been traced back to the Vedas (Singer 1972:157). Thus, the rise of devotional expressions of Hinduism in Bhubaneswar is not in itself a new phenomenon, but by being generally anti-caste and anti-intellectual, as well as more flexible and personal in orientation, such movements are better adapted to current conditions of urbanization and democratization in India. Perhaps, the vitality of the *sampradaya* and its associated *guru-shisya* relationship is attributable to the emphasis that it also places upon individuals and to its responsiveness to all socioeconomic groups. The crucial question, then, becomes whether these religious adaptations will continue to predominate or whether they will be reabsorbed at some later date into more ritualistic forms of Hinduism.

In conclusion, on the basis of these investigations in Bhubaneswar, let us offer three proposals for the study of urbanization and sociocultural change in India and elsewhere. First, it is clear that studies of sociocultural change must focus on the *adaptive* qualities of existant institutions. Even in the context of rapid urbanization and the abrupt introduction of new institutions and different values, as in the case of Bhubaneswar, old ways of life persist and it is to these old ways of life that we must turn to understand the processes of sociocultural change. As Singer (1972:384-85) has aptly noted, in India "traditionalism" provides a cultural ideology for sociocultural change. Such old institutions as caste, the joint family, *bhakti*, and the *sampradaya* have shown themselves to be highly adaptive. In addition, sets of individuals and families, as well as institutions, have demonstrated their flexibility and adaptiveness. For example, some traditional craftsmen in Cuttack, although they may not have acquired modern technology, have developed new management techniques and new ways of responding to changing market conditions. Similarly, Old Town temple priests, as well as other Bhubaneswar residents, have responded to changing educational and economic conditions by diversifying their interests: They are training some of their children for new forms of employment while directing others into traditional careers. Ultimately, as analysts of sociocultural change in India, we must examine the adaptive mechanisms inherent to traditional institutions and the adaptive strategies that families and individuals use when faced with rapidly changing conditions.

Whether or not India is unique in this regard is a question that should also be addressed. We think that it is not. While not all societies have the *known* long, rich cultural past of India, with its complex and adaptive institutions, all societies have a set of established institutions and associated patterns of behavior and values that must cope with innovation and change, whether it be introduced internally or externally. The adjustment of established institutions and ways of life may involve greater and lesser degrees of conflict, but it will rarely involve the total rejection of one sociocultural system for another. Thus, the bipolar model of "tradition *versus* modernity" is generally inappropriate for the study of sociocultural change. Rather, we need careful, comparative studies of the *strategies* that different societies adopt to contend with change.

Second, although there are clear continuities with the past in Bhubaneswar, there are also indications that more profound changes may well be underway—changes that may ultimately be more "systemic" than "recurrent" in character (Mandelbaum 1970:633-35). Some of these changes are similar to those that have been identified for other industrializing and urbanizing nations: e.g., movement toward a more flexible system of social stratification based more upon achieved rather than ascribed criteria; a concern with Western-style, formal education as a condition for social mobility and occupational flexibility; more egalitarian relations between the sexes and between generations; more focus upon the individual and individual decision-making; economic diversification; and movement toward more egalitarian expressions of religion. These kinds of forces may become the *parameters* for a new social system in India, although they will not necessarily *determine* the precise nature of that social system (Mandelbaum 1970:635). Such forces, however pervasive, will undoubtedly take their own form in the Indian context.

Finally, although long-term, multidisciplinary research *has* given us considerable insight into and understanding of the processes and directions of urbanization and sociocultural change in Bhubaneswar and its environs, more research from more theoretical perspectives and over continuing periods of time is needed. Only with further research can we achieve a yet more complete understanding of *how* such a microcosm as a small, sacred, temple town can be transformed into a contemporary administrative, educational, and cultural center. We continue to need careful, microscopic recordings of the processes of sociocultural change "as a potential guide, and, it is to be hoped, as a record, of the next turn in human affairs" (Du Bois 1978:7).

REFERENCES

Ames, Michael M. 1969. Class, Caste and kinship in an industrial city of India. *Asia* 15: 58-71.
Apter, David E. 1967. *The Politics of Modernization*. Chicago: University of Chicago Press.
Bendix, Reinhard. 1967. Tradition and modernity reconsidered. *Comparative Studies in Society and History* 9 (3): 292-346.
Chekki, Dan A. 1970. Social stratification and trends of social mobility in modern India. *Sociologus* 20: 146-163.
Du Bois, Cora. 1978. Foreward to H. C. Das, "Suburbanization of Two Orissan Villages 1950-1970." Unpublished manuscript.
Freed, Stanley A. and Ruth S. Freed. 1969. Urbanization and family types in a north Indian village. *Southwestern Journal of Anthropology* 25: 342-359.

Geertz, Clifford. 1963. *Peddlers and Princes: Social Change and Economic Modernization in Two Indonesian Towns*. Chicago: University of Chicago Press.

Goode, William J. 1963. *World Revolution and Family Patterns*. New York: The Free Press.

Gould, Harold A. 1968. Time-dimension and structural change in an Indian kinship system: A problem of conceptual refinement, pp. 413-421 in *Structure and Change in Indian Society*, edited by Milton Singer and Bernard S. Cohn. Chicago: Aldine Publishing Company.

_____ 1970. Occupational categories and stratification in the achievement of urban society, pp. 51-76 in *Urban India: Society, Space and Image*, edited by Richard G. Fox. Durham, North Carolina: Duke University Press.

Lerner, Daniel. 1964. *The Passing of Traditional Society: Modernizing the Middle East*. New York: The Free Press of Glencoe.

Levy, Marion J., Jr. 1966. *Modernization and the Structure of Societies*. Princeton, New Jersey: Princeton University Press.

_____ 1972. *Modernization: Latecomers and Survivors*. New York: Basic Books.

Mandelbaum, David G. 1970. *Society in India, Vol. Two: Change and Continuity*. Berkeley: University of California Press.

Myrdal, Gunnar. 1968. *Asian Drama: An Inquiry into the Poverty of Nations*. New York: Pantheon.

Rowe, William L. 1973. Caste, kinship, and association in urban India, pp. 211-249 in *Urban Anthropology*, edited by Aidan Southall. New York: Oxford University Press.

Rudolph, Lloyd I. and Susanne H. Rudolph. 1967. *The Modernity of Tradition: Political Development in India*. Chicago: University of Chicago Press.

Shah, A. M. 1974. *The Household Dimension of the Family in India*. Berkeley: University of California Press.

Singer, Milton. 1972. *When A Great Tradition Modernizes: An Anthropological Approach to Indian Civilization*. New York: Praeger.

Strinivas, M. N. 1966. *Social Change in Modern India*. Berkeley: University of California Press.

Weber, Max. 1958. *The Religion of India*. Glencoe, Illinois: The Free Press.

Index

Adaptation
  See Sociocultural change
Aiyappan, A., 68, 216
Aiyer, V. G. Ramakrishna, 106, 187
Ames, Elinor and Kalindi Randeri, 122
Ames, Michael M., 146, 269
Andhra Pradesh, 240
Apter, David E., 266
Ascetics, 83, 87, 89
Ashrama
  See Monasteries

Bailey, Frederick G., 13, 192, 194
Baragad village, 19, 20, 233
Bendix, Reinhard, 266
Bengal, 11, 13, 28, 87, 90, 91, 103, 238
Bengalis, 102, 240
Bhardwaj, Surinder Mohan, 106, 187
Bhubaneswar, 8, 55, 97, 100, 110, 121
  chronology of planning, 32-45
  description of 19-26, 185-186
  historical background, 12
  population, 1, 11, 19, 28, 30, 33, 70, 257
  research site, 1, 2
  site of new capital city, 18, 33, 37-38, 39, 54, 60
  See also New Capital; Old Town; Squatter Colonies; Urban Planning
Bhubaneswar Notified Area, 18, 30, 48, 50
Bhubaneswar Notified Area Council (NAC), 28, 36, 38, 52, 62, 178
Bihar, 11, 13, 18, 35
Biswal, Adikanda, 58
Bombay, 8, 34
British rule, 61, 71, 102, 103, 112, 264
Bronfenbrenner, Urie, 153

Calcutta, 8, 102, 103, 104, 143, 236, 238
Carstairs, Morris, 122
Capital city
  See New Capital
Castes, subcastes, and tribes

References to particular castes, subcastes, and tribes will be found under the entry "Castes, subcastes, and tribes."

275

INDEX

Astrologer (Jyotish), 27, 75
Bania, 27, 125, 187, 188
Barber (Barik), 27, 73, 76, 124, 187
Bauri, 77, 124, 187, 189, 191-94, 201, 202, 204, 205-07, 208, 210, 211, 223, 227, 228, 233
Blacksmith (Kamar), 27
Brahman, 19, 27, 68, 77, 78, 80, 107, 108, 123, 124, 125, 170-172, 177, 182, 187, 188, 192, 202, 209, 246, 261
Bricklayer, 124
Carpenter (Badhei), 27, 187, 188
Confectioner (Guria), 27, 75, 187, 188, 225
Cowherder (Gauda), 27, 187, 188, 220, 221, 225, 229, 233
Cultivator (Chasa), 27, 187, 188
Fisherman, 110, 187, 188, 192, 202
Gardener (Mali), 27
Karan, 27, 28, 125, 170-172, 177, 182, 187, 188, 219, 220, 229, 232, 261
Kayastha, 28, 125
Khandait, 27, 187, 188, 219, 220, 225, 232
Mallia, 106, 107, 108, 112, 114, 187, 189-191, 192, 193, 194, 201, 202, 204
Oil presser (Teli), 27, 187, 188, 192, 202, 207-209, 225
Potter (Kumbhar), 27, 71, 75, 187, 188
Saora, 220, 223, 226, 227, 228, 229, 231, 233
Sweeper (Hadi), 27, 80, 125, 147, 173, 187, 188, 194, 258, 262

Washerman (Dhoba), 27, 72, 75, 76, 124, 147, 152, 187, 258
Weaver, 74, 125
See also Temple priests and servants
Caste system
"administrative caste," 35
caste associations, 73, 78
caste solidarity and rivalry, 73, 78
change, 268-269
commensality, 73, 78
high caste landowners, 192
influence on occupational adaptations, 190, 191, 194, 259, 267
influence on school enrollment and attrition, 170-72, 174, 178, 180, 260, 261
intermarriage, 73, 78
jajmani relationships, 73, 76, 268
low caste, 177
middle caste, 177
outcastes, 19
personality and, 122
purity and pollution, 194
ranking of castes, 27-28, 187-188, 194
resilience of, 265, 267
scheduled castes and tribes, 28, 72, 257, 258, 260
service castes (Shudras) 19, 26, 39, 123, 268
tribals, 177, 180
untouchables, 28, 96, 109, 123, 171, 173, 177, 180, 189, 193, 206, 211
widening economic gap, 211-212
Central Town and Country Planning Organization,

INDEX

44, 45, 50, 51
Chandigarh, 37, 61
Chandi Temple, 96, 114
  charismatic priest, 104-105
  goddess worship, 103-104
  growth and popularity of, 101-103, 105, 106, 113, 265
  historical background, 100-103
  involvement of Cuttack merchants, 102, 265
Childrearing, 4, 120, 262
  care of infants and young children, 128-138
  dependence, training for, 122-123, 128, 134, 138, 141, 143, 145, 146, 150, 152, 262
  family organization and, 122
  fathers, 140, 147, 149, 151, 152, 206
  household size and composition and, 139, 147-150
  maternal nurturance, 138, 139, 141, 147
  maternal stimulation, 143, 147, 148
  methods of investigation, 123-128
  Old Town-New Capital contrasts, 121, 135, 138-139, 141, 145, 150-151, 262-263
  responsibility, training for, 142-143, 150, 160, 193, 263
  self-reliance, training for, 122-123, 128, 143, 145, 146, 152, 262, 263
  socioeconomic status and, 4, 123, 124-126, 140, 141-144, 146-147, 149, 150, 262, 263
  women's workloads and, 123, 141-143, 146
  See also Family organization
City planning
  See Urban planning
Chowduri, Nabakrushna, 55
Choudhury, Chief Minister, 59
Civil servants, 26, 33, 41, 125, 152, 165, 175, 177, 180, 268
  elite, 84, 93, 94
  officers, 1, 4, 41, 46, 48, 51, 53, 57-59, 64, 89, 90, 91, 92
  See also Monasteries, involvement of government elite
Civil service system, 76, 261
  administrative hierarchy, 26, 28-29, 40-41, 50, 121, 123
  expansion of, 56-58
Climate, 9, 111, 186, 239, 249-250
Cohn, Bernard, 194
Congress Party, 18, 86
Crozier, Michel, 64, 65
Cuttack, 65, 89, 96, 102, 106, 175
  commercial growth, 102
  commercial and industrial center of Orissa, 2, 11, 26, 33, 97, 259-260
  description of, 12, 13, 97, 100, 235
  industrial entrepreneurs, 234-252
  population, 11, 26, 97, 102, 235
  religious change, 113-114
  shift of government from to Bhubaneswar, 36, 37, 39, 46, 47, 59

278 INDEX

Cuttack District, 48, 50, 52, 55, 59
Das, Harish C., 216, 233, 259
Derrett, J. Duncan, 112, 115
Divine Life Society, 91, 93
Du Bois, Cora, vii, 1, 2, 233, 272

Economic development, 4, 26, 30, 37-38, 63, 211
  See also Industrialism; Kapileswar village; Nuapalli village; Occupational change
Education
  adaptiveness of the system, 181
  costs, 159, 160, 181
  caste and, 170-172, 174, 177, 178, 180, 260, 261
  daughters of, 165-166, 261, 269
  educational opportunities, 63, 156, 158, 181, 260
  employment and, 161, 162, 163, 164, 165, 167, 172, 263
  enrollment and attrition patterns, 146, 158, 159, 160, 179, 180, 260
  examination pass rates, 179
  father's occupation and, 176, 177, 180, 261
  intrinsic value of, 167-172
  planning for, 158-167, 181, 182, 260
  schools, 3, 63, 157, 164, 172-176, 178-180, 182, 260, 261
  study of, 4, 157-158

  socioeconomic status and, 160, 163, 166, 176, 179-181, 261
  Western-style schooling, 170, 263, 264, 269

Family organization
  change, 269-270
  household size and composition, 139 140, 147-149
  joint family ideals, persistence of, 265
  joint households, 121, 122, 124, 125-127, 150, 152, 262
  New Capital households, 145, 150, 262
  nuclear households, 121, 124-127, 265
  Old Town households, 123, 145, 149, 182
  personality and, 122
  sexual segregation, 127, 128, 269
  socioeconomic status and, 125, 128, 141, 146, 147, 262
  study of, 4, 262
  See also Childrearing; Education; Women
Ford Foundation Urban Planning Team, 18, 47, 48, 49, 63
Freed, Stanley A. and Ruth S. Freed, 269
Freeman, James M., 84, 96, 101, 109, 111, 115, 184, 189, 258, 259, 265
Freeman, James and James Preston, 94, 264
Friedman, John R. P., 64, 65

Geertz, Clifford, 146, 266
Gokhale, B. K., 32, 33, 59

Goode, William J., 269
Government officers
  See Civil servants
Gould, Harold A., 267, 268, 269
Government of India, 13, 18, 45, 49, 51, 174, 175, 239
Greater Bhubaneswar Master Plan, 45, 48, 50, 51, 52, 55, 56
Grenell, Peter, 8, 65, 257
Gross, Bertram, 64, 65
Gujaratis, 238
Gurus, 4, 84, 85-89, 91-94, 270

Harvard-Bhubaneswar Project, 1, 2, 3, 5, 19, 267
Hinduism
  adaptiveness of, 2, 85, 105, 112, 265, 270
  decline in temple rituals, 64, 76, 84, 264, 270
  devotional forms (*bhakti*), 265, 270, 271
  goddess worship, 83, 100-105, 109, 110
  guru-shisya relationship, 82, 84, 85, 86, 93, 264, 270
  popular religious movements, 109-110, 111-112, 265
  ritualistic forms, 2, 84, 270
  sampradayas, 85, 87, 91, 93, 94, 264, 270
  secularization, absence of, 109, 113, 114
  See also Chandi Temple; Kapileswar Temple; Lingaraj Temple; Monasteries; Rituals; Temple priests and servants
Hirschman, Albert O., 64, 65

Hunter, W. W., 107

Industrialism, 9, 11
  Cuttack industrialists and entrepreneurs, 237-251
  government influence, 241-242, 248, 260
  psychology of scarcity, 248
  tradition and modernity and, 245-247
Independence, 41, 60, 61, 64, 100-102, 245
Independence Movement, 33
Inkeles, Alex, 151, 251

Jagannath Temple, 11, 69
Jamshedpur, 18, 35
Jindel, Rajendra, 116

Kapileswar Temple, 4, 94, 96, 188
  decline of, 107-109 110-111, 265
  historical background, 106-107
Kapileswar village, 19, 20, 84, 96, 106, 258
  caste ranking, 187-189
  climate, 186, 209, 212
  distribution of wealth, 195-202, 209
  economic and occupational change, 186, 189-195, 209, 210
  population, 106, 186
  portraits of starvation and affluence, 204-209
  religious change, 109-112
Katju, Governor, 36, 58, 60
Kennedy, Beth C., 151
Khosla, Ajudhia Nath, 49, 60
Koenigsberger, Otto, 18, 32, 35, 36, 37, 40, 41, 45, 46, 48, 53, 54, 55, 57, 58, 63, 65

280 INDEX

Koenigsberger plan, 39, 46, 47, 48, 64
Kshetra
  See Old Town, sacred place
Kulke, Hermann, 103
Kutty, M. G., 53

Laxmisagar village, 19, 20, 233
Le Corbusier, 37
Lerner, Daniel, 251, 266
LeVine, Robert A., Nancy H. Klein, and Constance R. Owen, 153
Levy, Marion, 113, 266, 270
Lewis, Governor Sir Hawthorne, 33
Lingaraj temple, 4, 12, 19, 34, 38, 68, 108, 186
  categories of temple servants, 72-73, 74-75
  effects of the New Capital, 75-78
  historical background, 69-72, 79-80

Madras, 113, 236
Mahapatra, Laxman, 68, 216
Mahapatra, Manamohan, 68, 71, 94, 101, 103, 259, 264
Mahtab, Harekrushna, 18, 33, 34, 39, 47, 55, 59, 64, 79
Malamud, Bernard, 250
Mamdani, Mahmoud, 211, 212
Mandelbaum, David, 112, 266, 267, 269, 271, 272
Marwaris, 102, 237, 238, 240, 244
Matha
  See Monasteries
Mayer, Kurt B. and Sidney Goldstein, 250
Mehta, V. C., 35, 65

Mencher, Joan, 151
Miller, David, 82, 94, 264
Miller, David and Dorothy Wertz, 94, 101
Minturn, Leigh and John Hitchcock, 122, 134
Mishra, Kanhu Charan, 106
Misra, Bhabagrahi, 96 199
Misra, Sadasiva, 187
Mitra, Biren, 50
Mitra, Rajendralala, 79
Modernization
  See Sociocultural change
Monasteries, 4, 264
  disciples and patrons of, 86, 88, 89, 91-93
  involvement of government elite, 4, 84, 85-91, 93, 264
  monastic institutions in Bhubaneswar, 83-84
  Orissa Government and the, 89
  See also Ascetics; Gurus; Hinduism, *guru-shisya* relationships, *sampradayas*
Mukerjee, Prabhat, 79
Murphy, Lois, 122
Muslims, 237, 239, 240, 242, 249, 250
Myrdal, Gunnar, 113, 270

Nair, Armit Lal, 51, 52
Nehru, Jawaharlal, 54
New Capital, 3, 4, 15, 17, 21, 23, 25, 125
  administrative colony, 33, 37, 39, 59, 63
  children, 126, 143
  construction and development of, 37, 38 39, 50-57, 59, 62, 230, 257
  description of, 19,

121-122
educational and cultural center of Orissa, 1, 260
government quarters, 34, 40, 41-44, 45, 46, 47, 48, 52, 59, 62, 64
planned city, 1, 4, 31, 64
schools, 179
source of urbanization and sociocultural change, 4, 31, 69, 111, 185-186, 217, 233 257-265
transportation, 40
See also Family organization; Urban planning
New Delhi, 8
Nimkoff, M. F., 122
Nuapalli village, 19, 20, 216, 259
description of, 217
occupational changes, 217-233

Occupational adaptation, 75-76, 108-109 147, 257, 258
caste and, 190, 191, 194, 259, 267
See also Education and employment; Industrialism; Kapileswar village; Nuapalli village
Old Town, 3, 4, 14, 16, 21, 22, 24, 39, 58, 124
children, 126, 143
description of, 19, 85-86, 121-122
development of, 44-45, 60
effects of New Capital, 63
power hierarchy, 38
sacred place, 69, 70
schools, 179
See also Family organization; Lingaraj Temple; Monasteries

O'Malley, L., 109, 112
Orissa Government, 28, 31-65 *passim*, 89, 97, 101, 111, 174, 175
industry and, 9, 11, 238, 241-242, 248-249
restrictions on woodcutting, 228
See also Civil servants; Civil service system
Orissa Hindu Religious Endowment Act (O.H.R.E.A.), 69, 72, 73
Orissa Hindu Religious Endowment Commission, 101, 102, 105, 108, 112, 115
Orissa Legislative Assembly, 13, 44, 50, 59, 60
Orissa Legislative Assembly Debates, 50, 57
Orissa Legislative Assembly Proceedings, 18, 33
Orissa Province, 13
Orissa state
description of, 9, 11
historical and political overview, 13, 18
industrial development, 235, 236
landholders, 200
population, 9
Orissa State Planning Organization, 18
Orissa Town Planning Act, 36, 38, 48, 52
Orissa Town Planning Organization, 44, 49, 50, 51, 57, 58, 60, 62, 63, 65
Oriya language, 13, 87, 128, 145, 240
Oriya nationalist movement, 13

Panigrahi, K. C., 13, 79, 106, 186

282　　　　　　　　INDEX

Paradip Port, 11, 26, 49, 242
Partition, 41, 239
Patnaik, Bijoyananda, 47, 49, 50, 55, 59
Patnaik, D. R. K., 49, 51, 52, 54, 55, 58
Pilgrims, 11, 70, 73, 80, 81, 107, 109, 111, 112
Poggie, John and Robert Lynch, 146
Population
　See Bhubaneswar; Kapileswar village; Orissa state; Rourkela
Preston, James, 96, 103
Prothro, Edwin, 153
Princely states, 9, 13, 18, 33, 73, 101
Punjabis, 239, 240, 242
Puri, 11, 13, 69, 70, 89, 100
Puri District, 48, 50, 52, 55, 59, 199, 218

Ramakrishna Matha, 83, 84-89, 92-94
Ramesan, N., 106, 187
Randhawa, Mohinder Singh, 210
Redfield, Robert, 3
Regenstein Library of the University of Chicago, 2
Religion
　See Hinduism; Rituals
Reuben, Simon Solomon, 48, 158
Rituals
　Durga Puja, 103-105, 110, 111, 112, 113, 114
　firewalking, 109, 112
　Jagannath car festival, 80-81
　land sales and, 204
　lay initiation ceremony (*diksa*), 86, 88-89
　personal rites, 100
　sacrificial fire ceremony (*yajna*), 90
　Shivaratri, 107
　Trinath Mela (intercaste devotional songfest), 110, 112, 113
　See also Hinduism, decline in temple rituals
Rourkela, 11, 26
Rudolph, Lloyd and Suzanne, 114, 146, 266

Sable, Alan, 152, 156, 158, 260, 261
Sahu, N. K., 79
Schools
　See Education, schools
Seymour, Susan, 120, 262
Shah, A. M., 213, 269
Sharma, Hari P., 192
Shinohara, Miyohei, 247
Shivaite temple, 12, 69
　See also Lingaraj Temple
Singer, Milton, 113, 114, 146, 266, 267, 271
Sinha, B. N., 199, 200, 213
Siripur village, 19, 20, 28, 233
Slums
　See Squatter colonies
Sociocultural change
　adaptive strategies, 3, 271-272
　childrearing and, 151
　modernization, 83-85, 112-114, 146, 151, 185, 266, 267
　persistence of old institutions, 265-270
　recurrent and systemic change, 271-272
　religious institutions and, 2, 83, 96, 97, 112-114, 263-264
　study of Bhubaneswar, 1, 2, 145, 257, 272
　See also Tradition and

INDEX

Modernity; Urbanization
Squatter colonies, 26, 38, 39, 55, 62, 173, 258, 268
Srinivas, M. N., 2
Stein, Burton, 106, 187
Swatantra Party, 18

Taub, Doris, 234, 260
Taub, Richard, 60, 65, 84, 86, 93, 234, 260
Taylor, William S., 122
Temple priests and servants, 12, 27, 68, 71, 102, 104, 106-107, 170
  categories of, 72-74
  declining number and status, 76-77, 111
  secular employment, 75-76, 78, 84, 108-109, 113, 211, 264, 271
  traditional roles, 74
  See also Lingaraj Temple; Kapileswar Temple
Temple town
  See Old Town
Tradition, and modernity, 3, 106, 114, 143, 211, 246, 247, 251, 266, 267, 271
Tribes, 11, 28
Turner, John F. C., and Robert Fichter *et al.*, 8, 64

Untouchables
  See Caste system
Urbanization
  caste and, 195
  control of urban growth, 53
  persistence of old institutions, 266-270
  religious institutions and, 2, 64, 69, 97, 114, 184, 263-264
  study of Bhubaneswar, 1, 2, 257, 272
  village life and, 185, 189, 210-212
  See also Sociocultural change; Tradition and modernity
Urban planning, 4, 31
  chronology of planning for Bhubaneswar, 32-45, 50
  decision-making and, 37-45, 49, 57, 58, 60
  planning process, 45-62
  See also New Capital

Vaishnavite temple, 11
Vaz, Julius L., 34, 35, 46, 47, 55, 58, 63
Vidich, Arthur J. and Joseph Bensman, 250
Vidyarthi, Lalita, 106, 113, 187
Villages, 2, 26, 38, 39, 48, 50, 52, 59, 70
  See also Baragad; Kapileswar; Laxmisagar; Nuapalli; Siripur

Weber, Max, 113, 238, 247, 270
Wertz, Dorothy, 82
West Bengal
  See Bengal
Whiting, Beatrice B. and John W. M. Whiting, 143
Whiting, John W. M., Irvin L. Child, and William W. Lambert, 128
Wirth, Louis, 3
Women
  roles, Old Town-New Capital contrasts, 127-128
  work patterns, 126, 129, 146, 193, 223, 229, 244, 263
  See also Childrearing; Educational system, daughters